Anthropocene Childhoods

Feminist Thought in Childhood Research

Series editors: Jayne Osgood and Veronica Pacini-Ketchabaw

Drawing on feminist scholarship, this boundary-pushing series explores the use of creative, experimental, new materialist, and post-humanist research methodologies that address various aspects of childhood. *Feminist Thought in Childhood Research* foregrounds examples of research practices within feminist childhood studies that engage with post-humanism, science studies, affect theory, animal studies, new materialisms, and other post-foundational perspectives that seek to decenter human experience. Books in the series offer lived examples of feminist research praxis and politics in childhood studies. The series includes authored and edited collections—from early career and established scholars—addressing past, present, and future childhood research issues from a global context.

Also available in the series:

Feminist Research for 21st-Century Childhoods: Common Worlds Methods,
edited by B. Denise Hodgins
Feminists Researching Gendered Childhoods: Generative Entanglements,
edited by Jayne Osgood and Kerry H. Robinson
Theorizing Feminist Ethics of Care in Early Childhood Practice,
edited by Rachel Langford
More-Than-Human Literacies in Early Childhood,
Abigail Hackett
The Early Childhood Educator,
edited by Rachel Langford and Brooke Richardson

Anthropocene Childhoods

Speculative Fiction, Racialization, and Climate Crisis

Emily Ashton

BLOOMSBURY ACADEMIC
LONDON • NEW YORK • OXFORD • NEW DELHI • SYDNEY

BLOOMSBURY ACADEMIC
Bloomsbury Publishing Plc
50 Bedford Square, London, WC1B 3DP, UK
1385 Broadway, New York, NY 10018, USA
29 Earlsfort Terrace, Dublin 2, Ireland

BLOOMSBURY, BLOOMSBURY ACADEMIC and the Diana logo are trademarks of
Bloomsbury Publishing Plc

First published in Great Britain 2023
Paperback edition published 2024

Copyright © Emily Ashton, 2023

Emily Ashton has asserted her right under the Copyright,
Designs and Patents Act, 1988, to be identified as Author of this work.

For legal purposes the Acknowledgments on p. ix constitute
an extension of this copyright page.

Series design by Anna Berzovan
Cover image: © Lisa5201/ Getty Images

This work is published open access subject to a Creative Commons
Attribution-NonCommercial-NoDerivatives 4.0 International licence (CC BY-NC-ND 4.0,
https://creativecommons.org/licenses/by-nc-nd/4.0/). You may re-use, distribute,
and reproduce this work in any medium for non-commercial purposes,
provided you give attribution to the copyright holder and the publisher and provide
a link to the Creative Commons licence.

Bloomsbury Publishing Plc does not have any control over, or responsibility for,
any third-party websites referred to or in this book. All internet addresses given in
this book were correct at the time of going to press. The author and publisher regret
any inconvenience caused if addresses have changed or sites have ceased to exist,
but can accept no responsibility for any such changes.

A catalogue record for this book is available from the British Library.

A catalog record for this book is available from the Library of Congress.

ISBN:	HB:	978-1-3502-6238-6
	PB:	978-1-3502-6242-3
	ePDF:	978-1-3502-6239-3
	eBook:	978-1-3502-6240-9

Series: Feminist Thought in Childhood Research

Typeset by Integra Software Services Pvt. Ltd.

To find out more about our authors and books visit www.bloomsbury.com
and sign up for our newsletters.

Contents

List of Figures	vi
Series Editors' Introduction	vii
Acknowledgments	ix
1 Anthropocene Childhoods: Situating Speculative Child-Figures	1
2 Geontological Figurations of Anthropocene Childhoods	25
3 Infecting Whiteness: Child-Monsters at the End of the World	47
4 Becoming-Geos: The Stratification of Childhood	71
5 Monstrous Love for Regenerative Cyborgs	91
6 Parental Stewardship: Bionormative Care as Environmental Surrogate	115
7 Educational Imaginaries for Child-Climate Futures	139
Notes	154
References	165
Index	187

Figures

1	The Boy with the Bones	2
2	Becoming Boy-Animal-Monster	34
3	Kind-of Friends for the Anthropocene	41
4	Masking Monstrosity—Making Killable	49
5	Iconography of Abandonment	144

Series Editors' Introduction

The series Feminist Thought in Childhood Research considers experimental and creative modes of researching and practicing in childhood studies. Recognizing the complex neo-liberal landscape and worrisome spaces of coloniality in the twenty-first century, the Feminist Thought in Childhood Research books provide a forum for cross-disciplinary, interdisciplinary, and transdisciplinary conversations in childhood studies that engage feminist decolonial, anticolonial, more-than-human, new materialisms, post-humanist, and other post-foundational perspectives that seek to reconfigure human experience. The series offers lively examples of feminist research praxis and politics that invite childhood studies scholars, students, and educators to engage in collectively imagining childhood otherwise. Until now, childhood studies has been decidedly a human matter, focused on the needs of individual children (Taylor, 2013). In the Anthropocene (Colebrook, 2012, 2013), however, other approaches to childhood that address the profound, human-induced ecological challenges facing our own and other species are emerging. As Taylor (2013) reminds us, if we are going to grapple with the socioecological challenges we face today, childhood studies need to pay attention to the more-than-human, to the non-human others that inhabit our worlds and the in human. Toward this end, Feminist Thought in Childhood Research series challenges the humanist, linear, and moral narratives (Colebrook, 2013; Haraway, 2013) of much of childhood studies by engaging with feminisms. As a feminist series, the books explore the inheritances of how to live in the Anthropocene and think about it in ways that are in tension with the Anthropocene itself.

Emily Ashton's *Anthropocene Childhoods: Speculative Fiction, Racialization, and Climate Crisis* is the sixth volume in the series. As the title suggests, this book focuses on "racialized child-figures in speculative texts of literature and film that story the end of the world through some sort of climate related disaster." Ashton boldly asks "which child-figures have a future—are the future—in these times called Anthropocene?" Aligning with heterogeneous and sometimes incommensurable theories, *Anthropocene Childhoods* not only complicates the equation of the child with the future under climate crises conditions, but also thoughtfully argues how Anthropocene childhoods circulate through social and cultural texts in the shadows of ongoing colonialisms, anti-blackness, capitalism, and patriarchy. Thinking across feminist Black studies, feminist Indigenous studies, new materialisms, eco-criticism, feminist environmental humanities, speculative fiction theory, and queer theories of childhood, Ashton teeters between world-ending and world-building.

As it engages the equation of the child with the future, Ashton activates the concept of the Anthropocene as "a watchword" that glosses over "the material violences, temporal scalings, and incommensurable worldings that figure a 'shadow' behind the 'shine' of its current popularity." It is through its "apocalyptic trope" that Ashton challenges the reader to call into question the Anthropocene's "road to ecological and moral redemption in speculative texts" that "relies on figurations of terrorists and aliens via anti-blackness, territorial displacements and new frontier continuities of settler colonialism, and technoscience advancements rooted in capitalism, militarism, and imperialism that instead of devastating humanity will somehow now save it triumphantly." Yet, *Anthropocene Childhoods* does not refuse all speculative texts. As Ashton writes, it is the speculative texts that "engender imaginaries of not this, as in refusal of present systems and subjectivities; not yet, as in what might be to come; and what if, as in generative possibilities" that she is after.

Indigenous futurities and Afro-futurisms inspire *Anthropocene Childhoods* to argue that the child figures a radical potential for a different future in which the attributions of innocence and the need for protection and care are not only restricted to white children. As such, Ashton gives a compelling engagement of "the value of speculative fiction for thinking differently about children, childhood, and the future."

We are certain that *Anthropocene Childhoods* will be met with deep interest and enthusiasm by scholars and practitioners in feminist childhood studies.

Acknowledgments

This book project spans many years during which I have lived on the east and west coasts of Canada before finishing up in the middle on the prairies. Much learning in between those moves took place in Malawi. Respectfully, these are the lands of the Wolastoqey and Mi'kmaq peoples; Lekwungen, Songhees, Esquimalt, and WSÁNEĆ peoples; nêhiyawak, Anihšināpēk, Nakoda, Dakota, Lakota, and Métis/Michif peoples; and Chewa, Tumbuka, and Tonga peoples. I hope the ethics and politics expressed in this work might be received as one moment in a lifelong effort to be in good relation.

My Grampy always joked with me about my never-ending student status when he managed to leave school after grade 3 get a PhD, which, for a successful Grand Falls farmer, meant a Potato House Degree. Grammy left her small town for the big city as young teenager in order to get her high school diploma. She instilled in her children and grandchildren the value of education. The greatest lesson I learned from both of them however was the importance of family. To my family and friends, thank you will never suffice but I will keep saying it anyway. Playing, laughing, loving, and just being with my nieces and nephews strengthens my desire to think-with ideas of otherwise childhoods and otherwise futurities. Thank you, Sage, Levi, Harry, Merlin, Freddie, Arlo, and Iris for the inspiration.

I also want to extend a thank you to colleagues past and present who offer generous support and work to create a better world in small moments every day. Since my BEd at UNB, I have been privileged to have many feminist teachers whose fierceness, thoughtfulness, and kindness I greatly admire. That gift continues with the editors of this series—my sincere appreciation to Veronica and Jayne.

Portions of Chapter 3 will appear in an "Ecological Challenges with/in Contemporary Childhoods" special issue of the *Journal of Childhood Studies* as: Ashton, E. (2022). Speculative child-figures at the end of the (white) world. *Journal of Childhood Studies*. I thank the journal editors for their permission to reproduce parts of the article here.

1

Anthropocene Childhoods

Situating Speculative Child-Figures

Since beginning this project, I have practiced a daily routine of scrolling through news sites and taking screenshots of Anthropocene-related stories. I have quickly accumulated quite an archive. Browsing through my collection, I log that most of the climate headlines are dark, dim, and foreboding. I also notice an increasing number of announcements about the end of the world. Some punchy headlines of late include "The Earth Is in a Death Spiral" (Monbiot, 2018), "We Have 12 Years Left" (Nunn, 2018), "Climate Change: 12 Years to Save the Planet? Make that 18 Months" (McGrath, 2019), "Our House Is on Fire" (Thunberg, 2019), "Code Red for Humanity" (*The Independent*, 2021), and "Global Climate Crisis: Inevitable, Unprecedented and Irreversible" (Harvey, 2021). While it might seem bad form to date the opening of a book so strictly, the point I wish to make is that these headlines have become anything but exceptional. Announcements of end times are proliferating, and have only been amplified by the global Covid-19 pandemic. The exact wording may get shuffled around but climate change, extinction, and various geotemporal slights of hand make up the discourse of the Anthropocene—the new geological epoch marking destructive human impact on Earth system processes—and what in one of its more figurative iterations has been called the "Anthropomeme" (Macfarlane, 2016, para. 34).

Words are not the only things meming these days. The new Anthropocene normal also takes shape through the repetition and replication of images. A view of planet earth from space burning red, polar bears wasting away on melting icebergs, population graphs with rhapsodic hockey stick curves, and plastic islands polluting acidic oceans to name but a few. One particular image, however, has stood out to me. The colors are brown, the landscape is barren, the sky is dark, and the ground is cracking: it is a dying earth. In the foreground is a lone figure—a young boy sitting in the dirt, playing with the bones of the deceased livestock that once grazed his family farm (see Figure 1). When the 2018 Intergovernmental Panel on Climate Change study was released—the report that moved up the global over-warming threshold to 2030—this image accompanied summaries from *The New York Times* to the academic journal *Nature* to the *Black Science Fiction Society* blog. But, as I said, I have seen the image before. It was first used closer to its home as part of a series on the devastating effects of drought in Warrumbungle Shire, New South Wales, Australia, in June 2018, and later picked up in that context by *Newsweek* (Watling, 2019). Since then, the Boy with the Bones has achieved rapid international circulation.

Another viral success of seeming juxtaposition is a four-and-a-half-minute short film in which global conglomerate Unilever asks, "Why Bring a Child into this World?" (Falduit, 2014).[1] Since its multi-country launch on World

Figure 1 The Boy with the Bones. Harry Taylor, age 6, by Brook Mitchell @ Getty Images 2018.

Children's Day in 2014, the commercial has been viewed more than 70 million times on YouTube alone. The film-within-a-film captures an affectively amped process of doubt-reflection-hope as racially diverse sets of expectant parents in five different countries are recorded viewing a prenatal film. After the requisite close-ups of the we-are-all-the-same near-term bellies, parents express to the camera their worries and fears about the future. Next the couples watch the prenatal film while the camera pans between their reactions and the film itself. The film opens with horrifying scenes of destruction before quickly moving to overhead shots of pristine green fields, children splashing in water, and life-saving prophylactics being administered to toddlers. The reassuring voiceover tells a heteronormative love story that culminates in the instructive: "Our children will have better chances of meeting their great-grandchildren than we ever did . . . . Breathe calmly. Bring your child into world. There has never been a better time to create a future for everyone on the planet, for those yet to come." Then, through happy tears and soft touches, the parents narrate a renewed faith in tomorrow. It is emotionally manipulative, heavily moralized, subtly commercialized, and utterly compelling. It urges everyone to "make a change" because "there's never been a better time to create a brighter future. #brightfuture." But which child-figures have a future—are the future—in these times called Anthropocene?

The Boy with the Bones and #BrightFuture Child are the first two figures of Anthropocene Child in this book. They join with other child-figures in the chapters that follow to complicate the child-future relationship under conditions of climate crisis. They all inherit an ecologically damaged planet; they all inhabit a broken earth (Jemisin, 2015). They also exist in worlds differentially marked by ongoing colonialisms, anti-blackness, capitalism, patriarchy, and a host of other intersecting issues that pull the (im)possibility of the future into present view. The Boy with the Bones lives the impact of climate change now and his future is under threat; the #Brightfuture Child is under threat now but their future promises universal reprieve. Both suggest a larger Anthropocene-induced destabilization, a "converging of anxieties over planetary futures," what Nigel Clark (2017) names a "crisis of natality" (p. 12). Thinking crises in a temporality and imaginary of childhood (i.e., natality) means *we* cannot simply repudiate the child-future relation.[2] Instead, we can "stay with the trouble" of its de- and recomposition (Haraway, 2016); we can queer it rather than enact a straight disavowal (Taylor, 2013).

As a heuristic, Anthropocene Child has far reach. As he travels from Warrumbungle Shire to the global stage, the Boy with the Bones transforms from a located figure to a universalized one. He is abstracted from place and made to stand for climate crisis everywhere. At the same time, with animal bones as playthings, he marks an intimacy with the nonhuman world, perhaps gesturing toward a form of geontological conviviality that upsets human exceptional understandings of life. Still, I am reminded of Michel Foucault's famous biopolitical mantra of the "right to make live and let die"—the cattle can die, the green landscape can go dark, but the same fate for the young boy is too awful to type. Not all lives are valued. A movement of the particular to universal is also undertaken by the #BrightFuture Child as five countries become a single stage in an edited re-production of reproductive fears and futuristic dreams. What is happening in these movements of Anthropocene Child is a sort of "double duty in that these child-figures embody species survival" at the same time as they engage—through risk in the Boy with Bones and safety in #BrightFuture Child—the "human fantasy of reproduction" (Sheldon, 2016, p. 3). In other words, the child-figures are asked to secure not only the reproduction of the human in a generational landscape but also the reproduction of the species in an evolutionary one. While it may be true, as Unilever insists, that children today might have a greater chance of knowing their great-grandchildren—at least in the aggregated statistical form of life expectancy models—those great-grandchildren have a much smaller chance of ever encountering a pangolin, western prairie fringed orchid, or coral reef. As well as staving off human extinction, then, Anthropocene Child is asked to close the gap between the human and nonhuman world while continuing to elevate humans in the Great Chain of Being. These massive demands signify a shift in the dominant image of the child coinciding with the Anthropocene, a move "from the child in need of saving to the child that saves" (p. 2).

Many children today demonstrate an awareness of this transition from protected to protector. A prominent example is the growing number of students striking from schools on Fridays to protest global climate inaction.

This movement is growing every day. In an open letter released ahead of a Global Day of Action on March 15, 2019, the student coalition writes, in part:

> Climate change is already happening. People did die, are dying and will die because of it, but we can and will stop this madness. We, the young, have started to move. We are going to change the fate of humanity, whether you like it or not .... You have failed us in the past. If you continue failing us in the future, we, the young people, will make change happen by ourselves. The youth of this world has started to move and we will not rest again.
> (Global Coordination Group of the Youth-Led Climate Strikes, 2019, para. 1)

These young people understand that climate change is happening now, and they have no problem calling out adults who talk a big game but do little to address real problems. Additionally, among the youth activists there seems to be an intersectional awareness being advanced that runs counter to the mainstream.[3] This is especially evident in the work of youth of color activists who recognize that "there have always been, and will always be indigenous, black and brown youth at the forefront of creating systemic change and challenging injustice" (Martinez, 2019), and that "the climate crisis is everything. It's health care, it's racial justice, it's criminal justice—everything" (Hirsi, 2019). While these youth climate leaders are also figures of Anthropocene Child, the main focus in this book is on racialized child-figures in speculative texts of literature and film that story the end of the world through some sort of climate-related disaster. I argue that these speculative child-climate relations form an important part of the "public pedagogy of the Anthropocene" (Sheldon, 2016, p. 150).

Enter the Anthropocene

In the last few years, the Anthropocene has become a matter of intense scholarly concern. However, "its constitutive concerns—global warming, genetic technology, biodiversity loss, environmental racism" have been felt-lived for much longer (Leong, 2016, para. 3). As such, the Anthropocene is *more than* a proposed name for Earth system epochal change; it is *not only* a scientific marker. Temporal, ethical, and political challenges of thinking deep time, deep strata, and deep responsibility have encouraged scientists, politicians, artists, activists, writers, educators, and academics of all sorts to take-up the Anthropocene as a gathering term. This widespread interest, as reflected in the plethora of alternative nomenclature for example, entails a "complex web of significances—material, philosophical, scientific, ethical, political, textual" that are not always commensurable with one another (Saldanha & Stark, 2016, p. 433).[4]

Since its emergence (Crutzen & Stoermer, 2000), the Anthropocene concept has moved from the domain of Earth System Science to much wider usage.[5] It has become an important watchword. It signals to me to pay attention. It condenses immensely complex happenings under a single word. It blurs geologic time with human lifespan; it mixes planetary capacity with individualized responsibility. The Anthropocene is perhaps "the closest thing there is to common shorthand for this turbulent, momentous, unpredictable, hopeless, hopeful time—duration and scope still unknown" (Revkin, 2016, para. 1). As a watchword, however, invocations of the Anthropocene often gloss over the material violences, temporal scalings, and incommensurable worldings that figure a "shadow" behind the "shine" of its current popularity (Andreotti, 2012). Composing the shadow is a re-universalization, a sort of complementary pan-humanity, of the we-are-all-in-this-together sort, that does not always acknowledge differential distributions of safety and harm that accompany climate crisis.[6] Another concern is that a particular genre of the human (i.e., the figure of Anthropos) is extended world destructing powers that once and for all confirm its position atop the species hierarchy. This figuration of Anthropos has much in common with Sylvia Wynter's (2003) critique of the "overrepresentation of Man as the human" itself (p. 260).

With all of these complexities, it is hard to know what to make of the Anthropocene claim that the human species is now a geomorphic agent altering the atmospheric, stratospheric, biospheric, lithospheric, and hydrospheric conditions of the earth. Andreas Malm and Alf Hornborg (2014) note that an argument provided by some scientists for a species-based neologism, even given the recognition that humans are just one small part of the Earth system, is that "what really matters is that climatic disruption originates from *within* the human species, even if not *all* of it is to blame" (p. 65). Nevertheless, a question that lingers for critical scholars is if we can "really mend our ways with a concept that puts humans right back at the centre" (Hamilton & Neimanis, 2016, para. 4). One of the Anthropocene's more vocal critics, Ellen Crist (2013), is adamant in her repudiation because the "discourse of the Anthropocene refuses to challenge human dominion, proposing instead technological and managerial approaches that would make human dominion sustainable" (p. 129). Less carbon-dependent ways of life can be blocked from view in fast-paced pledges for techno-fixes and geo-engineering feats; multispecies interdependencies can be eclipsed by an overwhelming eco-anxiety which places human survival above all. Writ-large the Anthropocene covers over the humanity's profound interdependency on other species and nonlife existents, but that does not have to be the dominant narrative. What might happen to the figure of the Anthropos is that its exceptionalism may prove to be "delusional and self-sabotaging" (Taylor & Pacini-Ketchabaw, 2015, p. 6). What I am to show with the figures of Anthropocene Child in this book is that humans are "only made possible through a diverse network of technological, cultural, organic, and geological entities" (Palsson et al., 2013, p. 7). The speculative child-figures in this book are "human—*but not only*" (de la Cadena, 2014, p. 256). Bringing speculative fiction together with the Anthropocene discussion finds imaginaries not solely beholden to Man.

Apocalyptic Tropes of Speculative Fiction

I find quite provocative the observation that "fantasies of apocalypse are both a product and a producer of our current epoch—the Anthropocene" (Ginn, 2015, p. 352). The etymology of apocalypse as "revelation, disclosure" connects to this idea. The Anthropocene, or so the dominant narrative goes, finally reveals the detrimental effects of human consumptive and extractive practices on the earth. The recognition of humans as destructive agents—as producers of apocalypse—should hardly come as a surprise to those paying attention to how power has been exercised. So, in this way, while the Anthropocene "might seem to offer a dystopic future that laments the end of the world, imperialism and ongoing (settler) colonialisms have been ending worlds for as long as they have been in existence" (Yusoff, 2018, p. xiii). This bemoaning of the end of the world is nevertheless remarkable in both contemporary scholarly and popular discourse. Recall, for example, the news headlines that open this book. I have grabbed onto figurations of the end of the world as a way to engage the climate crisis, ongoing racisms and colonialisms, and child futurities. This is because "regardless of when the Anthropocene started, the ending of it is what is driving the current public preoccupation with it and marks its cultural significance" (Joo, 2018, p. 2).

Perhaps, most noticeably, apocalypse as a product of the Anthropocene manifests in the deluge of pop culture disaster film and cli-fi literature produced and consumed in recent years. This Anthropocene-allied genre "plays out a fantasy of human near-disappearance and redemption" where exalting life through survival is poised as the only goal (Colebrook, 2014, p. 197). Limited shelter, limited water, limited food, limited leisure, limited electricity, limited transport, and, overall, limited things make up the plot points and settings. Rarely is it considered that these same limits are the actual conditions many in the world face daily (Colebrook, 2018): Anthropocene imaginaries of future ends are the real worlds for many now. Alongside these pop culture texts are speculative non-fiction bestsellers that imagine humanity's end. Examples include *The World without Us* (Weisman, 2007), *The Sixth Extinction* (Kolbert, 2014), and numerous self-help preparation-preservation guides along the lines of "how to survive a zombie apocalypse" (e.g., Thomas & Thomas, 2009). Furthermore, apocalyptic thinking merges with politics when instead of being overrun by a tsunami in New York City (e.g., *The Day After Tomorrow*), or giant beasts after a nuclear meltdown (e.g., *Godzilla*), climate change migrants and refugees become the futurized "object-target" of "white affect" and fragility (Baldwin, 2016). In these examples, we may begin to see how the Anthropocene is produced and reflected as apocalyptic trope.

With regard to contemporary post-apocalyptic blockbusters there is a predictable narrative sequence to most speculative texts. First, a select group of humans led by a Man (e.g., family man, scientist man, military man, will-be-president man, Anthropos man) comes face-to-face with humanity's mistakes (e.g., hubris, ecological waste, gene manipulation) and realizes he must act. In many cases the actual disaster happens off-screen as a prequel event to the main story at hand. Another instigating action might be an apparent no-human-fault accident where nature is to blame (e.g., asteroid strike, giant wave, alien invasion), but in which planetary survival nevertheless becomes precarious. Urban centers are typically threatened, flooded, or destroyed, but a transport hub or military structure remains for temporary safety and world-saving meetings. The plot progresses as humanity comes closer and closer to the brink of extinction and a few good men are lost along the way. At the climax, and after just the right amount of earthly destruction, the hero and his ensemble save both the day and his family. Lastly, a proper humanity—not what caused the destruction at the beginning of the story—emerges (Weinstein & Colebrook, 2017), and oftentimes this is with/through/in the figure of a child. However, this road to ecological and moral redemption in speculative texts still often relies on figurations of terrorists and aliens via anti-blackness, territorial displacements and new frontier continuities of settler colonialism, and technoscience advancements rooted in capitalism, militarism, and imperialism that instead of devastating humanity will somehow now save it triumphantly. Summarized, the tropic plot line typically proceeds as follows: (1) humanity is in trouble, (2) humanity is near extinction, (3) humanity is saved, and (4) proper humanity is (re)becoming.

These are not the sorts of speculative stories I am overly interested in, but they do serve as a point of departure. Instead, the stories I pull on feature agentic child-figures who, in relation-with inhuman others, challenge whiteness, challenge injustice, and challenge an ethics of restoration for worlds built on violence. As a key hybrid-figure from the Broken Earth books featured in Chapter 4 offers: "Don't lament when those worlds fall. Rage that they were built doomed in the first place" (Jemisin, 2017, p. 7). Amidst the turmoil of these times, it is my belief that speculative fiction can apportion "windows into alternative realities, even if it is just a glimpse, to challenge ever-present narratives of inevitability" (Benjamin, 2016, p. 19). I do not mean this as a form of escapism where the climate crisis disappears from present concern, but that white supremacy, settler colonialism, fossil fuel extraction, and anti-blackness are not inevitable. The future is not (yet) written in stone. The speculative engenders imaginaries of *not this*, as in refusal of present systems and subjectivities; *not yet*, as in what might be to come; and *what if*, as in generative possibilities.

For my purposes, an important amendment follows this section's opening quotation. The sentence continues: "fantasies of apocalypse ... also take us beyond this epoch [to] what might be to come" (Ginn, 2015, p. 352). While what is "to come" is often depicted as an amplified intensification of the same, that is not the only vision available. Critical imaginings also exist as a form of "social dreaming that makes different futures possible" (Gergen et al., 2018, p. 5). These are speculative gestures that are an "Otherwise than this" (Crawley, 2015, para. 18). Much of this important work is found in Indigenous Futurisms and Afro-futurisms/Afrofuturisms.[7] While each genre has its own genealogy, artists, authors, theorists, and audiences—and the futures they animate might not be entirely commensurable—they do come together in that "whenever we envision a world without war, without prisons, without capitalism, we are producing speculative fiction" (Imarisha, 2015, p. 10). My contribution to these discussions is better understood to be in conversation with, and to be read alongside, Indigenous futurities and Afro-futurisms, wherein I turn my critical lens on those for whom the future is not necessarily a critical act of imagination but an accumulative continuation. This means having to ask hard questions of myself with regard to my social justice values and social positionings and how they impact my work in Childhood Studies. Summed up by Frank B. Wilderson III (2014) in the context of #BlackLivesMatter, and for which I am included in his "they": "Because what are they trying to do? They're trying to build a better world. What are we trying to do? We're trying to destroy the world. Two irreconcilable projects" (p. 20). Some speculative futures exist where settlerness and anti-blackness do not, and, as such, there are limits to my telling.

Situating Anthropocene Childhoods

I locate my work in the interdisciplinary field of Childhood Studies. As such, I am able to draw on a range of theoretical perspectives including critical theory, Black studies, Indigenous studies, environmental humanities, and feminist theory to think through ideas related to children and childhoods. Childhood Studies also has its own genealogy, short in duration compared with more traditional disciplines, but a field that has contributed much important scholarship since the mid-1990s. Its field-defining mantra in the early years was, "the immaturity of children is a biological fact of life but the ways in which it is understood and made meaningful is a fact of culture" (James &

Prout, 1997, p. 7). In this, we see two major forces at work: the biological and the social. We can also see how the biological is taken-for-granted as the raw stuff of childhood that is given meaning by culture. But this is not the only way the terms have been approached. By way of providing a context for the emergence of Anthropocene Child, I organize this section in terms of four themes: biosocial waves, childhood innocence, child-future joins, and the figure of the child as origin for a particular version of the human.

Biosocial Waves

A short history of Childhood Studies can be told as two movements or waves (Ryan, 2011). The first wave is recognizable by a strong emphasis on the social construction of childhood. Scholars put forth an understanding of childhood as a multifaceted phenomenon that differs over time and place. Discourse, language, and power were all key analytical values. There was also a push to appreciate children as agentic citizens valued for who they are in the here and now—as powerful social actors with unique cultures not solely beholden to adult desires—as beings and not just becomings (Qvortrup, 2009). The emphasis on social agency and social construction were, in part, a response to the dominance of child developmental science in child-related fields. Select psychological theories and methods were popularized that made claims to know the interworkings of children, reveal universal sequences of development, and provide pedagogical formulas for the right ingredients to grow children into productive adults. At this point, the biological largely became interchangeable with a form of positivistic child development knowledge that held up the figure of the "natural" child as subject and their interiority as object. The first wave set up a binary divide between the social and the biological (Lee, 2013; Lee & Motzkau, 2011), which took various forms, for example, nature/nurture or nature/culture, but the social drove research, theorizing, and publication.

What resulted from this first wave were two delimited positions: the first reduced childhood to an opposition whereby either biological or social understandings were dominant, and the second was additive in that figuring out an optimal combination of nature and nurture factors was the goal (Prout, 2005; Taylor, 2013). There were also critiques from within the field that the complexity of biological perspectives was reduced or at least left behind in an overwhelming emphasis on social constructionism (e.g., Lee & Motzaku, 2011; Prout, 2005). My understanding is that the critiques of developmentalism were not a rejection of the biological in total, but a challenge to any presumption that biological development is universal, fixed, deterministic, and teleological (e.g., Burman, 2017). While important, this emphasis did not always presume a full picture of how the biological is exercised, lived, and understood.[8] This is partly why I do not think the challenge to biological ontologies of childhood is complete—their power in shaping conceptions of the human continues. If anything, I think the biological subsumes the social in most child-related fields, and not the other way around, which is why I use the term bionormative in this book. Nevertheless, as the field of Childhood Studies developed, important questions were raised about the limits of dualistic thinking. A key challenge that signaled a second wave was whether "just two categories are enough to describe, let alone generate questions about, the great diversity of childhoods and children" (Lee, 2013, p. 19).

In advocating for a hybrid model of childhood, Alan Prout (2005) was a major instigating figure of the second wave. Instead of treating the biological and the social as separate entities, childhood is appreciated as a multiplicity of nature-cultures. What counts as natures-cultures is expansive and includes a heterogeneous "variety of material, discursive, cultural, natural, technological, human and non-human resources" (p. 3). Other binaries also proved to be limiting, including the supposed theory/practice divide, which, once dissolved, could draw "sensing bodies, matter and material environments—spaces and places" together (Lenz-Taughi, 2010, p. 3). This emphasis on matter and relationality is emblematic of the second wave shift away from postmodern and poststructural "deconstructive" analyses toward posthuman and new materialist "reconstructive" practices (Taylor, 2013). Prout's initial push has now been generatively and generously expanded upon in ways that decenter the child by shifting focus from hybrid childhoods to relational wordings (e.g., Cutter-Mackenzie-Knowles et al., 2020; Diaz-Diaz & Semenec, 2020).

The two waves story of Childhood Studies is a particular telling. It is condensed and glosses over the many specificities that make the field so enticing to me. Still, I am drawn to waves because they do not conjure up a process of discardment. A wave may run its course but as it laps up on shore it intermingles with what comes next: a second wave contains the first in its composition. I also like wave imagery because it opens up to diffraction (Barad, 2007; Haraway, 2004). If I throw rocks into the water, waves will redirect, bend, curve, and spread out. The ripples will crossover and remake each other. There is interference. I think diffraction might be a better characterization for much current Childhood Studies work rather than a third wave. Children's everyday relations with place, materials, animals, and other species coarsely summarizes important research and theorizing currently being undertaken, including scholarship from members of the Common World Research Collection (n.d.) that pushes beyond a bio-social mixing to "engage the relational webs in which children already live" (Kraftl, 2020, p. 7). This includes separate ethnographic works by Margaret Somerville (2017) and Karen Malone (2017) who each refer to their young co-researchers as "Children of the Anthropocene." These children are "born into a different understanding of the stability of the world, into a storied future of inevitable entanglement in the fate of the planet" (Somerville, 2017, p. 399). I am hopeful that my contribution can add another interference pattern to Childhood Studies, one that is left out of Prout's nature-culture listing above: geos.

I approach the Anthropocene as a condition of possibility for a geos-reconfiguration of contemporary childhoods. As an everyday example, I think we are comfortable enough with the fact that human bodies are made up of a lot of bacteria but we have been a little slower to acknowledge the mineral entanglements. It seems less well known that "we're also walking rocks" (Ellsworth & Kruse, 2011, "Zuihitsu 2").[9] With geos I signify not only the geological knowledge base and substance of the Anthropocene (e.g., rocks, minerals, mountains), but also how speculative child-figures "intra-act" with inhuman figures (Barad, 2007).[10] In this book, there are pathogens, zombies, cyborgs, and the earth itself who become with child-figures in ways that cannot be contained by a bio(socio)normative model of childhood. As variations of monster-figures, many of the speculative child-figures in these pages embody modalities of childhood that refuse a bionormative enclosure. How might a turn toward "geos be a refusal of the child development perspectives that shape" and delimit children's worlds (Nxumalo, 2017, p. 559)? My problematizing of bionormative childhoods is also intended as an opening into larger discussions about "our present culture's purely biological definition of what it is to *be*, and therefore of what it is *like* to be, human" (Wynter, 2000, p. 180). How might the Anthropocene "realize the child and the human in new ways" (Castañeda, 2002, p. 45)? Can figures of Anthropocene Child prompt us to "re-imagine human origins and endings within a geologic rather than an exclusively biological context" (Yusoff, 2016, p. 5)? Can an antagonistic relation of bios and geos further dissolve into an intradependent and generative relationship?

Child-Future Entanglements

Lee Edelman's (2004) queer theory classic *No Future* knots the figure of the child and the future together. The sacred, capital-letter Child of Edelman's "reproductive futurism" represents the symbolic encapsulation of a desired social order made through a desirable future: the figure of the Child is *the* "redemptive agent ensuring futurity" (Sellers, 2013, p. 71). Yet, the Child is a figure of the horizon—always ahead, always obscured, always out of reach. The Child as a universal, sentimental figure through which all matters of ethics and politics are articulated is wavering. It is not that ethics and politics are no longer spoken in their name, but that the child-figure's supposedly redemptive ability of "renewal of the barren world through the miracle of birth" is more and more difficult amidst the climate crisis (Edelman, 1998, p. 21). Deputized preemptively and perpetually as the future, the Child that Edelman rages against "now stands for a future out-of-date" (Gill-Peterson et al., 2016, p. 495). Edelman posits that the figure of the Child is "the pledge of a covenant that shields us against the persistent threat of apocalypse now—or later" (p. 18). But the world has changed since Edelman wrote his much-cited polemic: the apocalypse seems all the more imminent and for many it is already here or has already happened. In the Anthropocene, Edelman's "no future" is no longer an alternative to reproductive futurism but "a reflection of it under conditions of catastrophic climate change" (Out of the Woods, 2015b, para. 20). However, I want to question whether "no future," as a thought-experiment, is necessarily something to be refuted or if the end of the world might offer something different.

In a review of key feminist, poststructural, and queer theory texts that make use of the child-future join, Veronica Barnsley (2010) asks: "what happens if the child-image fails to suggest a future?" (p. 328). Rather than attempt a preemptory response, I want to add a follow-up question. My addendum: what if the future fails to suggest a child-figure? This question is just as difficult to answer because it first seems not to suggest any difference at all. Nevertheless, it does call the imbrication of the child and the future to account differently, in that, at minimum, the order of reliance is reversed. In other words, instead of the child-figure failing to suggest a future, the Anthropocene makes thinkable that there is no future for the child. So, in a bit of a twist, what if the appeal is not for the future or even for the child but for the end of the world? What happens when the child as dual figure of generational (familial) and species (human) survival encounters inhuman planetary limits (Sheldon, 2016)?

Additionally, the Child that stands for the future in Edelman's (2004) treatise was never all children everywhere. Edelman's Child is a privileged figure endowed with assurances of a future that are denied to racialized children. José Muñoz (2009) puts it succinctly: "The future is the stuff of some kids. Racialized kids, queer kids, are not the sovereign princes of futurity" (p. 95). Andrea Smith notes an incommensurability of Edelman's Child with Indigenous futurities. Smith (2010) quotes Colonel John Chivington of the 1864 Sand Creek massacre who told his fighters to not only kill the Indigenous inhabitants but "to mutilate their reproductive organs and to kill their children because 'nits make lice'" (p. 50). "In this context," Smith continues, "the Native Child is not the guarantor of the reproductive future of white supremacy; it is the nit that undoes it" (p. 50).

Exclusions within the category child also include, as Christina Sharpe (2016) articulates, how "Black children are not seen as children" (p. 89). Black children are either animalized, objectivized, sexualized, and/or adultized; they are positioned "outside of the category of the child" (p. 89). A growing body of empirical research confirms the unavailability of innocence to Black children: they are often thought to be older than their biological years; associated with animals, in particular, apes; and consistently judged as more culpable than white peers (e.g., Dancy, 2014; Dumas & Nelson, 2016; Ferguson, 2001; Goff et al., 2008, 2014; Ladson-Billings, 2011). Furthermore, Robin Bernstein's (2011) historical work in *Racial Innocence* maps the division of childhood into white and Black tracks in the early nineteenth century. At that time, "black children were libeled as unfeeling, noninnocent nonchildren" (p. 33), and white children became the embodiment of innocence. Bernstein argues that childhood and innocence came together as inseparable concepts wherein each re-invented the other, including their shared exclusions.

Childhood Innocence

The concurrence of childhood and innocence is pervasive in most child-related disciplines, even though the pairing has a slippery, complicated, and contested history. Much critical effort from scholars both in and outside Childhood Studies has been spent challenging the naturalness and normalness of this union rather than supporting innocence as something inherent to children or childhoods. For example, important work has traced the historical join of innocence and childhood to the invention of modernity (Aries, 1962; Cunningham, 2006); problematized the image of the innocent child in relation to early childhood pedagogies (Dahlberg et al., 2006); posited innocence as the binary pivot between adult and child in narratives of social reproduction (Katz, 2008; Malkki, 2010); located innocence as a geopolitical imaginary of Northern childhoods used to perpetuate paternalistic discourses about children elsewhere (Penn, 2007); and troubled the relation of innocence, desire, and sexuality from queer and psychoanalytic perspectives (Blaise, 2005; Davies, 1990; Kincaid, 1998; Robinson, 2008; Taylor, 2010; Stockton, 2009; Walkerdine, 1997). Less familiar to childhood studies are critiques of childhood innocence from perspectives of Black, Indigenous and environmental studies, with some key exceptions that I will address next.

For Bernstein (2011), it is not possible to hold childhood in one hand and innocence in the other because they are wholly sutured together. Since at least the mid-nineteenth century, "childhood was not understood as innocent but as innocence itself; not as a symbol of innocence but as its embodiment" (p. 3). And from the start this "innocence was raced white" (p. 3). Nevertheless, what typically happens is that the child-figure is wielded as a "human shield against criticism" where a "universalized conception of the innocent child effaces gender, class and racial differences, even if it holds those differences in place" (Jenkins, 1998, p. 14). As Bernstein's genealogical work makes clear, however, childhood innocence is not universally available—effacing difference may be the ideological intent but it is unfilled. Bernstein

(2011) names "racial innocence" as the performative ability "to make political projects appear innocuous, natural, and therefore justified" (p. 33). How does the Anthropocene perform racial innocence? And how does the figure of the innocent child work within environmental discourses of the Anthropocene?

Racial innocence transits from childhood through geology to the Anthropocene in situations where social categories like race, class, gender, ability, and location are said not matter to matter. Kathryn Yusoff (2018) demonstrates how attributing innocence to geology is a strategy to naturalize and neutralize anthropogenic climate change. The ongoing colonial theft of minerals, bodies, and lands gets reframed in positive terms of accumulation, modernization, and progress—a #BrightFuture. Yusoff challenges the "the racial blindness of the Anthropocene as a willful blindness"—and therefore a performance of forgetting that Bernstein suggests accompanies innocence—that relates to the normalization of geology as a field of study whose objects of knowledge (e.g., rocks, soil, minerals) exist naturally outside of politics. What this idea overlooks are the intimate relationships of racialized peoples with inhuman matter, which are discussed more fully in Chapter 4. Critical work in Childhood Studies notes how developmental discourse acts as a recapitulation theory in that the child's development "is compared to the development of the species (with the child as nature, as the origin of the species) from 'savage' to 'civilized'" (Murris, 2016, p. 81). Read with Yusoff's re-framing, the perceived innocence of a geology that relies on divisions of human/inhuman, nature/culture, and savage/civilized recapitulates childhood into an unexpected surround.

Anchoring the Human

Due to its tangled relationship with innocence and nature, children and childhood have long been used to promote a certain understanding of humanity. Succinctly stated, the child "is conceived as the origin of the human" (Bignell, 2005, p. 380). Early childhood reconceptualist scholars Gaile Cannella and Radhika Viruru (2004) argue that "part of the definition of what it means to be human has been a construction of what is not human—humans are not *animals*, humans are not part of the *earth*, humans are not *inanimate*, and so forth" (p. 35; emphasis added). What is most interesting to me is how the child fits spectrally into this listing as a "not-quite human being" (Lury, 2010, p. 284).

From Darwin's daddy diary to Rousseau's romanticism of nature-as-teacher, the child has been positioned close to nature, including modern-day picture books and films that show the child as intimate kin with animals (Taylor, 2013). Tyson Lewis (2012) explains, "children have always been precariously placed in a zone of indistinction between 'not yet' fully human and 'no longer' simply animals" (p. 285). However, all this boundary play is only tolerable when the innocent white child is the referent. The child as not-quite and less-than fully human takes on other meanings when anti-blackness, colonialism, and Indigeneity are considered. In a world where #BlackLivesMatter faces such potent resistance, the Black child *is* animal, the Black child *is* primitive, the Black child *is* non-sentient—as in impervious to pain. Not *close* but *is*. And unlike the white child, the Black child cannot develop or mature out of it. I do not intend this as the truth of Black children but the "truth for" a particular understanding of the human today that is based in anti-blackness (Wynter, 2003). Similarly, though not thought through enough in my work, the figure of the Indigenous child shares much of this spacing with the Black child. As one note of difference, however, the Indigenous child is not *close* to nature and animals but *too* animist in their kin relations.

Working in a deconstructive historical mode, Wynter (2000) understands stories as narrating a "specific genre of being human" into reproductive circulation (p. 196). These stories are not the truth of the human but the "truth-for" a specific version of the human—not humanity in toto but "partial humanisms" (p. 196). These stories—for example, the story of positivistic child development science—provide a framework through which humans are initiated into worlds and then make sense of themselves within these worlds: children are born(e) into stories and live these stories into temporal existence. What this also means is that the story of the Anthropocene and the figure of Anthropos have inclusions and exclusions already built into the script; however, the story is not determined once and for all. It is possible to "give humanness a different future" (Wynter & McKittrick, 2015, p. 9), and to write new genres and new worlds into being. This is why it is important for Wynter and her followers to speak of genres of "being human as praxis" and "as performative enactment," rather than take the human-as-Man as given and timeless (p. 31).

Wynter (2000) traces the current genre of the human to "the history of the expansion of the West from the fifteenth century onwards" (p. 198). Wynter

(1995a) argues that colonialism insisted upon a species account of humanness, which entailed a move away from theology toward biology in constituting the human and rationalizing conquest. This new bio-based humanity found its origin story in Darwin's evolutionary narrative which parses humans into naturally selected and dysselected categories (Wynter, 2003). In Wynter's words, this is "our present Darwinian dysselected by Evolution until proven otherwise descriptive statement of the human on the biocentric model of a natural organism" (p. 267). In other words, since Darwin, the dominant story about the human is that "we are biological beings" (Wynter, 2005, p. 361). What follows as a logical outgrowth from the "biocentric conception of the human" is "race and racism" (p. 361). This "descriptive statement" of the human maps onto current biopolitical differentiations of whiteness/blackness and settler/Indigenous, and continues to become-with histories and practices of violence, genocide, slavery, extraction, and coloniality (Wynter, 2000, p. 198). It also maps onto childhood as a recapitulation theory.

Wynter points to the importance of Darwin in creating the biocentric human through the story of evolutionary theory. Darwin is also an important figure in the institutionalization of the study of childhood; he published the first diary of infant development in 1877 (Burman, 2017; Mayall, 2013). In part, Darwin's evolutionary ideas were developed through observations he made about his own children. In them, he perceived that "having had little time to learn, [children] were close to nature and so provided a route into adult understanding of what it is to be human" (Prout, 2005, p. 4). Darwin tracked development patterns of his children which were then scaled up to indicate the development of the human species as a whole, or, better said, the racialized and hierarchical story of the human. Another way of stating this is ontogeny recapitulates phylogeny, explained as "individual development repeats, in foreshortened time, the development of the species" (Ryan, 2011, p. 448). The result is a racialized, paternalized, and hierarchical story of the human where so-called primitive races are said to stall at the level of development of a small child.

This biocentric genre of the human has become, as expressed by Wynter (2015), "the overrepresentation of Man as the human itself," and, therefore, understood as "truth-in-general" instead of a "genre-specific order of truth through which we know reality" (p. 32). As noted, Wynter does not accept the

Overrepresentation of Man as the human as inevitable and "offers a different origin narrative possibility" (p. 31). To do this, Wynter extends Franz Fanon's work to redefine the human as a hybrid being, both *bios* and *mythoi*, which might "draw attention to the relativity and original multiplicity of our genres of being human" (pp. 31–2). Another way to say this is that "besides ontogeny and phylogeny stands sociogeny" (Fanon, 1967, p. 11). Human beings "exist not as purely natural or biocentric beings or selves, but also are inscribed as specific modes or genres (types, kinds) of being human" (Kromidas, 2019, p. 68). Loosely translated, this human is biology and story—we are *homo narrans* (Wynter & McKittrick, 2015), which adds a layer of analysis to my exploration of speculative child-figures and texts in the chapters to come. Bios and mythoi entangle to make the human: "Human beings are magical. Bios and Logos. Words made flesh, muscle and bone animated by hope and desire, belief materialized in deeds, deeds which crystallize our actualities … And the maps of spring always have to be redrawn again, in undared forms" (Wynter, 1995b, p. 35).

Part of me is tempted to connect this emphasis on social and story back to the constructionism and hybridity of the two waves of Childhood Studies. However, this would ellipse the openness and situatedness of Wynter's (2005) invitation for a new counter-poetics. Stories, genres, and descriptive statements are inscriptive, and they are lived out adaptively in "response to the ecological as well as to the geopolitical circumstances in which we find ourselves" (Wynter, 2005, p. 361). Additionally, the social, does not only have to signify Man or even the human; there are versions of "more than-human sociality in which nonhumans are also seen as fully social, as beings engaged in webs of world-making relations" (Palsson & Swanson, 2016, p. 151). These narrative possibilities are geostories, which encompass humans and earthly actors of all sort including the geologic, and stand for a return to story "back to the ground" (Latour, 2014, p. 17). Geostories grapple with openings that can extend enough for new worlds, new relationships, and new humans to be imagined (Haraway, 2016). These stories can rewrite the frames of how the world is normally understood; for example, the child-orogenes of Broken Earth exist in symbiosis with geological forces rather than only biological ones. Geostories have implications for Childhood Studies, the Anthropocene, and the remaking of the human.

Chapter Outlines

Each chapter in this book performs a close reading of a speculative geostory through directed attention to figures of Anthropocene Child. A close reading, in my terms, is not unequivocally faithful to its original in that I foreground certain frames more than others. Bringing texts and figures together can also produce something new that was not there originally. I do try to respect the speculative texts I draw from by treating them as theory—this does not mean that I do not engage and respond, but that the plot points, dialogue, character, and setting contribute important commentary on the Anthropocene. My main emphasis will be on how the child-figures engage with the end of the world—in its various formations—in order to re-imagine geos-futurities.

In Chapter 2, "Geontological Figurations of Anthropocene Child," I look to how geos-inspired reconfigurations of childhood might stand up to biocentric formulations of the human. While I do not want to disavow the child's entanglement with bios—as if such an eclipsing were possible—I do want to complicate it as an entrenched mode of knowing childhood. To do this I draw on Elizabeth Povinelli's (2016) work on geontology as a way to figure forth alternative childhood imaginaries that engage with divisions of life and nonlife. According to Povinelli, geontology breaks with a biopolitical assumption that power works via tactics of making live and letting die and is instead concerned with maintaining the division of life from nonlife. The three figures Povinelli finds illustrative of this form of governance are the Desert, the Animist, and the Virus. In this chapter, I pursue how speculative child-figures intersect with Povinelli's geontological figures. The Boy with the Bones makes a reappearance in this chapter in a discussion of the Desert as the infiltration of nonlife into the lively domain of childhood. Hushpuppy from *Beasts of the Southern Wild* (Zeitlan, 2012) is a key Animist figure in my assessment of geontology as she forefronts concerns about multispecies relations, racialized structures of abandonment, and the ethical harms of locating hope for the future in the precarious child-figure. Additionally, I turn to Métis author Cherie Dimaline's (2017) speculative novel *The Marrow Thieves*, in which the child-figures care for each other and their more-than-human kin in order to endure another settler apocalypse. There is no heroic individual in this text and no kin are abandoned; there is a multigenerational, multi-Nation, viral form of community wherein Indigenous children set in motion a liveable future through resurgent relations to language, land, and each other. The generative premise and promise of geontological childhoods carry through the remaining chapters in this book.

In Chapter 3, "Infecting Whiteness: Child-Monsters at the End of the World," I spotlight Melanie, a zombie child called a "hungry" in the novel and film *The Girl with All the Gifts* (Carey, 2014; McCarthy & Carey, 2016). Melanie troubles the strict bionormative construction of a human child. She is a hybrid-child who is infected by a fungal pathogen that has made mindless, flesh-eating zombies of the rest of humankind. Hungry-children are not typical zombie-figures; they are conscious yet imprisoned because their child-bodies hold a potential cure. Importantly, between the novel and film Melanie racebends. The film's visualization of Melanie as a young Black girl-figure allows me to problematize allocations of humanness. This includes how Melanie must symbiogenetically become-with pathogen in order to survive, how a world on fire instigates processes of regeneration, and how an otherwise world not defined by human exceptionalism might arise in the wake of destruction. Throughout the chapter, I foreground the work of Black Studies scholars who theorize the end of the whiteness as a means to create different systems, forms of belonging, and futurities.

In Chapter 4, "Becoming-Geos: The Stratification of Childhood," my speculative companion is Nassun, a child-orogene in N. K. Jemisin's (2015, 2016, 2017) Broken Earth trilogy. Orogeny is a geologic term that refers to how mountains are made overtime by seismic displacements in an upward folding of the earth's crust. Orogenes in Jemisin's world have geos-powers derived from the earth. An example of their abilities is that they can quell or cause earthquakes. This chapter continues the task of reconfiguring bios-geos childhoods by looking at how the biological and geological subtend each other. Orogene abilities derive from an innate biological embedment in their brain stems, which allows them to affect and be affected by the earth's forces. Transposed as an Anthropocene geos-subjectivity, orogenes are recognized as becoming-with strata (Yusoff, 2016). The final section of the chapter considers how Jemisin frames the end of the world as not a singularity but a multiplicity. Apocalypse in Broken Earth is a recurrent phenomenon which mirrors what this world has been for many racialized peoples. It is catastrophe on repeat.

I take seriously the provocation that as one world ends another begins. This impetus to rebuild after the end of the world puts a shudder into teleological announcements of end times.

The fifth chapter, "Monstrous Love for Regenerative Cyborgs," brings together a mismatch of contemporary theorists and figures. The chapter opens with Bruno Latour (2011) and his re-reading *Frankenstein* as an analogy for the Anthropocene condition. Latour argues that Dr. Frankenstein's true sin is neither invention nor hubris, but that the doctor abandoned his creature to the world. The figurative leap Latour makes is that "we" should treat technoscience creations like children and "love our monsters." From my Childhood Studies standpoint, the equivocation of technological invention and child caretaking raises concerns that are examined in this chapter as a way to foster a speculative ethics of critical feminist care. The central speculative text in this chapter is Ruha Benjamin's (2016) "Ferguson is the Future," which is a short story that gives Black Lives Matter an Afrofuturistic face in the techno-scientific regeneration of young Black lives ended prematurely by police violence. The story's main characters take the names of children who have been killed in this world and who are re-born as child-cyborgs in Benjamin's speculative world. In the story, a political reparations movement has been advanced alongside scientific stem cell technologies so that Black children murdered by police are given a second life. This again complicates a straight-forward understanding of biological determined childhoods. In re-imagining cyborg figures that test divisions of life and nonlife, Benjamin's story encourage critical scholars to "anticipate and intervene" now in racialized "logics of extinction" (p. 22).

Chapter 6, "Parental Stewardship: Bionormative Care as Environmental Surrogate," shifts focus from the child-figure to the parental relationship within conditions of climate crisis. My concern is how bio-care and environmental stewardship interchange for one another in the Anthropocene. In other words, I aim to make problematic "parental love as the antithesis and antidote to environmental destruction" (Johns-Putra, 2016, p. 521). To do so I look to parental figures, mothers specifically, in *The Handmaid's Tale* television adaption of Margaret Atwood's (1986) novel who refuse to abandon their offspring. This refusal comes at a price as the parents make all else secondary. It may seem at first that this kind of intense parental care is a refusal of Sheldon's (2016) swing from the child in need of protection to the one who does the saving, but, while these texts put the relation in tension, I do not think they void the transition. Instead, racialized heteronormative fertility, preservation of the human species, and the threat of a dying earth reinforce the figure of the child as futurity. In apocalyptic texts of this sort, I contend that child survival becomes a metonym for species survival and parental love becomes analogue to "planetary stewardship" (Steffen et al., 2011). As such, it is the bionormative parent-child relationship that is the focus of this chapter rather than a specific child-figure per se, and how the devastation of this bio-bond reflects "anxieties surrounding the demise of white supremacy" via the family form at the end of the world (Joo, 2018, p. 4).

In the final chapter, "Educational Imaginaries for Child-Climate Futures," I challenge Edelman's (2004) declaration that the figure of the Child must not "be confused with the lived experiences of any actual ... children" (p. 11). I do not think the lines between child-figures and children are so clear cut; instead, they are entangled. It is not a 1:1 correspondence, but it is a relationship. As such, I try to keep Povinelli's (2013) cautionary words in mind when working with child-figures: "Why don't we ever ask what it is like to be this figure?" Some related questions that move between worlds and challenge any borders between them include: What is it to be a toxic-child? What is it to be "born pre-polluted" (MacKendrick & Cairns, 2019)? What is it to be the one who is supposed to save? Can thinking-with child-figures at the end of the world grapple with the kinds of conditions, resources, and imaginaries required to capacitate lives actually capable of flourishing? To engage these concerns, I consider the value of speculative fiction for thinking differently about children, childhoods, and the future. It can be both an exercise in cruel optimism (Berlant, 2011) and a "necessary experiment" in living and relating otherwise (Nxumalo & ross, 2019). I also gather figures of Anthropocene Child from earlier chapters together in order to think-with speculative proposals for educational futures from the Common Worlds Research Collective (2020) in hopes of learning to live well together with life and nonlife.

2

Geontological Figurations of Anthropocene Childhoods

Initiated by Michel Foucault (2003 [1976]), analyses of contemporary forms of governance tend to map a shift from sovereign power (i.e., "take life or let live") to biopower (i.e., "make live and let die") in order to explain how power is structured and lived today (p. 241). The central figures of these formations have always been humans: our institutions, our heath, our behaviors, our sexuality, our economics, our education. However, for Elizabeth Povinelli (2016) and geontologies, a different relation subtends sovereign, disciplinary, and biopolitical divisions, that of life and nonlife. Whether taketh and giveth, life and death occupy the same side of the governmental equation: *Life (Life {birth, growth, reproduction} v. Death) v. Nonlife* (p. 9). Life and death are differences in degree, but not differences in kind. Understood in geontological terms, life instantiates a "biontological enclosure of existence" (Povinelli et al., 2017, p. 171), which necessitates that a difference be made and stayed between lively/inert, sentient/unfeeling, animate/inanimate, organic/inorganic, and bios/geos. What is being exposed by the climate crisis and the accompanying Anthropocene discussion however is the "trembling architecture" of this division (Povinelli, 2016, p. 16). There is growing awareness of human impact and reliance on nonlife—nonlife also has a major effect on human well-being. That said, bios and geos have never been wholly separate—it is biosgeos all the way down.

As a strategy of governance, the life versus nonlife division has been deployed destructively and racializingly as an "attribution of an inability of various colonized people to differentiate the kinds of things that have agency, subjectivity, and intentionality" (Povinelli, 2016, p. 5). In terms of settler colonial techniques, an alternative ontological understanding of nonlife provides an ongoing rationale for casting Indigenous peoples within "a premodern mentality and a postrecognition difference" (p. 5). In other words, Indigenous difference can be acknowledged (both as *less than* and as *different than*) so long as it does not disrupt dominant arrangements of settler colonial governance (Povinelli, 2011). Nonlife can be kin, can be sentient, so long as settler superiority is not altered. Povinelli (1995) shares a story of a government official attending a speech by her Indigenous friends about a sacred Dreaming site named Old Man Rock. At one point during the talk, a friend turns to Povinelli and asks: "He can't believe, eh, Beth?" (p. 505). Povinelli answers, in part, "He doesn't think she is lying. He just can't believe himself that Old Man Rock listens" (p. 505). The snippet provides an example of how the "cunning of recognition" operates in ways in which a belief is acceptable but an analytics of truth is not (Povinelli, 2002). Nothing has to change if the official believes these women believe what they say, but if it were accepted as truth that Old Man Rock listens then the Dreaming could not be destroyed for mining or other extractive economies. Different modes of existence, relationship, and responsibility would be necessary. That Indigenous peoples believe rocks can listen, and that politicians believe Indigenous peoples believe this, poses no real threat to late liberal modes of settler colonial governance. Such recognition actually supports these modes in the sense that a multicultural space can be provide for the expression, and even celebration, of alternative beliefs, while nonlife can still be dug up, polluted, and destroyed.

Generating Geontological Childhoods

In *Geontologies: A Requiem to Late Liberalism*, Povinelli (2016) lays out variations in how the division of life and nonlife has been performed. Life and nonlife often take form as that "which supposedly arrives into existence inert and that which arrives with an active potentiality" (p. 173), for example, the sort of difference between a stone and a baby. When I hear the last clause of the quotation—active potentiality—I am taken to the figure of the child as the dominant imaginary of life. In the formula presented above, *Life (Life {birth, growth, reproduction} v. Death) v. Nonlife*, the bionormative child is perhaps the superlative embodiment of the first polynomial expression. Each bracketed term of Life—birth, growth, and reproduction—is foundational to the child's developmental constitution as origin of the human. This includes how power operates in late liberalism, particularly by linking the child to the future (Edelman, 2004). The equation might be even be rewritten *Life (Child v. Death) v. Nonlife*. The figure of the child's placement on side of life is not only due to its biological beginnings but also to its social constitution. This involves the dominant ideas of Childhood Studies outlined in the last chapter: childhood is a social construction and children are social actors. The relations of biological and the social with child-related disciplines can be summarized as: *Nature + culture = childhood?* and *Childhood = the biological +/– the social?* (Ryan, 2011, pp. 443 & 446). The first is an additive approach where nature and culture exist as "incommensurable entities that are then seen as contributing a distinct proportion of the material that goes into the making of childhood" (Prout, 2005, p. 3). The latter expression aims to capture how "Western childhood is at once a biosocial process of formation and a biosocial mode of power" (Ryan, 2011, p. 446). Analytically and heuristically the biological and social can be pulled apart in the (re)making of childhoods, but in actuality their contributions are undividable and remain solidly on Life's side.

My interest is not to heavily dissect the components of the childhood equations but to point out that each expression of bio-social dualism (Lee & Motzkau, 2011), and even its hybridization (Prout, 2005), still generates a formula of *Life=Childhood*. Life then becomes a condition of possibility for childhood, whereas nonlife, for the most part, gets pushed out of view or is made oppositional. Edelman argues that the figure of the Child is the symbolic-referent around which the entire political enterprise turns. "The Child," Lee Edelman (2004) writes, "has come to embody for us the telos of the social order and came to be seen as the one for whom that order is held in perpetual trust" (p. 11). The figure of the child as such, made possible in the above equations (i.e., figurations), depends on its tie to life and life depends on it. The future that the child epitomizes, and that Edelman rallies against, is not possible if the child is attached to nonlife. The provocation I want to offer is *Life (Child) v. Nonlife (Child)*, where the versus is less of an opposition and more of a relation. The child in this expression is always intra-acting with something and/or someone else.

The biosocial child is when, where, and whom "the appeal of life—in it's newness, it's potentiality, it's vulnerability—is at its most intense" (Clark, 2017, p. 4). Nigel Clark (2017) posits that precisely because of this intensity is a potential to "begin thinking beyond biological life" (p. 4), which entails thinking beyond human exceptionalism as well. A disarticulation of bios from the human might open up to forms of otherwise existence. As mentioned in the introduction, my touchstone for an understanding of bionormative childhoods is a rich body of work from Childhood Studies that problematizes an image of the child as a naturalized developmental subject (e.g., Burman, 2017; Canella, 1997; Fendler, 2001; Pacini-Ketchabaw, 2011; Taylor, 2013). This child-figure is rendered knowable by deficit-based scientific theories and constructed as an incomplete and disempowered becoming who is acted upon by adults.[1] This child is the center of much research and pedagogy. Also contained within the bionormative frame is a narrow conception of family based on a heterosexist parental regime of shared genetic code (Baker, 2008; TallBear, 2019). While a bionormative imaginary has long structured work in child-related disciplines, I want to add speculative forms of geos to the equation and shift the child from a center position toward emplacement with more worldly relations.

In thinking-with figures of Anthropocene Child, I move through a three-tier framework that engages with geontological provocations. This arrangement builds on Rebekah Sheldon's (2016) noticing of a shift from the image of the child in need of protection to the child tasked with doing the protecting, but add a layer of resistance to the heightened demand. Firstly, child-figures reflect problematics of the contemporary world without interrupting dominant patterns of thought, materiality, and governance. Here, the child is the future and the future is the child. The figure of the child upholds a biosocial dualism, even in its contestation. Secondly, child-figures are tasked with protecting a world in which they have been made disposable. This incites critical questions about distributions of racialized harm and also exposes the limits of survivalist logics. These child-figures struggle with the versus in the geontological formula (Life vs. Nonlife); it disciplines, it racializes, and it consumes them. Thirdly, child-figures refuse current arrangements of existence and set in motion new worlds, even if the contours, forces, and politics cannot yet be fully described. These are child-figures who are in symbiotic relations with nonlife, and therefore cannot be solely positioned on the side of life, especially when the end of the world is their timespace. These child-figures largely maintain the agency that biosocial understandings attribute to them, but it gets refigured and redistributed as relationality is their true superpower. Taken together, this framework allows me to grapple with speculative geontological figures and figurations of worlds that are *not this, not yet*, and *what if*.

Figures of Geontology

To recap, geontology is a contemporary mode of governance concerned with maintaining the division of life from nonlife. This perceived rift is under increasing pressure by the climate crisis, which is to say that geontology is not so much new as newly visible (Povinelli, 2016). The three figures Povinelli finds illustrative of geontology are the Desert, the Animist, and the Virus. For Povinelli these figures are not escapes from power but symptoms of how it works and also where it fails. Povinelli's three figures "represent the nodal points in contemporary struggles to make sense of a current destabilization of this foundation division" between life and nonlife, including the Anthropocene defining proclamation of humans as a geologic force (p. 16). The figures can be summarized as follows:

> The Desert stands for discourses and strategies that re-stabilize the difference between life and nonlife by asking how we can stop the drift of life into the inert; the Animist discounts the difference between nonlife and life by claiming everything is alive with potentiality; and the Virus uses and ignores the division for the purpose of diverting its energies in order to extend itself.
> (p. 173)

Returning again to the formula cited earlier assists my explanation: *Life (Life{birth, growth, reproduction}v. Death) v. Nonlife*. Applied to the figures, the Desert reaffirms the versus between life and nonlife, the Animist dissolves it, and the Virus jumps back and forth over it. Povinelli presses on the point that these figures are neither exits nor escapes from power, nor are they the answer to anthropocentric climate change. They are symptoms, not solutions; for example, the take-away is not to all become animists now. Importantly, these figures are also "not subjugated subjects waiting to be liberated" (p. 16).

They already engage otherwise worlds even as they have to wade through the environmental, economic, social, political, racial, and colonial destruction of this one to endure.

Povinelli offers up the geontological figures with two caveats. The first is that these figures are not seeking inclusion in dominant way of knowing and being (i.e., life). These figures displace and confuse hard divisions of life/death and bios/geos. They are expressions of a formation of power and "windows into its operation," and "not a repressed truth of human existence" that if only widely known and accepted then things would automatically change (p. 15). In settler capitalist societies in particular, much has been invested in keeping life and nonlife epistemologically and ontologically separate. So to care about and for geontological figures is not to (re)emplace them in the current order of things, or to reverse relations of dominance (i.e., nonlife over life), but to understand them "as a way station for the emergence of something else" (p. 15). These figures are not entirely free from current governmental structures yet are not completely enclosed within them either. They indicate possible worlds otherwise than late settler liberalism and biopolitical rule.

Povinelli's second provision is that the Desert, Animist, and Virus "are tools, symptoms, figures, and diagnostics" of late liberal settler governmentalities that are not universally applicable or fixed. While Povinelli's figures of geontology find resemblance and connection with the speculative child-figures I study, I am curious if texts and authors from other places and with other genealogies would imagine differently. Late liberal settler modes of governance rely on divisions of bios/geos but there are worlds in this world "in which these enclosures are no longer, or have never been, relevant, sensible, or practical" (p. 16). This has resonance with Claire Colebrook's (2018) suggestion to rethink the Anthropocene's "concern with ends" by looking "to literary experiences of what it is like to be already without a world, to have already experienced social death" (p. 276). This alternative might generate something other than a narcissistic imperative of "we ought to be saved" because the post-apocalypse "might offer them a chance for existence" (p. 277). Colebrook is careful to submit literary experiences as a source rather than literal ones, but she also extends outside the text to peoples and communities who struggle "with the experience of near-extinction well before the vogue of the post-apocalyptic" (p. 277). I pull from these ideas that figures of governance might be different in non-settler nations and economies, as they might be for communities that have already had their worlds ended (Todd, 2015).

Figures of Anthropocene Child give heed to Povinelli's geontologies. What follows in this chapter is not about aligning child-figures absolutely into Povinelli's schemas but seeing what is possible when potential connections are mapped out. There are many points of connection between the speculative child-figures in the coming chapters and Povinelli's three figures of geontology. In this chapter however I overlay Povinelli's figures with my three-tiered arrangement by revisiting the Boy with Bones as a figure of the Desert (Miller, 2018), Hushpuppy from *Beast of the Southern Wild* as a figure of the Animist (Zeitlin, 2012), and a multi-age, multi-Nation group of Indigenous child-figures in *The Marrow Thieves* as a figure of the Virus (Dimaline, 2017).

Playing Desert: The Boy with the Bones

Povinelli's figure of the Desert encapsulates the anxieties surrounding the end of the world. By this I mean the disappearance of life—not only or even mainly in relation to death—into nonlife. An Anthropocene-related term for the ultimate withdrawal of vitality is extinction. For Povinelli, the Desert "dramatizes the possibility that Life is always at threat from the creeping, desiccating sands of Nonlife" (p. 19). The figure of the Desert stands for life lost, life at risk of being lost, and also life that can be regained "with the correct deployment of technological expertise or proper stewardship" (p. 17). This is the kind of save-the-world mentality that motivates techo-utopic, survivalist fantasies played out in Hollywood disaster blockbusters but that are also evident in ecomodernist discourse. Nonlife awaits defeat in these worldings. For the ecomodernists, a group I turn to in Chapter 6, deserts have not yet been brought to life because humans "have not yet found an economic use for them" (Asafu-Adjaye et al., 2015, p. 19). Povinelli makes a distinction between the desert as a barren landscape and the figure of the Desert as an affect that arouses a deep desire for liveliness, but the overlap is often difficult to tease apart. An example of this would be the ongoing technoscience research seeking to colonize Mars and the speculative films that imagine life lived abundantly on this formerly barren frontier (e.g., *The Martian*, *The Space between Us*).

An alternative example of the Desert from earlier in this book is the Boy with the Bones (see Figure 1, Chapter 1), otherwise known as Harry Taylor, who is pictured against a barren landscape playing with the bones of his family's dead livestock after a prolonged drought.

Photographer Brook Mitchell (2019) recounts the story of Harry and his family after revisiting them a second time about a year after the first photoshoot. The initial visit was ten months on from the New South Wales state declaration that the region was in severe drought. At that time, some places had received a bit of reprieve, but the town of Coonabarabran was still severely affected. Mitchell described the scene at the family-run Windy Hill farm as dire: "the dams were empty, the paddocks littered with the rotting carcasses of fallen stock. Clouds of dust whipped up as cattle rushed for scarce rations hand fed by the family" (para. 11). Harry was six years old at the time and had recently asked for rain as his birthday wish. He did not get it. It would be six more months until rain drops hit the dry soil. Harry made the same wish at seven. This time heavy winter rains poured down on the farm. Greenery was back—nonlife was life again. The headline from a local newspaper which ran the updated pictures from Mitchell's second visit read, "From dust bowl to lush green land" (Wood, 2020). The new shots include Taylor standing amidst waist-height healthy crops.

I found my thoughts wandering back to the Boy with Bones again given how hard Warrumbungle Shire, New South Wales, was hit by fires in January 2020. More than five million hectares were destroyed in the region, including more than 2000 homes (BBC, 2020). A cycle of drought, regrowth, and fire is the temporality the Boy with the Bones inherits and inhabits. Furthermore, I am concerned about how drought brought about the end of the world for much livestock and other nonhuman existents on the farm, and the fire may have brought another catastrophe. Who among them survived the drought only to have their world ended by the fires? What happened to the bones—did the Boy's playthings burn up? I am also thinking about what cannot die because they are never considered to have lived in the first place; in other words, the rocks, air, streams, and landscapes that have been altered by climatic events. I recognize the Boy with the Bones as a figure of the Desert because his world is where there was once much life but now that vitality is severely reduced only to come back and be threatened yet again.

Povinelli's figure of the Desert is where life might regenerate, particularly given the right technoscience inventions. Windy Hill farm was renewed with rainfall this time, but what will happen in the future if/when droughts or fires return. What if Harry's wish does not come true? Within this context, the child-figure "signifies the future we (adults) threaten, the connection to nature we (adults) have corrupted and the human spirit whose ingenuity will overcome the (adult-made) disasters of the present" (Sheldon, 2016, p. 39). This is to ask the Boy with the Bones to become protector against ecological destruction and take-up premature death as his playthings. I have my doubts about the likelihood of technoscience innovation to overcome anthropogenic climate change, but that does not mean that creativity and resourcefulness do not happen in smaller moments. In a way, looking back at the photo of the Boy with the Bones, I imagine him having retained joy in play amidst destruction. As a viewer of the photo, however, I wonder if my interpretation falls back upon an image of the innocent child and their intimacy with the natural world that has always been "raced white" (Bernstein, 2011, p. 8). Can my sentimentality acknowledge that "joy is not innocence; it is openness to caring" (Haraway & Tsing, 2019, p. 20)?

José Muñoz (2015) notes that "poor people of color, Indigenous people, and people in the global South are punished and pathologized for their improper engagement with nature/animals, namely, for survival and sustenance rather than recreation or companionship" (p. 211). Have I been reveling in thinking-with the Boy with the Bones within this formulation? In another photo in the same original series, the Boy with the Bones is shown against the same dark, dusty backdrop. However, this time he is standing tall and in front of his face he is holding up a full-faced horned skull of a sheep. In the caption, Mitchell explains that the Boy with the Bones calls this his "monster hat" (see Figure 2). I am quite taken by this photo of becoming-boy-becoming-animal-becoming-monster (Deleuze & Guattari, 1987). Yet, while I see the posthuman potential, I am nevertheless uncomfortable with how I am privileging the vitality of the Boy with the Bones over the dead sheep and dying landscape. If I were to ask myself whose life is more valuable, it would largely be a rhetorical exercise. I continue to grapple with these uncertainties in Chapter 3 with Melanie and with Hushpuppy from *Beasts of the Southern Wild* in the next section.

Figure 2 Becoming Boy-Animal-Monster. Photo by Brook Mitchell @ Getty Images 2018.

Saving the World: Burdens of *Beasts*

With the figure of the Desert, Povinelli (2016) captures "the drama of constant peril of Life in relation to Nonlife" (p. 15), whereas a different drama is embodied by the Animist. The difference between life and nonlife is not significant to the Animist "because all forms of existence have within them a vital animating, affecting force" (p. 15). There is no nonlife, not really. A caricatured exclamation of the Animist is: "everything is alive and we are all related." The foremost figure of the Animist in the popular imagination is Indigenous peoples. However, Indigenous peoples' relations with more-than-humans have been used as a rationale for discipline in late liberal settler governmentalities. Making kin with land and animals has not been respected. It has been used as a rationale for discounting Indigenous ways of knowing and being with the world, which, under dominant governmentalities, have been described as illogical and as childish. Child psychologist Jean Piaget claimed that very young children attribute feeling and intentions to inanimate objects, like their teddy bears, but grow out of this belief as they progress through stages of cognitive development and develop more sophisticated thinking. I am not saying Indigenous understandings are the same as the children Piaget observed, but drawing a parallel to the bigger discussion the figure of the Animist encapsulates: who can be animist? A question I have about the Anthropocene moment is whether this discounting of animism is shifting. For example, Indigenous caretaking practices are now being sought out as harm-reductive ways of caretaking for the planet. Is this recognition, adaptation, assimilation, extractivism, honoring, or something else? The figure of the Animist is not locked to Indigenous peoples in Povinelli's formulation either—New Age spiritual practitioners, new materialism/vitalism theorists, and individuals who are neurodiverse like Temple Grandin are other representatives of the Animist (p. 17). In sum, Animist figures are "those who see an equivalence between all forms of life or who can see life where others would see the lack of life" (p. 18). Examples from later chapters include the orogenes of Broken Earth and their geos-powers. However, here I think-with Hushpuppy as a figure of the Animist who reminds me that racialization needs to be taken into account in posthuman suppositions.

Benh Zeitlin's (2012) *Beasts of the Southern Wild* (hereafter *Beasts*) is ecological fairy tale, magical realism, and a romanticization of survivalism made more severe by environmental, racial, and economic inheritances. The film opens with Hushpuppy (actor Quvenzhané Wallis) sculpting a sandcastle-like structure for a chick in the dirt. She holds the chick up against her cheek and hears the heartbeat of the whole world before softly lowering the tiny being onto its new abode. The camera pans out and the audience realizes that the play is happening inside a ramshackle structure—Hushpuppy's own dirt castle. There is not much difference between Hushpuppy's home and the scrap yard outside, nor with her father's tin-sheet shack that is located 100 feet away from her solitary encampment. Hushpuppy is six years old. This is a "throwaway world" (Yaeger, 2013). In a uniform of stained white tank top, underwear, and rubber boots, Hushpuppy checks the vitals of the pigs, roosters, and dogs nearby. Without any fear of getting cinched, she presses a crab flat to her face in order to hear its muted pulse. Later, she will do the same for a leaf and her sick father. Hushpuppy is also the story's narrator, philosophizing off-screen about her actions on-screen, she tells us: "All the time, everywhere, everything's hearts are beating and squirting and talking to each other" (2:26). In Hushpuppy's world, everything is alive, and everything is connected. Hushpuppy is at one with animals and "at one in and with the dirt" (Sharpe, 2013, para. 5). Hushpuppy's animist oath is "the whole universe depends on everything fitting together just right" (21:30).

Hushpuppy's father, Wink, makes sporadic appearances. Wink's drunkenness and neglectfulness co-exist with his love of place and hyper-masculinist ambition for his daughter to "beast it." Wink also suffers from a terminal blood disorder that impacts his heart health. After disappearing for days Wink returns just in time to pluck Hushpuppy from her shack that is ablaze. Terrified of her father's anger, Hushpuppy runs off only to be caught and struck down by Wink's hand. Hushpuppy rises, closes her first, and hits Wink in the chest. As Wink falls to the ground, Hushpuppy fantasizes about the polar icecaps crashing into the ocean and a band of ancient aurochs awakening from extinction. Simultaneously thunder rumbles in the distance signifying an impending storm. Both the tempest and the beasts are moving toward her in ways in which mysticism and realism meld into one another. Hushpuppy seems to think that her punch set off this cascade of world ending events: "Sometimes you break something so bad that it can't get put back together" (33:25). Familial dysfunction and climate disaster are intertwined with the distribution and disposability of life in The Bathtub.

The Bathtub is an isolated bayou community literally sinking into the waters of a post-Katrina world. Everyone and everything share space here: dirt, animals, humans, ghosts, and the discarded possessions of capitalist materialism that wash ashore. The Bathtub is cut off from the mainland by a levee system. Only instead of keeping water out in a protective mode that failed in Katrina, these levees are keeping the water in. When the big storm hits there is nowhere for the water to go: The Bathtub is drowning. Much critical reception of the film ignores the complexity of precarity and praises the portrayal of a multi-racial, anti-capitalist community who just manage to make do. A multi-award winner on the festival circuit, *Beasts* is heralded as "sheer poetry on screen: an explosion of joy in the midst of startling squalor" (Lemire, 2013), "beautiful, funny, timely and tender" (Wise, 2012), and "a blast of sheer, improbable joy" (Scott, 2012). Conversely, all I can think about is a society with no sustained chance of much of anything let alone flourishing. The Bathtub's inhabitants have to leave or die as the waters rise, and this inevitability stalks "the film's ambition to valorize feral human nature" (Nyong'o, 2015, p. 251).

There are scenes that distract from the effort, endurance, and exhaustion of survival (Povinelli, 2011), and facilitate the audience and critic applause. For example, Hushpuppy tells us that The Bathtub has more holidays than anywhere else on earth. Their celebrations are joyful—there are drinks, fireworks, music, laughter, and dancing in borderless fields. They often feast together on bottomless volumes of fresh seafood, unburdened by formal dining etiquette that might otherwise insist on plates and cutlery. On the film's promotional poster, Hushpuppy runs through the grass with massive bursts of firelight pouring from the sprinklers in her hands. She seems magic. The children go to school when they want; they play together and with animals whenever they desire. Despite these moments, or maybe because I know they cannot last, I share with Tavia Nyong'o (2015) an overwhelming "anxiety about cinematic depictions of black (and other subaltern) people as primitives on a continuum with nonhuman animals" (p. 251).

This leads me to the reception of *Beasts* in scholarly circles, which can be gathered under two broad characterizations. First, much like the press reviews, scholars render a story of multi-racial climate change resilience and resistance—what Patricia Yaeger (2013) praises as "dirty ecology." Second, *Beasts* is received as relishing in a "romance of precarity" wherein any attention to racialization makes the triumphant aspects of point one impossible and irresponsible (Brown, 2013; Sharpe, 2013). In its most generative moments, *Beasts* asks viewers to re-examine humanity's relationship to the more-than-human world and how all existents are altered by climate change. Perhaps though what I am most drawn to is the displacement of biological kinship as the center point of relationships. The Bathtub is "a mixed-race, multi-generational community that realizes humans are not at the top, or the center, of the world" (Joo, 2018, p. 79). However, there is little time and space for animacy hierarchy in a world so engrossed in everyday survival. This is why I hesitate to hold up The Bathtub as some sort of bastion of alter-kin making. Hushpuppy tells a stranger, "I can count all the times I've been lifted on two fingers" (1:18:35). Valorizing non-bionormative kin-making in these circumstances overlooks the fact that Hushpuppy is abandoned multiple times by multiple people and multiple systems. While *Beasts* is "thoroughly critical of the idea of the biological family as natural" (Joo, 2018, p. 80), its precarious patchworking of kin is not an antidote to biocentric idealizations.

A particularly intriguing assessment of *Beasts* comes from Yaeger (2013) in her conceptualization of "dirty ecology." Yaeger begins her analysis by noting that *Beasts* serves as a synecdoche for America's history of environmental racism. However, after mentioning these racial politics, Yaeger moves on to other things. In doing so, Yaeger argues that *Beasts* "refuses the realism of social critique and advances instead into hubris land, into a new realm of myth making for the twenty-first century" (para. 3). For Yaeger, the kinds of critiques suggested in her opening lines, and which I detail next from Black feminists, are "eloquent" but "off the mark" (para. 9). For Yaeger, the mythic triumphs over the racial and political:

> *Beasts* is not a slice of life or a realist screed; its business is mythological: it proffers a sacred narrative with overtones of awe and cosmic investigation. Querying the social order, it offers strange pedagogies about how we should live in a melting world.
>
> (para. 9)

On the one hand, the "strange pedagogies" Hushpuppy learns are self-taught lessons of self-reliance and self-sufficiency. They are about how to survive on a broken earth and endure the everyday slow violence of climate change. The Bathtub's school teacher, Miss Bathsheba, instructs "Y'all better learn how to survive now" (9:32), and a big part of that message is a reconfigured relation to nonlife. I can get behind Yaeger's critique of a pristine, beautiful nature and call to care for brutalized landscapes. However, I cannot fully back *Beasts'* pedagogical implications in ways Yaeger celebrates. For example, at a rare "feed-up time" provided by Wink he tells Hushpuppy to "share with the dog" (2:50). For Yaeger, this dinner scene in *Beasts* contradicts the main message of the Anthropocene that tells humanity to "see themselves as a geologic force preying on the planet," and instead Wink teaches Hushpuppy "to know ourselves as a species dependent on other species" (para. 7). In that ephemeral moment of caretaking, I can see Yaeger's meaning, but I cannot forget another scene a few minutes later when after days of being left to fend for herself, Hushpuppy blows up her shack. The cause? Hushpuppy was heating herself a meal of tinned cat food to eat on her propane stove. So, while there may be much truth to another of Miss Bathsheba's teachings that "Meat. Meat. Every animal is made out of meat. I'm meat. Y'all asses meat" (8:30), I am uncomfortable with the juxtaposition of food scenes and even more so with Hushpuppy's repeated abandonment.

After the big storm, Hushpuppy and Wink float through a submerged Bathtub looking for signs of life. Most of the residents, although reluctant, left before the storm. There are only a few survivors now, human and nonhuman, and this number will lesson as the days go and the water cannot recede. As they float along in their derelict boat made from a truck bed and empty oil drums, Hushpuppy peers down at dead animals submerged beneath the water's surface: "They're all down below trying to breathe through the water. For animals that didn't have a Dad to put them in the boat, the end of the world already happened" (29:05). I think there is an argument that the end of the world is ongoing for Hushpuppy as well: her father is dying, her home is burnt, her community is drowning, her future seems determined. As the days go by more plants and animals die from the salinized waters, Wink also gets sicker, and the aurochs come closer. Yaeger interprets this differently than I do. She understands Hushpuppy as "an early avatar of who we need to become" in the Anthropocene (para. 18). In the slippage of the figural to the literal, I hope Hushpuppy's life is not the fate of children today. The question I hold onto is: "How does a little black girl child orphaned and abandoned become a vision for climate resistance for so many people who watched the film?" (Sharpe, 2013, para. 8).

The film's source material is a play called *Juicy and Delicious* which features a white ten-year-old boy as lead, and the setting is Georgia rather than the Louisiana bayou (Alibar, 2013). How does this revisioning of location and the presence of a Black girl-figure alter the optics of survivalism? Several Black feminists argue powerfully that making the protagonist a young, precocious Black girl "is not at all accidental" (Nyong'o, 2015, p. 262). Hushpuppy's blackness is necessary because "how else could … the violence of extreme poverty, flooding, the violence of a six-year-old girl child living alone in her own ramshackle house with no mother or father, be inspiring and not tragic?" (Sharpe, 2013, para. 7). Blackness naturalizes precarity in ways that displace history and deimagine futurity. Audiences do not ask how or why Hushpuppy got in this situation because her poverty fits into pre-established racial narratives. Christina Sharpe (2013) explains that "at least part of the disaster on view here is everyday Black life lived in the wake of slavery and neither this film nor many of its viewers actually account for that life as disastrous" (para. 6). bell hooks (2013) situates Hushpuppy as yet another representation of "abused and abandoned black children, whose bodies become the playing fields where pornographies of violence are hidden behind romantic evocations of mythic union and reunion with nature" (para. 21). The film is grounded in a "Western fantasy of the primitive" that encourages audiences to celebrate Hushpuppy as a "brave survivalist" battling not only the elements, her father, and her imagination, but a mainstream societal order that would dictate how she should live and behave (Brown, 2013, para. 4). To see Hushpuppy as a redeemer figure is to ignore the thousand things that should otherwise make us shudder. hooks argues, "it is truly a surreal imagination that can look past the traumatic abuse Hushpuppy endures and be mesmerized and entertained" (para. 19).

As a figure of Sheldon's (2016) Anthropocene-related slide in the image of the child, Hushpuppy is protector of the wild, which includes her father and The Bathtub residents. Additionally, as a figure of the Animist, Hushpuppy understands that everything and everywhere is connected. She has an uncanny ability to commune and communicate with animals. One particular scene stands out for me here. The Bathtub residents flee a state shelter that housed them after the flood and escape home in time to meet the arrival of the aurochs (see Figure 3). The adults recede from view and Hushpuppy comes to the front. Hushpuppy and the giant beasts come face-to-face and after sharing intense looks the aurochs bend a knee, lower their gaze, and leave the bayou. Hushpuppy says to the aurochs, "You're my friend, kind of" but "I've gotta take care of mine" (1:22:05).

In connecting with the beasts, Hushpuppy "claims responsibility for the devastation embodied by the aurochs and manifested in the land, and for her whole community's future" (Cecire, 2015, p. 166). Innocence is not available for the Black child (Bernstein, 2011); she is responsible for her community's survival. As figure of the Animist, Hushpuppy not only sees life in the most reduced circumstances but she's able to communicate with a range of multispecies existents. The film closes with Hushpuppy's narration: "I see that I am a little piece of a big, big universe, and that makes it right" (1:26:30).

Nyong'o (2015) finds problematic that the figure of a Black girl is "asked to perform the work of imagining the survival of a civilization that has abandoned

Figure 3 Kind-of Friends for the Anthropocene. Film still from *Beasts of the Southern Wild*, directed by Benh Zeitlin @ Fox Searchlight 2012. All rights reserved.

her" (p. 251). This points to the pitfalls in elevating Anthropocene Child as a figure of the protector. In my attempts to think-with Hushpuppy I keep returning to the questions: what is it to be this figure (Povinelli, 2013)? Why do theorists, and I am complicit here, locate a potential otherwise in those most precarious? Why is suffering assumed as resistance and the basis for a new way of being in the world? In a powerful essay titled, "In Defence of the Wastelands: A Survival Guide," nēhiyaw writer Erica Violet Lee (2016) begins contouring a pedagogical response that I am reaching out toward:

> To provide care in the wastelands is about gathering enough love to turn devastation into mourning and then, maybe, turn that mourning into hope.... Hope, then, is knowing there is more to living than surviving; believing that some worlds must exist for us beyond survival. Even when we must piece those worlds together from gathered scraps, slowly building incandescent ceremonies out of nothing but our bodies, our words, and time.... When we make a home in lands and bodies considered wastelands, we attest that these places are worthy of healing and that we are worthy of *life beyond survival*.
>
> (paras. 33–4; emphasis added)

It is not that The Bathtub or its residents are unworthy of care, but that there is no form of care made available that can match up to the classed, racial, and ecological damage. No matter how much Hushpuppy wants to protect her kin—animal, land, and human—she cannot face down the Anthropocene. In contrast, *The Marrow Thieves* provides a speculative imagining of care in the wastelands of post-apocalyptic Canada that gestures at *life beyond survival* within community—survival because of community.

Viral Contagion: Care for Collectives

Hushpuppy is a geonotological figure of the Animist and also a figure for whom the inheritance of environmental racism is extreme. The weight of the future will be too much for Hushpuppy in the long term, in part because she bears the heaviness alone, as was exemplified in her encounter with the aurochs. The final child-figure I think-with in this chapter is not an individual child but a group of Indigenous children from different Nations that come together to build a common world. With them, I shift from singular child-figures (even when in relation) and take a step toward refusing "the centrisms of the individual child and foreground the enmeshed and heterogeneous common worlds that children inherit and inhabit" (Taylor, 2013, p. 87). *The Marrow Thieves* is a multilayered, speculative, and decolonial story about "collaborative survival in precarious times" (Tsing, 2015, p. 2). Instead of the more expected attachment of Indigenous characters with the Animist, I associate this band of *survivants* with the figure of the Virus.[2] It is a speculative story told from within an ongoing apocalypse, where life and nonlife are in constant interplay. *The Marrow Thieves* is about how life and nonlife nourish each other: the Indigenous children's survival depends on what is typically characterized as nonlife—for example, Story and ancestors and land—and these existents depend on the children and elders carrying them along for their survival.

Povinelli (2016) explains that the defining difference between the Desert and the Virus is the former's passiveness and the latter's intentionality. In other words, the Desert awaits a technoscience fix from elsewhere while the Virus "is an active antagonistic agent" making moves (p. 19). Furthermore, the Virus is distinguished from the Animist because it muddies the oppositions of life/death and bios/geos rather than assuming everything is alive as a starting point. For Povinelli (2016), the Virus has as "its central imaginary … the Terrorist" (p. 19). The Virus is what the Desert and Animist become if radicalized (p. 19). Figures of the Virus for Povinelli include Ebola, nuclear power, zombies, and eco-activists who—depending on perspective—are often called terrorists (p. 19). In present-day Canada, this includes Indigenous land defenders and other anti-petroleum protestors who stand up against pipelines being installed through Indigenous territories. An example is the Wet'suwet'en peoples, particularly the Unist'ot'en clan, who for years have been preventing Costal GasLink from finishing their pipeline. If completed 2 billion cubic feet per day of fracked gas will pass through their traditional territories. Many land protectors have been arrested; their camps have been raided repeatedly; many have their social media illegally monitored—all of this by state police who are rarely referred to by such an incendiary term as terrorist. The Virus transgresses "the borderlands between activists and terrorists across state borders and interstate surveillance" (Povinelli, 2016, p. 19). The Virus is an *international* activist-terrorist, which takes on additional meanings in consideration of how Indigenous peoples navigate nation-to-nation relations among themselves and outside state enclosure and colonial borders. However, to be the Virus is to always be "under attack" (p. 19), which plays out speculatively in *The Marrow Thieves*.

Métis author Cherie Dimaline's (2017) *The Marrow Thieves* is a post-apocalyptic speculative story set in Canada in the year 2050. An environmental apocalypse has destroyed all that is taken for granted about modern life. Dimaline describes the situation as follows: "The earth was broken. Too much taking for too damn long, so she finally broke. But she went out like a wild horse, bucking off as much as she could before lying down" (p. 136). There were melting ice caps, tsunamis, tornados, earthquakes, and the pipelines "snapped like icicles and spewed bile over forests, into lakes, drowning whole reserves and towns" (p. 136). The population reduced by half and those remaining were on the move as "the shapes of countries were changed forever, whole coasts breaking off like crust" (p. 136). This speculative world is not wholly Desert but quickly becoming one. Apart from Indigenous peoples who have some sort of immunity, the settler population has lost the capacity to dream. Without dreams they are going mad—drugs can only haze away so much. The Canadian government—supported by Science and Church—believes that Indigenous bone marrow holds the cure to their dreamless nightmare. The exact pathogen causing the loss of dreams is unknown and unnamed, and, like

Melanie in the next chapter, those excluded from the category human hold the promise of a cure.

In an effort to acquire research subjects, the government first asked for Indigenous volunteers. Rightly suspicious of settler state politeness, the solicitation efforts failed to garner enough experimental subjects. So next "they turned to the prisons. The prisons were always full of [Indigenous] people" (p. 129). After running through the captive population, there still was no cure and the state needed more experimental bodies so "they turned to history" for advice on how best to keep Indigenous peoples "warehoused, how to best position the culling" (p. 129). History had the solution in the re-implementation of residential schools. As the schools rematerialized there were rumors about a technoscience breakthrough—an instrument had been invented that could extract dreams from Indigenous peoples' bones. The rationale behind the first rollout of residential schools was to "kill the Indian in the child," but this reincarnation had no such pretence.[3] To harvest the bone marrow was to literally kill the Indian *and* the child; Indigenous peoples were "little more than a crop" (p. 36). Settler history taught Indigenous peoples to be distrustful of state medicine and schools so those who were able took to the land and headed North. Their Indigenous history held the teachings necessary for survival. However, their escape was made more difficult by a new police force called Recruiters who were tasked with tracking and capturing them for dissection.

The main action kicks off when a young Métis teenager named Frenchie has to flee an urban center after Recruiters capture his brother, mother, and, assumingly, his father. Exhausted after days on the run, Frenchie passes out in the forest to be found by Miigwans, an adult member of a mismatched, thrown-together band of seven Indigenous children and an elder named Minerva. The child-figures include Anishinaabe, Métis, and nêhiyawak belongings and they range from seven to seventeen years old. Each character is introduced in a separate chapter through a "coming-to" Story. They have all experienced trauma, loss, abandonment, and pain, but suffering will not be the main story of their lives. They heal through regenerative relations of collective care and thus the coming-to signifies a new strength and resilience in community, even at the end of the world. Throughout the text are words in nêhiyawêwin, as Minerva is a fluent speaker who shares with the child-figures Story, song, ceremony, and teachings inherent in the language itself. For the children who do not know the language, like Frenchie, they desire it more than any other comfort of a lost world. Importantly though, while they long for language and "the old-timey," *The Marrow Thieves* does not dwell on some nostalgic idealization of a pristine past or romantic wilderness (p. 29). This crew is engaged in creating futurities. The child-figures learn to hunt and build camps. They listen to traditional stories, perform ceremony, strengthen plant and animal relations, and share their own histories and tragedies in ways that allow them to grow together. "We needed to remember Story," shares Frenchie (p. 142). The heart of this speculative story is caretaking and kin-making.

The common world the child-figures and their teachers create in the woods is not one of heteronormative family, patriarchal leadership, or generational segregation. Everyone is cared for. Physically, Minerva slows them down and often has to be carried, but she is a highly valued member of the group. Although her body is failing, Minerva's spirit is strong, and the children never abandon her. The same goes for the youngest group member, RiRi, whose size prevents her from making the same contributions as the teenagers. Yet she is not disposable. The lesson, "No one is more important than anyone else" (p. 58), which applies to the Indigenous characters as much as the more-than-humans they encounter on their journey. Cherokee scholar Daniel Heath Justice (2018) writes in *Why Indigenous Literatures Matter* (2018) about the importance of being in good relation:

> *Relationship* is the driving impetus behind the vast majority of texts by Indigenous writers—relationship to the land, to human community, to self, to the other-than-human world, to the ancestors and our descendants, to our histories and our futures, as well as to colonizers and their literal and ideological heirs—and that these literary works offer us insight and sometimes helpful pathways for maintaining, rebuilding, or even simply establishing these meaningful connections.
>
> (p. xix)

The end of the story brings about a direct clash with settler Recruiters and Minerva sacrifices herself so the others can escape. But instead of running away they regroup and plan a rescue. The attempt does not go according to plan and Minerva is shot by police. At this point, we learn that when the scientists tried to harvest her dreams, she set the residential school on fire with her nêhiyawêwin songs. Over the course of the text, the child-figures come to recognize and respect the power of their language. Language is a Virus in that it ignores the division of life and nonlife "for the purpose of diverting its energies in order to extend itself" into the surrounds and save (Povinelli, 2016, p. 173). Language is also immunity rather than pathogen; it is what protects the Indigenous peoples from losing the ability to dream. The child-figures also learn what outlives bionormative bodies—a sense of geontological existence that cannot be killed—Minerva's ongoingness is language and Story and ceremony and kin and land. Dreams are in all these relations and not like the settlers assume a bio-substance in bones. The anguish of Minerva's death is tempered by the joy of an unexpected reunion. Miigwans reunites with his partner Isaac, who has escaped capture, and who is also a fluent speaker. Although Isaac does not yet have the worldly experience of an Elder like Minerva that is fine because "the key doesn't have to be old, the language already is" (p. 227).

The child-figures in *The Marrow Thieves* do not walk alone. Nor is any single individual made responsible for the ruined earth or for saving it. Like the Virus, they are under assault because their bone marrow may be a bio-fix but also because their worlds are not organized by life and nonlife divisions. They are also terrorists in the sense that they resist and refuse settler futurities. *The Marrow Thieves* is clear that climate change and settler colonialism go hand-in-hand and that to regenerate worlds requires renewed relations with land, more-than-human kin, and each other. Language—and everything entangled with and embedded within it—was their immunity and their future. *The Marrow Thieves* encourages me to consider how the end of the world can mean otherwise: it can be the end of apocalypse, the end of settler colonialism, the end of anti-Black racism, the end of extractivism, and the flourishing of Anthropocene Child in common worlds. These otherwise possibilities are provocations for the chapters that follow. I think that speculative fiction and speculative figures, particularly *The Marrow Thieves* and its Indigenous youth, offer a glimpse of what otherwise might feel, look, and be like.

3

Infecting Whiteness

Child-Monsters at the End of the World

There is no shortage of critical and popular work that upholds the figure of the child as the epitome of futurity. This futurity depends on a particular formation of life that is defined by a "metabolic imaginary" (Povinelli, 2016), which is recognizable by biological processes of birth, growth, development, and reproduction.[1] This imaginary is perhaps most fully encapsulated in the biocentric image of the child in all its potentiality (Arendt, 1958; Castañeda, 2002). The provocation I want to delve into is if foregrounding geos-childhoods can put under pressure "our present culture's purely biological definition of what it is to *be*, and therefore of what it is *like* to be, human" (Wynter, 2000, p. 180). This definition has long disciplined humans and inhumans via racialized hierarchies of life. Life, in this sense, takes meaning from what it is not—life is that which is not nonlife—life is sentient, energetic, and active. It is also what is under threat in the climate crisis, or, at least, what is behind much ecoanxiety: extinction is nonlife forever. This chapter (re)tells a geostory about Melanie from the speculative novel and film titled *The Girl with All the Gifts* (hereafter *Gifts*) (Carey, 2014; McCarthy & Carey, 2016). Melanie is a zombie-child called a "hungry," who, unlike the prototypical zombie, is conscious, caring, and agentic. However, Melanie and her kin-kind are also imprisoned and experimented upon because their bodies might hold a cure for a global pandemic. Melanie is "human—*but not only*" (de la Cadena, 2014, p. 256): she is child, she is pathogen, she is racialized, she is monster—she blurs any easy cuts between life and nonlife.

I structure this chapter by way of several overlapping deliberations. First, Melanie brings into question what constitutes the properly human subject. Melanie problematizes racialized allocations of humanness through her visual embodiment of both blackness and monstrosity. Second, I explore how the end of the world for Melanie is the end of the racialized and militarized systems of oppression that did her violence. Melanie invites me to consider a series of questions about the end of the world, including: for whom might the end of the world not be a cause for mourning (Wilderson, 2015)? What if the end of the world is a renunciation of anti-blackness and "settler futurity" (Tuck & Yang, 2012)? What possibilities emerge when refusal and resistance are the child-figure's response to saving the world? Third, as a figure of both child and virus, Melanie troubles divisions of life/nonlife, immunity/exceptionality, and innocence/responsibility that govern the present and are put under increasing pressure in the Anthropocene. Melanie and the pathogen exist in a symbiotic relationship wherein each needs the other to thrive. Lastly, drawing on the work of Sylvia Wynter (2000), Melanie and the child-hungries provide a new origin story for a hybrid, "counterhumanism" of Anthropocene Child.

Fungal Pathogens: Infecting Whiteness

For the most part *Gifts* plots along like any other post-apocalyptic zombie film, that is, until the very end. The setting is a world much like this one, London specifically, in the near future. A mysterious fungus has infected nearly everyone on earth turning them into mindless, flesh-eating zombies. The few remaining humans—mostly female scientists and military men—have gathered on an armored base where the scientists among them search for a cure. Everyone who comes into direct contact with the pathogen becomes infected, except for a mysterious group of children who were born to infected mothers. Melanie and these other "second gen" hungries have retained the ability to think, feel, and care. They attend school and are learning to read and write imaginative stories. However, they are also locked in cells at night and have their heads, arms, and legs strapped to wheelchairs when outside solitary confinement. If these child-hungries smell or touch humans they transform into ravenous, instinctual zombies just like the others. Nevertheless, why

I argue this story matters is that one particular child-hungry sets off the end of the world. Before this happens though the number of child-hungries on the base gets fewer and fewer. Their biology—their bodies—holds the possibility of a vaccine. The research process entails dissecting the child-bodies in ways in which they cannot survive. The day Melanie is taken for dismembering, a large horde of hungries attack the base allowing her to break free from the operating table. Dr. Caroline Caldwell, Miss Helen Justineau, Sergeant Parks, and a handful of soldiers manage to escape with Melanie in tow.

The debate about whether or not the child-hungries are human or monster continues throughout the duration of both the novel and film. Never is it considered that there are possibilities of existence outside these dualistic oppositions. Perhaps debate might be too strong a descriptor as everyone but Justineau conceives of the child-hungries as inhuman monsters. If there is any lingering doubt about the child-hungries' species-status it is primarily because they outwardly resemble any other ten-year-old child. In spite of their appearance, however, the Sergeant is keen to remind his colleagues that "not everyone who looks human is human" (Carey, 2014, p. 29). The publicity posters and preview clips for the movie feature Melanie wearing a full-faced, clear muzzle type of mask, which the survivors insist she wear for their protection once they flee the invaded base. This mask serves as a persistent reminder of her monstrosity (see Figure 4). Not only is it the sort of guard that

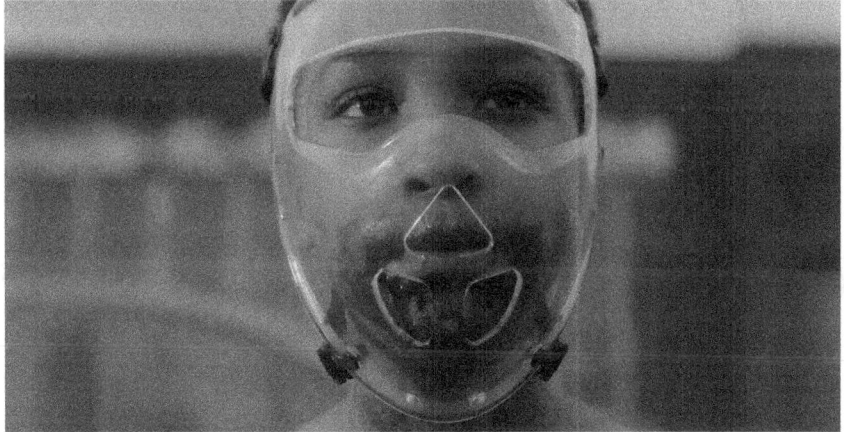

Figure 4 Masking Monstrosity—Making Killable. Film still from *The Girl with All the Gifts* directed by Colm McCarthy @ BFI Film Fund 2016. All rights reserved.

I imagine is used to constrain animals, but its transparency allows Melanie's blackness to remain visible. With it, Melanie's "form remains identifiably human, but recognizably monstrous" which is a tactic of "making-killable" in contemporary culture (Gergen et al., 2018, p. 11; see also Haraway, 2008).

Caldwell, on the other hand, takes a hard-line approach to making-killable but disguises it behind the neutrality of science. Caldwell's view is that "the moment of death"—meaning a geos-zombification in this context and not a biological-metabolic death—"is the moment when the pathogen crosses the blood–brain barrier. What's left, though its heart may beat, and though it speaks ... it is not the host" (Carey, 2014, p. 63). The species battle line is thus drawn between human and fungus, despite their coexistence in the child-hungries. The second gen hungries have formed a symbiotic relationship with the pathogen—the fungus and the child collaborate to survive and are inseparable from one another. Melanie and the fungus have found ways to work together, not always in equal or nonviolent ways, but not always in conflictual ones either. Child and fungus are a practice of "becoming with" (Haraway, 2008) that designates the child-hungries as a figure of Anthropocene Child.

The child-hungries most dedicated defender and favorite teacher is Justineau, a military-trained psychologist who both reads the students stories and keeps anecdotal records of their behaviors. Justineau and Caldwell constantly battle about the humanity of the child-hungries. Justineau shames Caldwell for dissecting the children without anesthetic. Caldwell's response is that "they don't respond to anaesthetic....Which in itself ought to tell you that the subjects' ontological status is to some extent in doubt" (Carey, 2014, p. 80). While Justineau purposefully refers to the child-hungries as children rather than monsters, what counts as human for Caldwell is an ability to feel pain. Sentience, as a marker of the human, has a long anti-Black history that merges the speculative world of hungries with this world. Its specificity traces back to the denial of sentience to create the slave as property (Wilderson, 2010). In brief, the dominant narrative was that enslaved Black persons did not feel pain—therefore they could be worked to the bone, beaten, and assaulted—but after the abolition of slavery these racist tropes needed a new place to land. In *Racial Innocence,* Robin Bernstein (2011) reveals how the "libel of insensateness" was regrafted onto "children's culture" after abolition in the form of the unequal allocation of childhood innocence (p. 51). In this refiguration, whiteness equals innocence and blackness equates insensateness. Childhood becomes "a cover under which otherwise discredited racial ideology survives and continues, covertly, to influence culture" (p. 51).[2]

At stake in a perceived ability to feel pain is "inclusion in the category of the child and, ultimately, the human" (p. 36). The last conversation Melanie has with Caldwell is telling in this regard. Melanie asks, "We're alive?" and Caldwell responds, "Yes. You're alive" (McCarthy & Carey, 2016, 1:36:05). Even the admission of aliveness from Caldwell does not mean that she thinks the child-hungries should be exempt from the scientific experiments that end their lives. One can be alive—can be a form of life—without being human, which is why sentience is important to keep in mind. In *Gifts*, the child-hungries bio-exceptionalism makes them capable of living-with the pathogen but it does not translate into a worthiness for life. In this case, their exceptionality means that they are too far removed from the bionormative human, which, as mentioned earlier, makes them killable.

In the transition from page to screen a few characters in *Gifts* racebend, meaning the characters' race changes as the medium does. Included are the two main characters of Melanie and Justineau. Their race is reversed in the film: Melanie (played by Sennia Nanua) is Black and Justineau (Gemma Arterton) is white. The concept of racebending was popularized as a term of protest against the casting of white characters in the live-action film adaptation of *Avatar: The Last Airbender,* although it is a longstanding Hollywood practice (Racebending.com, 2011). Nowadays it mostly involves casting decisions that have a discriminatory effect on a minority group or unrepresented community. I write *mostly* because, at least in the case of Melanie, the change makes *Gifts* something more than a traditional zombie story. As a small point of personal sharing, I do not actually like zombie movies—the blood, gore, and violence are not something I count among my preferred leisurely or scholarly activities. Without this casting change I doubt I would have given *Gifts* a second thought and I certainly would not be writing about it here. Novel and screenplay writer Carey has said in interviews that the casting choices were race-neutral, meaning that the parts went to the best actors for the job (Weisberger, 2017). But his apparent color-blindness has unintended consequences.

Carey insists that race is not consequential to the book so it should not matter in the movie either. I disagree. In the first chapter of the novel are multiple racialized descriptions of the two protagonists. On the first page, we are told, "Her name is Melanie. It means 'the black girl,' from an ancient Greek word, but her skin is actually very fair so she thinks maybe it's not such a good name for her" (Carey, 2014, p. 9). Melanie prefers the name Pandora, an important point I will revisit in a later section. On the second page, we get a further description of Melanie as "ten years old, and she has skin like a princess in a fairy tale; skin as white as snow. So she knows that when she grows up she'll be beautiful" (p. 10). This phrase is so loaded with racialized tropes that I think matter a great deal. I sincerely doubt the child-hungries are afforded the movie-going privileges of Disney consumption on the military base, yet white-princess-power still somehow becomes a point of self and societal worth in a zombie story. A few pages later is a description of Justineau from Melanie's point of view:

> Miss Justineau's face stands out anyway because it's such a wonderful, wonderful colour. It's dark brown, like the wood of the trees in Melanie's rainforest picture whose seeds only grow out of the ashes of a bushfire, or like the coffee that Miss Justineau pours out of her flask into her cup at break time. Except it's darker and richer than either of those things, with lots of other colours mixed in, so there isn't anything you can really compare it to. All you can say is that it's as dark as Melanie's skin is light.
>
> (p. 23)

This description is how Carey alerts the reader to Justineau's blackness without ever having to write out any racially explicit terms. While it is a welcome reprieve from many productions in that the novel equates blackness with beauty, nevertheless, the up-front textual position of these racialized descriptions—whether positive or negative—conveys to me at least some significance. My stance is that race and racebending are pivotal to the story's overall impact and to the significance of refiguring geos-futurities in the film.

After the military base is attacked, the humans who escape must rely on Melanie to guide them undetected through the hordes of hungries in the city center. While out collecting food for her captors, Melanie makes two important discoveries. The first is that fungal seed pods that house the pathogen have grown to cover one of London's highest and most phallic shaped buildings. The second discovery is a group of feral child-hungries much like her, only they have not yet learned to speak. Returning to the temporary shelter Melanie learns from Caldwell that if the seed pods were to open then the pathogen would become airborne and infect all remaining humans. After some careful thought Melanie decides that she does not need or want to die to save a few remaining humans who have treated her as inhuman-instrumental other. To cite a particularly powerful moment, Melanie says to Caldwell: "Why should it be us who die for you?" (McCarthy & Carey, 2016, 1:36:10). Next Melanie leaves the lab and sets ablaze the fungal tower of spores. The fire opens the seed pods thus effectively ending the world, or, more carefully stated, ending *a* world. As the pods burn, Melanie has one last conversation with the Sergeant who had been injured nearby. The Sergeant wails, "It's over. It's all over." Melanie responds, "It's not over. It's just not yours anymore" (McCarthy & Carey, 2016, 1:41:05).

The End of the (White) World

Melanie chooses to destroy the world instead of scarifying herself to it. In doing so, she brings possibilities for a new world into existence. This also brings into alignment, even if momentarily, the world of speculative fiction and anti-blackness in this world. Hari Ziyad (2017b) shares their surprise and delight at the ending:

> Because I am so used to humanity being granted a sanctity it does not deserve, I fully expected Melanie ... to sacrifice herself for her human captors .... When juxtaposed with the argument put forth by some Afro-pessimists that humanity is reliant upon the subjection and enslavement of Black people, Melanie's refusal of humanity is in clear contrast to what we are taught about Black people's possibilities. We, the living dead in America (for what else but death is a life that doesn't #matter?) are told that we can only try (and always fail) to become more human or sacrifice ourselves and our communities for the continuation of human society.
>
> (para. 9)

Instead of a limited form of inclusion in a white-supremacist-militaristic-human-biocentric society, Melanie sets in motion a more "liveable world" by "fac[ing] up to the outrage of human exceptionalism" and delivering a deadly blow (Haraway, 2008, p. 106). The liveable world for the child-hungries has to be the end of the human-exceptional world, otherwise they will remain hunted specimens for a potential human cure. If the humans were to find an antidote, all indications suggest that the child-hungries would be eliminated once and for all. They would be of no more use to humans. The co-existence of humans and hungries is never entertained as a viable option.

In most speculative stories, monsters await defeat by humans—the relationship is simplified as a battle between bad versus good. We know who is supposed to win. Monsters are analogous to those who embody difference in this world. Often, the monster figures are explicitly racialized. This is a preemptive strategy to rationalize the violence they will face. It is what is expected, "for it mirrors the spectacle of symbolic violence against the Dark Other in our own world" (Thomas, 2018, p. 1). However, "when people read fantastic texts from the perspective of the monster … they find themselves in completely different terrain" (p. 3). "*Gifts* dares to imagine a happy ending for its monsters, and that is simply amazing," journalist Sherronda Brown (2017) excites (para. 6). A story in which whiteness "becomes dismantled through the intentional action of a Black child enhances the theme of decolonization that is already present in the zombie narrative" given its African and Haitian origins (para. 6).[3] Melanie is a figure of the terrorist from the point of view of human exceptionalism and whiteness: she is "the face of decolonization from the perspective of the interests and entities that decolonization threatens" (Kawash, 1999, p. 238).[4] For the likes of Caldwell, the Sergeant, and the institutions they represent (i.e., Science and Military), Melanie is a threat but also a potential savior—the complexities abound. Tiffany Lethabo King (2019) writes about "grammars of suffering" that violently and perpetually unmake Black and Indigenous lives in the making and sustaining of the human. Melanie is able to refuse this grammar and flip it—suffering is not her end story. *Gifts* ends up potentiating a world that does not require Black death in order to exist. And this fact snaps apart the overlap of speculative and real worlds that I just mentioned.

Gifts puts in motion an end of the world as an end to "humanity as whiteness," as Ziyad (2017a) phrases it (p. 143), meaning that the end of the world for Melanie is the end of the systems of oppression that did her violence and that elevated the bionormative child and biocentric human (Wynter, 2003) above all other forms of existence. The end of the world is not the end of all life in

Gifts—the figure of Povinelli's (2016) Desert is not the child-hungries future. Instead, there is a possibility of regenerative reworlding. At the end of *Gifts*, wide-panned camera shots of a hungry-filled London cityscape show greenery already taking back space in abandoned concrete structures. These images also happen to be actual drone footage of the ghost town of Pripyat in Ukraine near Chernobyl—a literalization of the regeneration possible after disaster and after humans have gone (IMDb, 2016). This is the "possibility of life" and nonlife ongoing together "in capitalist ruins" (Tsing, 2015).

Blackness has long overlapped with ideas of monstrosity; however, recently, "the figure of the monster has been reclaimed by Black subjects" (Bey, 2016, p. 51). In this vein, Joy James (2013) offers the Black rebel cyborg as an inhuman figure who, drawing on Frantz Fanon, "sets out to change the order of the world" (p. 65). To be a Black rebel cyborg means no longer seeking inclusion in the white supremacist state. The Black rebel cyborg "relinquishes the unachievable goal: striving for a socially recognized humanity" (Vargas & James, 2013, p. 200). This was one of the lessons Melanie learns. For much of the film, she longs to be accepted by her captors—to be counted as human just like them. But in ultimately refusing to sacrifice herself and her child-hungry-kin, Melanie comes to understand the human as a figure of "Settler/Master(Human)" that is never going to be otherwise (Wilderson, 2010). More than just a refusal of whiteness, however, Melanie comes to "refuse blackness-as-victimization and reconstitute blackness-as-resistance" (James, 2013, p. 68). This adds a layer to Sheldon's (2016) proposal about the slide of the child-figure from protected to protector in the Anthropocene. Rather than saving the world, Melanie generates another option: she refuses, she resists, and she destroys. She opens up an otherwise that privileges multispecies becomings.

I am not promoting *Gifts* as some sort of manual for revolution. I share it as a thought-experiment. For me, the take-away from *Gifts* is not about there being no humans in this world, but it is about the structures and institutions of systematic oppression that keep whiteness at the top by way of rendering others inhuman, less-than-human, nonhuman, or any other arrangement that maintains whiteness as the supremacist referent. Another articulation I am leaning on to make this argument comes from the Combahee River Collective (2002) and their classic "A Black Feminist Statement," which reads in small part: "If Black women were free, it would mean that everyone else would have to be free since our freedom would necessitate the destruction of all the systems of oppression" (p. 215). I think about this in line with the vision proposed by the Black Lives Matter Global Network: "We fight for our collective liberation because we are clear that until Black people are free, no one is free" (BLM, 2016, para. 11). This points to how flourishing is a collective undertaking. Melanie rearranges the world in ways in which Wynter's (2003) Man is no longer omnipotent: she is free and so are her fellow child-hungries. In ending a world not only does Melanie achieve freedom from incarceration and experimentation but so to do her kin-kind (and some other more-than-humans too). The overhead shots of rewilding that close out *Gifts* begin with a close up of the child-hungries. Melanie has returned to the military base to free the child-hungries from their cells and we see them sitting together among the feral child-hungries. They are a multiaged, multiracial, multispecies squad.

Community through Contagion

While Melanie may appear to commit a solitary act when she sets the seed pod tower ablaze, her each movement and thought depends on a synergetic relation with the pathogen. The Melanie-pathogen relation helps me appreciate "that no one stands or acts alone, that all human lives are inextricably enmeshed with others (human and more-than-human) and that all human actions are implicated with and have implication for others (including nonhuman others)" (Taylor, 2013, p. 117). The fire and its releasing of the pathogen will end the world for humans but for other species it will be regenerative. These differential reverberations are especially pertinent today considering the coronavirus, including how marginalized communities have been further disadvantaged and disproportionally infected/affected. Covid-19 makes clear that humans are not the only actors on the stage and that survival is difficult, necessary, and never enough (Shotwell, 2020). In this section, I want to linger with the enmeshment of human and virus. All humans are part virus—it has always been in our DNA (Tsing, 2015, p. 143). Humans are full of microbes—they outnumber human cells by a rate of ten-to-one (NIH, 2012). "Everyone carries a history of contamination," Tsing insists, "purity is not an option" (p. 27). The contributions bacteria make is crucial for human survival, we could not live (e.g., digest our food) without them. The virus is entangled with other species; it needs others to endure. So do we.

As introduced in the last chapter, Povinelli (2016) theorizes the Virus as a key figure of geontology that disrupts and confuses the antagonism of life versus nonlife amplified by the Anthropocene. For Povinelli, the virus is not definable by either term because each uses the other to extend themselves. The preeminent pop culture formation of the virus is the zombie, which Povinelli summaries as "Life turned to Nonlife and transformed into a new kind of species war—the aggressive rotting undead against the last redoubt of Life" (p. 16).[5] To this *Gifts* adds a complex layer as Melanie is not in a state of either existential or corporeal decomposition, but re-enlivened through an imaginary akin to what Ashleigh Wade (2017) theorizes as "viral blackness." Wade (2017) proposes a "theory of world making through viral blackness" that challenges associations of the virus solely with the spread of harmful pathogens (p. 34). Instead, Wade figures virality as the transmission of generative compositions like #BlackLivesMatter. In today's anti-Black and settler colonial world, Wade points out, "containment is extremely important for maintaining control, but the viral cannot be contained" (p. 35). Neither could the pathogen in *Gifts*. It moves, it spreads, and it mutates. Andrew Baldwin (2016) argues that "the guarantee of white supremacy lies in its capacity to contain the excess" (p. 84), and, since viral blackness is always in movement, it is in excess of repossession, and a future for whiteness becomes uncertain. Despite scientific and militaristic efforts in *Gifts*, neither the child-hungries or the pathogen could be fully controlled. Yet to be the virus, Povinelli (2016) insists, and as we saw with *The Marrow Thieves* in the last chapter, is to always be "under attack" (p. 19).

For me, the pathogen in *Gifts* is especially intriguing as a figure of contagion because it interrupts the cycle of virality as something inherently malicious and oppressive. Melanie and the pathogen need each other in a relational equation not set on conquest. Additionally, Wade importantly moves the figure of the virus from individualized bodies to collective ones. With the protests that followed Michael Brown's murder in Ferguson as her case study, Wade traces how viral blackness moved from online spaces to the streets and back and forth again and again. Viral blackness configures community in ways supportive of the viral as a "deterritorializing mode of subversion to white supremacist systems" (p. 36). I read this into Pricilla Wald's (2008) work on contagion that reframes the virus as "not inherently about killing but rather about changing" (p. 139). This perspective understands the virus as an embodiment and enactment of worldmaking.

The main focus of Wald's (2008) work on contagion is unpacking the taken-for-granted literariness of the "outbreak narrative," which includes attention to its rhetorical devices and storytelling strategies in both scientific press, news articles, and blockbuster films. Wald notes a dominant pattern whereby "conventions of horror and myth" reduce the complexities of pathogenic emergence to "an apocalyptic battle between heroic scientists and the hybrids who embody the threat" (p. 257). The outbreak narrative follows a predictable pattern which includes identifying the virus, naming the disease, outing its carriers, tracing its travel routes, developing prophylactics, and curing the disease and dis-ease. What starts as a horror story of human versus pathogen ends as a "timeless and ritualized story of renewal in which Humanity is reaffirmed as it is redeemed by Science" (p. 260). Not all pandemics fit this narrative structure, however, especially those that do not have a cure and/or cannot be easily contained. In these cases, for example, Covid-19, SARS, and HIV/AIDS, responsibility gets recirculated from "science to society" (p. 255).[6]

As documented earlier, *Gifts* has the lab, scientists, and hybridity of the outbreak narrative but also challenges many of the conventions outlined by Wald, especially the triumphalism of science. Nevertheless, it is from science that part of *Gifts*' horror emerges. The scientific story of the *Ophiocordyceps unilateralis* fungus provides a realistic, scientific frame from which the speculative story in *Gifts* grounds itself. Known colloquially as the zombie-ant fungus, *Ophiocordyceps unilateralis* takes over the central nervous system of bullet ants in tropical rainforests causing the ants to leave their colony, bite down in a "death grip" on a leaf which induces paralysis, and then sprout fungal stem-like spores from their exoskeleton (Hill 2013). This description mirrors the immobilization of expired hungries on the London streets; blooms exude from decomposing bodies as life and nonlife combine. In *Gifts,* this real-life fungus has found a way to jump the species-barrier, which makes it new yet still familiar (recall the making killable discussion). Melanie and her hungry-friends have similarly broken the species line: both fungus and child have mutated—are mutants. While the child-hungries are pathologized, they are also protected because they are necessary for a cure. Given my film-spectatorship training, I assumed that science would triumph, and humanity would defeat the zombie threat. I fully expected a cure. Wald cites this form of anticipatory confidence as a means of "sanction[ing] the status quo" so that "social existence" does not have to be significantly rearranged (p. 268). Both the Anthropocene discussion and the outbreak narrative pull on "the promise and authority of science in the heroic service of a threatened Humanity" (p. 257). This is where *Gifts* makes another impact: the status quo *is* challenged, science fails to provide a solution, humanity does not survive, and a serious refiguration of global existence is set in motion.

In making apparent the narrative organization of pandemic performances, Wald highlights shared links between communicable, communication, and community, which could be used to "evoke a profound sense of social inter-connection" (p. 12). Neither disease, sickness, nor infection were the original associations of the term contagion. Wald points out that contagion literally means "to touch together" and it first "referred to the circulation of ideas and attitudes," for example, "revolutionary ideas were contagious" (p. 12). This connects again with Wade's (2017) theorizing of viral blackness that moves between virtual spaces and physical places in the constitution of resistant communities. There is a disruptive and transgressive potential inherent to pathogens: the virus needs others to endure. Contagion has similar qualities: transformative, fluid, hard to control, and disrespectful of boundaries. With contagion, human individualism and exceptionalism are again challenged. Tsing (2015) expresses how we are undoubtably "contaminated by our encounters; they change who we are as we make way for others. As contamination changes world-making projects, mutual worlds—and new directions—may emerge" (p. 27). What might be possible if we grab onto the notion of "contamination as collaboration" in ways that re-make community and care for those humans and nonhumans most vulnerable (Tsing, 2015, p. 27). What tentative "alliances in the Anthropocene" might allow for "collaborative survival in precarious times" (Tsing, 2015, p. 2)? How can these relationships be cultivated in ways that respect difference, diversity, and incommensurably?

Otherwise Origin Stories

While the repetitive structure of the outbreak narrative can help us anticipate the way pandemics unfurl in this world, Wynter's attention to stories demonstrates the power of narrative in the overall making of worlds. Wynter understands origin stories as narrating a specific genre of being human into reproductive circulation. These stories are not the truth of the human but the "truth-for" a specific version of the human—not humanity in toto but "partial humanisms" defined by a "descriptive statement" (Wynter, 2015, p. 196). Origin stories provide a narrative framework through which humans are initiated into worlds and then repeatedly make sense of themselves within these worlds. What this also means, for example, is that the figure of biocentric Man has inclusions and exclusions already built into the script; however, the story is not determined once and for all. It is possible to "give humanness a different future" (Wynter & McKittrick, 2015, p. 9), and to write new genres and new worlds into being. This is why it is important for Wynter and her followers to speak of genres of "being human as praxis" and "as performative enactment," rather than take Man as the human as given and timeless (p. 31).

Cathy Peppers (1995) reads Octavia Butler's *Xenogenesis* trilogy (also known as *Lilith's Brood*) through Haraway and Foucault to reassert a value for origin stories outside hegemonic narrative patterns. Butler's trilogy stories the "genesis of an alien humanity" wherein the complications and complicities of a new beginning for humans and more-than-humans are considered (p. 47). The first book, *Dawn*, begins after an earthly apocalypse brought on by nuclear war and a few remaining humans are "rescued" by an alien species of Oankali. The human subjects are put to sleep for years and unconsciously prodded, tested, sampled, and studied before being awoken to the "choice" of reproducing with the Oankali or being made sterile. *Xenogenesis* is a therefore an origin story but not one in which humanity as it has been survives. It "is a story with difference ... reproduction with a difference, the (re)production of difference" (p. 47). This is not an innocent story either. Humans and aliens do not escape legacies of forced consent and miscegenation. Peppers' argument for revaluing origin stories like *Xenogenesis* proceeds with a close reading of Haraway:

> While Haraway claims in "A Cyborg Manifesto" that "the cyborg has no origin story in the Western sense," it is important to note that she does not

say that cyborgs have no origin stories. She makes a distinction between traditional Western origin stories, which are based on "salvation history," and are "about the Fall" ... and cyborg origin stories, which "subvert the central myths of origin of Western culture" by focusing on "the power to survive, not on the basis of original innocence, but on the basis of seizing the tools to mark the world that has marked them as other."

(p. 47)

With support from Haraway, Peppers calls to account the "anti-essentialist, anti-origins attitude taken up by mainstream" critical theorists who fail to recognize that those "whose stories have been written out of the dominant accounts have different stakes in the desire to re-write origin stories" (p. 48). It is only possible to disavow origin stories when you have them; it is only safe to reject foundations when you are already on solid footing. This why otherwise origin stories matter. What are the origin stories of the child-hungries?

Before the drama of the military base escape, viewers are offered a series of stories within the bigger story of a zombie apocalypse. The first is the myth of Pandora's Box that is read to the hungry-children by Justineau, the second is a creative story shared by Melanie as part of a classroom exercise, and the third is a version of Schrödinger's cat in a box—one of a series of thought experiments that Caldwell shares with Melanie in order to test her reasoning abilities. I want to dwell with these stories through concepts offered by Wynter (2000, 2003, 2005), including origin stories, hybrid beings, and *homo narrans*. While on a superficial level "boxes" thread these stories together, what also knots them is a potential entrapment within a hegemonic form of humanism that instead of proving inevitable are possible to rewrite, renarrate, and live otherwise.

Viewers first encounter the child-hungries all together in a classroom. They are arranged in rows and strapped down in their chairs. The lesson we drop in on has the children reciting the periodic table back to their teacher. Thankfully, this rote learning does not last long. Soon Justineau enters, having finished her regression analysis, and takes her place as head teacher. The children are pleased and immediately request a story. Justineau warns she might get in trouble for veering off the curriculum so the children suggest that Greek myths count as history and therefore story is permissible. Justineau picks up a book and reads them the story of Pandora. The film cuts between Justineau reading in the classroom and the recitation of the story as background soundtrack to Melanie wishing a pleasant evening to her armed captors as they lock her in her cell for the night. The guards respond to her polite gesture by calling her "Cujo" and "it," and, in other moments, a "friggin' abortion."

As for the story Justineau reads, we hear that Pandora's creation is tied up with Zeus's wish for revenge, Hephaetus's obedience, and Epimetheus' weakness. But neither the child-hungries nor I am particularly interested in those figures—we want to hear about Pandora. Given my interests here, I cannot help but linger with how Pandora is made of clay—composed of the earth itself—a geontological figure from a different time and place. Pandora is ordered made by Man, remade by Athena and Aphrodite as desirable according to the male gaze, and then given a box as she is sent off to live among men. She is warned that the box (or jar, depending on the translation) can never be opened or severe consequences for humanity will result. Pandora eventually opens the box "whereupon every plague and tribulation, every misfortune and evil thing in the world came pouring out, and they have afflicted mankind ever since" (McCarthy & Carey, 2016, 05:28). Pandora realizes what is happening before the box empties and closes the lid with one thing left inside: hope. The myth is meant as cautionary tale. Like Eve in a related origin story, qualities inherent to women (e.g., curiosity, disobedience, lack of impulse control—characteristics also often attributed to the child) cause all the trouble. The idiom "don't open Pandora's box" warns against starting something new and unknown as there might be unwanted consequences.

In most versions of the myth, hope remains inside the box. Pandora is therefore accused of making another mistake by trapping what is good inside: she condemns humanity to suffering forever. In Justineau's telling, Pandora "lifted [hope] in her hands and set it free. Hope is the good thing that makes you able to stand all the bad things" (06:30). For most of the film, the child-hungries embody hope for the human exceptional world: they are a potential cure, and for that they endure dehumanizing treatment. But instead of hope for inclusion in the world as is, Melanie makes a new world possible with her fiery act of refusal. Hope can be a form of cruel optimism wherein we are complicit in desiring something that "is actually an obstacle to our flourishing" (Berlant, 2011, p. 1), an idea I revisit in the book's conclusion, but, for now, it is important to note that hope can be otherwise—hope is a gift to the child-hungries from a fellow geontological friend named Pandora. In the novel, Justineau tells the child-hungries that Pandora "was a really amazing woman. All the gods had blessed her and given her gifts. That's what her name means—'the girl with all the gifts.' So she was clever, and brave, and beautiful, and funny, and everything else you'd want to be" (Carey, 2014, p. 27). Melanie thinks similarly: she voices concern about the unethical blame placed on Pandora, wishes that Pandora was her name, and is curious about the secrets being hidden from the child-hungries, including the story of their origins.

A day or two passes and viewers are taken again to the classroom to hear the second story I want to highlight which is written by Melanie. At this point, we still are not sure why these children are restrained and there is not much in the history of zombie films that prepares us for what we will see next. Child zombies are rare. If present at all, they take the form of "changelings ... monsters who have been swapped in for child; even though they may look like children, talk like children, and act like children, they really aren't children at all and therefore don't deserve to be treated like children" (Renner, 2016, p. 12). This is how the soldiers and scientists treat the child-hungries, but I am far from convinced that the child-hungries can or should be expelled from the category child altogether. As we enter the classroom, we watch the students struggle to translate their imagination onto paper. The camera zooms in on a few of their hands holding pencils—we see different pincer grips, different levels of handedness, different stages of motor control. After a period of quiet composition, Justineau asks for volunteers to read aloud their stories. Melanie's hand shoots up. She begins:

> Once upon a time, in ancient Greece, there was a woman. She was very beautiful, the most beautiful and kind and clever and amazing woman in all the world. One day, she was walking in a forest when suddenly she was attacked by a monster. It was a friggin' abortion and it wanted to eat her. The woman was really brave. She fought and fought, but the monster was big and fierce. She couldn't kill it. She broke her sword and her spear. The monster was about to eat her but then a girl came running up .... She fought the monster and killed it and cut of its head and went galumphing back. And the woman.... The women said, "You are my special girl. You will always be with me and I'll never, never let you go." And they lived .... They lived happily together ever after.
>
> (11:52)

The story brings Justineau to tears and Melanie profusely apologies thinking that she has told a story incorrectly. Justineau comes over to Melanie and softy touches her on the head. This causes the Sergeant to rush into the room, scolding Justineau as he does. Parks decides to rub off the blocker ointment from his arm and stick it beneath the nose of a child-hungry. The blocker gel is to mask human smell and once removed we see the child-hungries transform for the first time. They foam at the mouth, they gyrate in their chairs, they snap their teeth—they change from a prototypical child-figure to something more. The Sergeant snaps at Justineau, "You think something's human because it's vaguely the right shape" (15:15).

Wynter draws on Césaire and Fanon to put forth her theory that humans are not only biological beings but are a "storytelling species … the human is *homo narrans*" (Wynter & McKittrick, 2015, p. 25). From Césaire, Wynter plays on his "science of the Word," which means that "the study of the Word (the mythoi) will condition the study of nature (the bios)" (p. 18). From Fanon, Wynter builds on his theory of sociogeny to conceive of the human as a hybrid being. For Wynter (2015), "our 'stories' are as much a part of what makes us human … as are our bipedalism and the use of our hands" (p. 54). Drawing from the sciences, Wynter also forwards the idea that storytelling allows for autopoiesis, a form of self-(re)generation that attends to "the ways life comes into being" (Erasmus, 2020, p. 50), and/or the "capacity to turn theory into flesh" (Wynter, 2000, p. 51). This means that humans "constitute themselves as subjects within specific physical, historical, psychosocial and power formations that are themselves shaped by human design" (Erasmus, 2020, p. 51). So, it is not only that child-hungries are the "right shape" to be recognized as human, but that they have storytelling capacities within which they (and others) story themselves as human (or are storied out of being human). This storytelling capacity "has been used to uphold and reinforce the dominant world order, it also has the potential to rupture humanism from within" (Truman, 2019, p. 1).

As the film proceeds, we understand better why Melanie's story is remarkable. The child-hungries' origin story is revealed in a way that makes the "friggin' abortions" nickname particularly crass. The Sergeant and his squad used to leave the base to do retrieval and supply runs in nearby towns. On one of those trips, they discovered newborn child-hungries inside an abandoned hospital maternity ward. The assumption is that the mothers became infected while pregnant and passed on the pathogen to their embryos. The mothers' corpses were found "cored"—all organs around their mid-sections were gone—the child-hungries "ate their way out" (51:50). This is an awful image to visualize: the origin story of the child-hungries is violent. The military convoy transported the infant child-hungries to the base where they have been locked up ever since. Melanie, nevertheless, has learned about forests, monsters, swords, spears, bravery, murder, and to desire a maternal kind of love. These were things she had not experienced, but they become the story of her hungry-self. Melanie was not the monster in her story either; she was a survivor—the hero—because "they lived."

Until the Sergeant made the child-hungries transform, Melanie seemed unaware of their hungry form. Yet from the story we can glean that it was not necessarily biology that Melanie supposed made her human—in this case, being the "right shape"—but her constitution in and through story. Melanie's alternative origin story matters. Wynter explains, "In this case we are no longer, as individual biological subjects, primarily born of the womb; rather, we are both initiated and reborn as fictively instituted ... kin-recognizing members of each ... referent-we" (Wynter & McKittrick, 2015, p. 34). Taking seriously Wynter's homo narrans as "a function that made us who we are as a species, this very 'mechanism' can be used speculatively to rewrite the human" (Truman, 2019, p. 5). Melanie and the child-hungries are not determined by their awful entry into the world, their origin story can be otherwise. Is this the gift that *Gifts* offers us? Is this what Melanie's story-within-a-story about love, compassion, violence, and hope also performs? Is the origin story the world on fire—a world not yet written?

The third story I want to recount also concerns the child-hungries emplacement within a bios-mythoi worlding. Caldwell uses logic problems to test Melanie's ability to think both rationally and creatively. The particular thought experiment I want to focus on is a version of Schrödinger's cat experiment, which is told without the details of quantum superposition being a point of interest. Instead, the biocentric question of concern is whether the cat is alive or dead. Caldwell explains the problem to Melanie as, "There's a cat in a box. It could be alive or dead. Fifty-fifty. How would you find out?"

(08:51). Melanie's quick response is that she would open the box (perhaps forgetting—or not—the lessons of Pandora from earlier) and take a look. Caldwell replies that seeing, listening, or disturbing the box in anyway is not permitted. Intrigued, Melanie responds that she would like to consider it further and get back to her. Caldwell agrees and scribbles in her notebook, "Exquisite mimicry of observed behaviours," which recalls the behaviorist school of child development. In this way of knowing, children are said to learn best by watching and listening to adults as a form of observational learning (e.g., Bandura, 1971), and Melanie is excelling. Caldwell then asks Melanie for a number between 1 and 20 and Melanie responds 13. We hear Caldwell call "transit" as the scene ends and cell door opens. The next day in class, Melanie keeps looking around and asking about Kenny. We learn that Kenny was in cell 13, and we wager he has been taken away for experimental dissection. Later on, Melanie is asked again for a cell number and she responds 4, which is her lockup unit. Melanie has figured it out and the next day she is brought to Caldwell for experimentation. While we have no reason to foresee the fiery ending of seed pod dispersion, this is an early indication that Melanie will not sacrifice her kin-kind for the humans that incarcerate them. When Melanie enters the lab, Caldwell ask again, "Is the cat alive or dead?" Melanie responds, "The cat's not in the box," to which Caldwell returns, "The standard answer is ... it's both. Alive and dead and the same time. But it's what you came here for, isn't it? The answer to the mystery. It's you, Melanie. In this analogy you open the box ... and you find yourself there. I'm sorry." (22:43). Melanie is not only the cat—both alive and dead, human and pathogen, child and monster—but also Pandora—she releases a plague on humanity, which simultaneously instantiates hope for the child-hungries. The future Caldwell was trying to achieve was incompatible with Melanie's, and so, at the end of the film, Melanie materializes a new origin story for a world shaped by contagion. This new origin story is not one of autopoiesis but sympoiesis.

While Wynter draws on the concept autopoiesis in her work, I do not intend to lock her down into an individualistic frame of interpretation.[7] Wynter's work continues to be theorized and reconceptualized, for example, by Zimitri Erasmus (2020) and Bedour Alagraa (2021), as more relational and intradependent. Instead of autopoiesis as something humans perform alone, Erasmus reinterprets this process as the "making of the world as a symbiotic and relational process ... a way of knowing—not only the human, but life—which postulates that human, animal, and organic life-systems co-create the world in this technological and information age" (p. 52). Taking this further, and toward what I take as a gesture of nonlife's intra-active capacities, Erasmus reads the hybridly human (i.e., "biological/organic and symbolic/myth-making") as "sym-bio-lic being" (p. 52). The sym is meant to highlight the symbolic (i.e., logos and mythoi), but I think it can be doubled up to embrace the symbiotic—life and nonlife in mutually co-constitutive relationships, something explored in more detail in the following chapter. In the case study at present, sympoiesis find form in the intra-action of pathogen and child:

> *Sympoiesis* is a simple word: it means "making with." Nothing makes itself; nothing is really autopoietic or self-organizing .... *Sympoiesis* is a word proper to complex, dynamic, responsive, situated, historical systems ... Sympoiesis enfolds autopoiesis and generatively unfurls and extends it.
> (Haraway, 2016, p. 58)

In a description fit for pathogens and child-hungries, Haraway presumes, "critters do not precede their relatings; they make each other through semiotic material involution, out of the beings of previous such entanglements" (p. 60).

Origin stories told through the figure of the child find theoretical affinity with Hannah Arendt's (1958) concept of natality. Natality is a note of optimism in her large corpus of work most recognized for incisive accounts of totalitarianism and the banality of evil.[8] Arendt describes natality as when "something new is started which cannot be expected from whatever may have happened before ... so that with each birth something uniquely new comes into the world" (p. 177). Each child is "unique, each capable of new initiatives that may interrupt or divert the chains of events set in motion by previous actions" (p. xvii).[9] Recalling the discussion in Chapter 1, Clark (2017) flips Arendt's hopeful concept on its head by suggesting that the Anthropocene encapsulates a looming "crises of natality: a waning of that resurgent hope attending the coming into the world of new life" (p. 159). However, Clark also holds onto something generative in Arendt's insistence that natality "stresses that the birth of a child has a miraculous potentiality, repeating—as it does each time—the improbable of emergence of organic life from the domain of inorganic matter" (p. 164). Clark therein extends natality from biopolitical reproduction to geontological possibility. The crisis that Clark gestures toward includes dangerous levels of greenhouse gasses, rising temperatures, and toxic waste, for example, that have increased anxiety about "spectres of mutation, pollution, proliferation, and dehiscence" that feed into an "apprehension of nonhuman agency" (Sheldon, 2016, p. 177). Rebekah Sheldon (2016) argues that the figure of the child is called to "bind [nonhuman agency] back, reconsolidating liveliness within the charmed circle of human futurity" (p. 177). Through the figure of the child, the damaged Earth system—including uncontainable pathogens and pandemics—can be brought back to human auspice, thereby reiterating the ideological elision of continuing ecocide. Melanie and the child-hungries upset this possibility. The dominant image of the child has long been "a redemptive agent ensuring futurity" (Sellers, 2013, p. 71), but Melanie insists on a follow-up question and response: future for whom?

In this chapter, I have tried to spotlight how *Gifts* gestures toward what otherwise origins and otherwise survival might look, feel, and be like. As explained, this otherwise is not an innocent undertaking in *Gifts* and involves a world on fire where destruction and regeneration coincide. Thinking with Melanie and the pathogen has been in an effort to grapple with belonging, anti-blackness, questions of the human, damaged landscapes, and pathogenic disturbances, while staying open to *not this, not yet,* and *what if* of speculative possibilities. While I have tried to highlight Melanie's becoming-with pathogen in ways that trouble the image of the child as an innocent, individualistic hero figure, I am aware of slippages. My worry is that conceiving of Melanie as a "brave survivalist" (Brown, 2013, para. 4) places undo responsibility on a Black female child-figure to claim responsibility for the end of the (white) world and the survival of her hungry-kin in a new world (Cecire, 2015; Nyong'o, 2015). It is an ever-present danger in the movement of the figure of the child who saves to one doing the protecting, surviving, and, even, destructing. A concern emerging from this work that requires more engagement is how we might think with speculative child-figures at the end of the world in ways that grapple with the kinds of conditions, resources, and imaginaries required to capacitate lives actually capable of flourishing in this one.

I hope a takeaway from this geostorying of *Gifts* is not that a speculative figure or fiction can "save us—but it might open our imaginations" (Tsing, 2015, p. 19). What is most generative about speculative fiction is its capacity to "experiment with different scenarios, trajectories, and reversals, elaborating new values and testing different possibilities for creating more just and equitable societies" (Benjamin, 2018, para. 31). What happened to be most just for the child-hungries was the end of a world. Otherwise origins and ends are possible, and story has a major role to play. The next chapter foregrounds a speculative series that engages with what might emerge in the wake of the end the world. It also continues questioning the value of survival for survival's sake in worlds that elevate a particular genre of the human above all other forms of existence. Whereas *Gifts* ends with a world on fire, however, N. K. Jemisin's Broken Earth trilogy begins with the end of the world. The first words of the series capture this difference: "Let's start with the end of the world, why don't we?" (Jemisin, 2015, p. 1). As such, Jemisin never lets readers sit comfortably *in potentia* of a new world. The child-figures in the series are not granted any assurance of futurity either. This is a world that ends again and again and again.

4

Becoming-Geos

The Stratification of Childhood

In the last chapter, a figure of Anthropocene Child ended a world to begin another that might not be so cruel to her kin-kind. The world Melanie insisted upon was one where a fellow speculative species—the orogenes of N. K. Jemisin's Broken Earth trilogy—might not only survive, but, along with the child-hungries, come to thrive. Neither hungries or orogenes are the sort of companion species that humans show themselves capable of living-with (Haraway, 2008); they are "incompanionate" species "with whom interspecies relating may not be so obvious or comfortable" (Livingston & Puar, 2011, p. 4). Some call them monsters in the pejorative, but I am not so quick to turn away from what is different or difficult. "You may be a monster," the narrator of Broken Earth surmises, "but you are also great" (Jemisin, 2015, p. 232). Jemisin's award-winning trilogy is supportive of my continued efforts to de-amplify a particular genre of the human as Man (Wynter, 2003), anchored in place as it is by the figure of the bionormative child. Jemisin aids this effort by foregrounding geos in the constitution of both beings, relations, and worlds.

Geos Beings and Becomings

In Jemisin's worlding, orogenes have geos-powers derived from and shared with the earth. Orogeny is a concept from geology that refers to how mountains are made overtime by tectonic displacements—a slow upward folding of the earth's crust. Orogenes have the ability to connect with and redirect earthly energies—they can symbiotically produce or negate seismic movements like earthquakes, frost freezes, or tidal waves. With orogenes as protagonists what counts as human is not taken-for-granted in the world of Broken Earth but is up for geos-refiguration. This can be read into Kathryn Yusoff's (2013) figuring of the Anthropocene "as a provocation to begin to understand ourselves as geologic subjects, not only capable of geomorphic acts, but as beings who have something in common with...geologic forces" (p. 781). The child-figures in this chapter, particularly a child-orogene named Nassun, embody and enact these provocations in ways that may have anticipatory significance for this world.

My understanding of geos-powers is indebted to key feminist teachers. First, Elizabeth Grosz's geopower is "the force, the forces, of the earth itself" that exceed human control, despite our best efforts (Grosz et al., 2017, p. 135). This challenges an Anthropocene recentering of the human atop the species hierarchy—as if we are acting alone on the world stage. Second, Elizabeth Povinelli's (2016) geontopower captures the tactics, strategies, knowledges, and practices that maintain the division of life (bios) and nonlife (geos) in late liberal capitalist economies of difference. This includes disregarding the agentic potentiality of those who are nonlife (e.g., rocks, minerals, chemicals), and governing humans who are too close to nonlife (e.g., Indigenous peoples and their more-than-human kin). Third, Yusoff (2018) brings together both theorists to figure geopower as "both the inhuman context in which biopolitical life is organized and as a concept that opens thinking towards cosmic forces" (p. 205). This includes how the humans exist in an ecological web that depends on nonhuman matter, and also that there are relations between inhuman existents that impact planetary systems in ways not delimited by the Foucauldian mantra to make live and let die. Thought with Broken Earth, geos-powers emerge from the intermingling of bodies, stones, energetic threads, and earth. In so doing, "Jemisin critiques divisions between life and nonlife to reveal the contiguity of geological, biological, and imaginary worlds that transcend" the human as Man (Dowdall, 2020, p. 161).

Geos-Figuring Speculative Worlds

In the world of Broken Earth multiple temporalities and perspectives are simultaneously at play. The epic fantasy moves between deep planetary time and human lifespans. The temporal juxtaposition of human life and earth life is remarked on by the narrator, a creaturely figure of inhuman timespaces themselves: "human beings, too, are ephemeral things in the planetary scale. The number of things that they do not notice are literally astronomical" (Jemisin, 2015, p. 150). What the Broken Earth novels do, attributable to Jemisin's layered world-building, is help me notice geos-spatiotemporal scales and relations, and thereby begin to think of space, time, and earth as quasi-characters themselves.

The background to the apocalyptic event that opens the Broken Earth series is that forty thousand years ago humans tried to extract all of Earth's energy and ended up driving the Moon out of orbit. This is explained as follows:

> Then people began to do horrible things to Father Earth. They poisoned waters beyond even his ability to cleanse, and killed much of the other life that lived on his surface. They drilled through the crust of his skin, past the blood of his mantle, to get at the sweet marrow of his bones.
>
> (Jemisin, 2015, p. 379)

Reminiscent of the description of the destruction of Mother Earth in *The Marrow Thieves*, this also connects to causal descriptions of the Anthropocene in that mass fossil fuel and mineral extraction have destroyed the relative stability of the Earth system. In Jemisin's series the Moon is Father Earth's child. Father Earth's response to his child's atmospheric expulsion is to implement the Seasons, which are apocalyptic climatic events like volcanic eruptions, floods, and earthquakes that end the world for a while but not for once and all. Storying a planetary existence in paternal terms might seem overly anthropomorphic save for the fact that humans have never been the center of this world, so all qualities and relations cannot be attributed back to them. The world of Broken Earth is a supercontinent called the Stillness that has always homed inhuman existents; the inhabitants of this planet are acutely aware of their multispecies intra-dependence.

The lifelike qualities that define the human, particularly children in the prime of development, are those most often denied to geologic forms. For example, nonlife does "not seem to participate in social life … they do not seem to have interiorities, they do not strive, they do not metabolize, they do not reproduce or seem to respond" (Palsson & Swanson, 2016, p. 152). Jemisin troubles this set of exclusions with her set of speculative creatures that include orogenes, stone-eaters, and Father Earth. Immediately, Earth as Father is set up as atypical; Mother Earth is the more familiar figure, a feminine nurturer and site of life. Yet it was Father Earth who took care of everyone for a long time: "he crafted even, predictable seasons; kept changes of wind and wave and temperature slow enough so that every living being could adapt, evolve" (Jemisin, 2015, p. 37). Father Earth now inflicts destruction out of revenge, out of pain of losing his son. He has interiority; he has motive. Earth has agency, lots of it. Humans realize this too late, after they have selfishly taken too much. They mistakenly thought, Jemisin makes clear, that "someone must suffer, if the rest are to enjoy Luxury …. Better the earth …. Better to enslave a great inanimate object that cannot feel pain" (Jemisin, 2017, p. 334). Much like the case with the child-hungries in the last chapter, this is not true. We also learn that Father Earth's attachment to his child is stronger than the parental bio-bond of the more human characters in the series. Theirs is an intimacy and sustained trauma that transgress the short timeframe of human lifetimes. Father Earth will not be ignored if the end of the world is ever to end. He demands a response. In the Stillness, humans are instead "with and of the earth, and the biotic and abiotic powers of this earth are the main story" (Haraway, 2016, p. 55).

Geostorying a Broken Earth

The first novel is called *The Fifth Season* (Jemisin, 2015) and recounts the stories of three orogenes: Essun, a middle-aged woman; Damaya, a newly discovered child-orogene; and Syenite, a teenage student trained at the Fulcrum, which is a government school for orogenes that has more in common with the military base in *Gifts* than the infamous magic of Hogwarts. Before the main characters are introduced, the narrator tells of a great and powerful orogene so disgusted with how his kin-kind have been used and abused for centuries that he fractures the Stillness along its most vulnerable fault line. What is suggested is that this could be the start of how "the world ends. For the last time" (p. 14). Essun feels the shockwaves of the ground being ripped apart, so she runs home to her children, who also happen to be orogenes, not that anyone in their "comm" (i.e., community) is aware that they have been living among these feared beings. In an excruciating scene, Essun discovers the dead body of her toddler son, killed at the hands of her husband, and quickly realizes her daughter, Nassun, has been kidnapped, also by her husband. Her world ends twice in mere moments—ecocide and grief. Essun's search for Nassun is the narrative thread that carries the three novels forward. However, there is much more than a straight temporality at work. Near the end of the first novel, the three figures of Essun, Damaya, and Syenite are revealed to be the same person at different stages of their life.

In the second and third books, narrative attention redirects toward Nassun. Nassun is eight years old when the story begins. She has untapped geos-powers of enormous potency. As an orogene, Nassun exists in excess of the nature/culture divide that traditionally delimits childhood. She is both bios and geos, and not a mixing of two mutually exclusive components either but biosgeos—one. Donna Haraway's (2004) "naturecultures" would be a close parallel. Even more apt, Nassun is a Chthonic one, the "powers of Terra" form in, through, and with her (Haraway, 2016). Upon discovering Nassun's orogeny, her father insists that they find a cure and they travel to a place rumored to know of an antidote. This search is the focus of the second book called *The Obelisk Gate* (Jemisin, 2016). Once they arrive, however, Nassun learns to accept her orogeny as a gift rather than a "disease" or a "poison" (p. 114), much like Melanie in this regard. Nassun's control and refinement of her geos-abilities grow quickly under the watchful eye of a Guardian—who, unbeknownst to her, is the same being who almost forty years ago found her mother and brought her to the Fulcrum. Guardians are members of the ruling class who are tasked to "track, protect, protect against and guide orogenes" (Jemisin, 2015, p. 409). Guardians are particularly cruel figures in that they speak of love while exercising authoritarian control over the young, oftentimes resorting to violence.

As Nassun battles within herself about her orogeny, she also grapples with the implications of broken bio-bonds on a broken earth. Nassun's mother has been tough on her, trained her secretly in orogeny, and withheld the affection that Nassun most desired. Her father murdered her brother, cannot accept her geos-powers, and longs for her to become someone much less extraordinary. These bio-relations are linked up to systemic oppression in the Stillness. The despicable way society treats orogenes is felt-lived in intimate moments between parent and child. Jemisin pays attention to "the impact of structural oppression on parents and children—how the pressure to keep her children alive in a world hostile to their existence drives Essun, and how Nassun experiences that pressure as a child" (Oler, 2018, para. 8). And while I am not going to rationalize the father's behaviors, it does show how a historicized conditioning of hate and fear gets acted out on those not considered fully human. Jemisin has repeatedly said in interviews that her formulation of oppression is influenced by anti-Black racism and settler colonialism. The trauma Essun experiences as a child-orogene has intergeneration effects on Nassun in ways that reflect what happens in this world, particularly in the context of residential school survivors. I return to this point later.

The third book, *The Stone Sky* (Jemisin, 2017), ventures way back in geological time to trace how the Seasons unfolded and how the subjugation of orogenes was normalized over the centuries. In this way, the colonization of the orogenes is intertwined with that of the earth in a Mobius strip-like relation. In an Anthropocene connection, this illustrates Yusoff's (2018) argument for the co-constitution of the inhuman wherein both earthly materials and subaltern bodies are formed in relations of negation to what counts as proper humanity. Nevertheless, unable to be fully controlled, both orogenes and earth contain "within them the same potential to shatter the control that has been so painstakingly, and brutally, constructed by the [human] majority" (Oler, 2018, para. 7). The climax of the trilogy occurs when Nassun and Essun finally reunite. However, they meet on opposing sides. Should the world end once and for all and with it the systems of governance that have kept orogenes enslaved, as Nassun desires? Or should orogeny be used to return the Moon to the Earth's orbit and end the Seasons once and for all, as Essun wishes? Like Melanie, Nassun is not a child-figure in need of saving: she can protect the world *as is*, become its destroyer in an affirmation of *not this*, or instigate a future of *what if*.

Geos-Powers in Inhuman(e) Worlds

As noted, Essun/Damaya/Syenite and Nassun are inhuman figures called orogenes or roggas in the derogatory slang of the Stillness. Like its semantic equivalent in this world, the use of the rogga "slur is deliberate. A dehumanizing word for someone who has been made into a thing" (Jemisin, 2015, p. 140). Orogenes are able to gather energy from the earth and other lively matter: they can "manipulate thermal, kinetic, and related forms of energy" (p. 462). They have enormous power, for example, they can reach down to sediment underneath the ocean floor and raise it up into mountains. In short, orogenes have the power to bring about the end of a world but mostly they stop the end from happening—orogenes quell much more than cause. The lines between what is sentient and inert are blurred to such an extent that everything in the ironically named Stillness has vital potential.

Orogeny has a biological base in that geos-powers depend on the sessapinae, which are "paired organs located at the base of the brain stem" (p. 343). This bio-embedment allows orogenes to "sess" the earth's movement—think of this as a kind of ongoing earthly relational awareness. Additionally, orogenes symbiotically draw upon the earth's energetic forces—think of this as a sort of becoming-geos-with. Orogene abilities are innate, present from birth, and at first instinctual: bios and geos always already exist intra-actively in orogene children. Because orogeny can easily kill, orogenes become targets for being killed. Damaya is told by her Guardian that she is one of the lucky ones. Though locked in a barn as a child by her Still (i.e., human) family she was given just enough food and shelter to survive, and, unlike many other orogene children who are abandoned, she never accidentally kills anyone. Orogenes who survive early childhood are brought to the Fulcrum to be trained by Guardians. Through indoctrination and discipline—what Guardians count as care—orogene children are taught to control their powers. For example, Damaya "learns how to visualize and breathe, and to extend her awareness of the earth at will and not merely in reaction to its movements or her own agitation" (p. 197).

Jemisin says that she modelled the Fulcrum school system on the Stolen Generation of Indigenous children in Australia (Hanifin & Jemisin, 2015), but these schools were a technology of genocide in most settler colonial states. Like with the Fulcrum, many Indigenous children in Canada were taken from their families, stripped of their language, given new names, and made to be ashamed of their culture's gifts. Not everything is transposable though. Some orogene children become breeders for the Fulcrum. Even though orogeny is not a guaranteed genetic inheritance the odds do increase when two orogenes reproduce. So, while orogenes are hated, they are also desired; this reproductive insistence splits orogene-children from equivocations of Indigenous children in settler states. The goal of settler colonialism is elimination, not reproduction (Simpson, 2011; Smith, 2010; Wolfe, 2006). The Fulcrum also hires out orogenes for assignments in which they move earth in productive ways, for example, clearing a harbor of coral so ships can enter and trade. Whatever the form of labor—reproductive or economic—the orogenes are made slaves and the Guardian/Fulcrum masters. This relates to critical questions of who and what counts as human in the novels. Alabaster tells an inquiring Syenite: "But each of us is just another weapon, to them. Just a useful monster" (Jemisin, 2015, p. 143). Later he tells her: "That we're not human is just the lie they tell themselves so they don't have to feel bad about how they treat us" (p. 354). Identifications of monster and human do not stay still but shift from abject to admired, and condemned to desired.

In press for the series, Jemisin relays that Essun/Syenite/Damaya and Nassun would be seen in this world as Black, and, as such, she purposefully wrote the series as a "Black female power fantasy" (Hurley & Jemisin, 2018, p. 470). Blackness is not mainly an exteriorized feature in the Stillness, which connects with Hartman's (1997) explanation of blackness as an aspect of "social relationality rather than identity... a contested figure at the very center of social struggle" (p. 57). Blackness is much more than skin deep. Jemisin (2015) describes the orogene children of the Fulcrum as "all different: different ages, different colors, different shapes" (p. 193). Physical features adapt to environmental conditions in the Stillness, and Jemisin developed markers along these lines. Orogeny in Broken Earth is a means for Jemisin "to question widespread cultural assumptions about the 'natural' divisions between race, species, and matter that underpin hierarchies of the human" (Dowdall, 2020, p. 151). Orogenes do not share skin color, which challenges the externalization of biological racism. Nevertheless, they are the "dysselected" ones (Wynter, 2003)—beings racialized as naturally inferior by another biological feature (i.e., sessapinae). Without skin color to rely upon, orogene-children are made recognizable as a racial group by other means (e.g., black uniforms), and they are a hated, feared, and violently oppressed one at that. While orogenes' symbiotic earth powers are not overly familiar to this world, the oppression that they face is entirely recognizable. While race in the Stillness may be color-blind, it is just as systemically real as racism in this world. The Stillness is structured by "racializing assemblages" that jive with contemporary governmentalities, including state policies, government schools, segregated communities, surveillance technologies, selective histories, and micropolitical aggressions (Weheliye, 2014).

The oppression of orogenes has been naturalized over time and space in such ways that the very existence of the Stillness depends on the sacrifice of some orogene lives for the benefit of human lives. Orogenes—those not economically or reproductively valuable—are made disposable and in being made disposable maintain their usefulness. What I intend by this claim is rendered apparent in one of the trilogy's most affective scenes. Syenite, accompanied by Alabaster, has been sent on an assignment for the Fulcrum. Deep into their travels they feel the earth shake and they can tell its source is orogeny. The Fulcrum assigns unruly orogene children or those brought to school too late to be properly educated (i.e., controlled) to the position of node maintainer. Node maintainers are stationed at outposts across the Stillness and their job is to quell any seismic activity that may arise in their vicinity in order to protect the nearby villages and villagers. Syenite had assumed that the node maintainers were just "poor fools assigned to tedious duty" (Jemisin, 2015, p. 119), but what she discovers unbalances her worldview:

> The body in the node maintainer's chair is small, and naked. Thin, its limbs atrophied. Hairless. There are things—tubes and pipes and things, she has no words for them—going into the stick—arms, down the goggle—throat, across the narrow crotch. There's a flexible bag on the corpse's belly, attached to its belly somehow, and it's full of—ugh. The bag needs to be changed.
> (p. 139)

Because orogeny is instinctual, the Fulcrum keeps the child-body and discards the rest. These children are reduced to "nothing but that instinct, nothing but the ability to quell shakes" (p. 141).

This makes me want to push the move Sheldon (2016) makes in theorizing a shift in the image of the child from protected to protector. This orogene-child did much saving of humans while strapped to a machine; however, this node maintainer also found a way to resist and caused a quake. In doing so he ended his suffering along with the lives of nearby humans that contributed to it or were complicit with the system of injustice that required it. He moved from saving the world to destroying it, which is a form of justice from the perspective of those who are persecuted. What Jemisin offers, especially in scenes such as this, is a speculative and serious engagement with structures of oppression that mirror this world, arrangements that might be otherwise, and cautions about locating the potential for an otherwise in a subaltern subject. Who are the node maintainers in this world? What is required of them? Is their resistance possible? Syenite resolves that "survival is not the same thing as living" (Jemisin, 2015, p. 441), and this is a question the Anthropocene discussion has largely avoided engaging according to Colebrook (2014):

> The post-apocalyptic is best read as a question posed: just as the human species starts to approach the real possibility of its actual non-existence ... there is a barely perceived and half-articulated problem of how and whether humans ought to survive. What is it about humanity that one would want to accept?
>
> (p. 190)

The Broken Earth trilogy engages these provocations and more. The emergence of a new "modality of the human"—the orogene—is dangerous and violent (Weheliye, 2014, p. 8). It is monstrous.

Inhuman Monsters, Inhuman Natures

Picking up on a theme from the last chapter, post-apocalyptic speculative fiction is full of inhuman monsters of various sorts. There are abundant examples of cyborgs, zombies, vampires, robots, and anthropomorphic animals that fill books and screens. Often in such stories another key inhuman figure is a feral nature set as adversary, for example, viruses, tsunamis, and earthquakes. The inhuman can also signify human cruelty and violence, as in the inhumanity of humans. Yusoff (2019) outlines two figurations of the inhuman that extend this figuration further: first, the inhuman as matter—the earthly substances that geology takes as its proper object, for example, rocks and minerals; second, the inhuman as in the making of racial categories and persons, particularly those subjected to the violences of slavery and settler colonialism. In other words, the inhuman as a technology of "unhumaning" (Sharpe, 2018, p. 172).

Yusoff (2089) explains that there is a material economy that travels across these compositions—the inhuman doubling composes the extractive and accumulative logics of the Anthropocene. For example, this brings to mind the Gold Coast, which was the colonial British name for what is now Ghana. The Gold Coast was rich in gold, petroleum, and other minerals; it was also rich in bodies—Black Africans for enslaved labor. The Anthropocene can therefore be understood as an inhuman assemblage where inhuman substances (e.g., gold, diamonds) and inhuman bodies (e.g., enslaved persons, miners) are entangled. What is mined from the earth cannot be thought apart from the human labor that extracts it and the geographical territories from which it is taken. Contemporary examples are also plentiful, including the De Beers diamond mines and Keystone pipelines running through Indigenous territories in what is currently Canada. Often the lines of difference between the various senses of inhuman are important to untangle, but, in this chapter, I look at how they are remade in relation.

In bringing both racist structures and extractivist practices together, Jemisin illustrates the double sense of the inhuman outlined by Yusoff. The trilogy slowly unravels how the exploitation of the earth and the racialized oppression of orogenes are intra-related. The consequences of both are a broken earth:

> It is a powerful way of evoking our own relationship to energy during the Anthropocene; an Afrofuturist projection that sees connections between various imperial projects of resource extraction. Whether it is the geological labor of the planet of the biological labor of black bodies, the Empire works for the assumption of a right to life in all its forms.
>
> (Dowdall, 2020, p. 162)

Importantly, life in the Broken Earth is not just that which is biologically (i.e., metabolically) alive. It is "life-that which is alive, or was alive, or even that which was alive so many ages ago that it has turned into something else" (Jemisin, 2016, pp. 360–1). Life is mineral too. It is geontological perplexity.

Possibilities for inhuman sovereignty lie with Nassun. She must choose her kin-kind over her parental bio-bonds. Nassun turns her father to stone in order to free herself and begin to fully intra-connect with earthy forces in ways that Fulcrum trained orogenes cannot; she also has to battle her mother to end the oppression of orogenes once and for all. Her geos-powers are raw and undisciplined. They have not been schooled. Nassun can feel and visualize silver threads—what she calls magic—which are the forces of life and nonlife combining all around her: "Magic is everywhere in the world ... cultivated in every flower bed and tree line and grapevine-draped wall" (Jemisin, 2017, p. 209). Magic winds bios and geos together into a network of life and nonlife:

> A web of silver threads interlacing the land, permeating rock and even the magma just underneath, strung like jewels between forests and fossilized corals and pools of oil. Carried through the air on the webs of leaping spiderlings. Threads in the clouds, though thin, strung between microscopic living things in water droplets.
>
> (Jemisin, 2016, p. 361)

Nassun recognizes and learns to become-with these threads in *geosocial* relations: "the inscription of human activities in geologic matter and the inscription of the geologic in living beings" (Palsson & Swanson, 2016, p. 167). In the reciprocal exchanges between life and nonlife, Jemisin "opens up a down-to-earth form of geopolitics .... by attending to different geologic scales—to living bodies, human and nonhuman; to solid rock; and to the planet itself" (p. 151).

The inhuman creatures that I listed atop this section as monsters are not necessarily how some critical theorists define the monstrous. In an interview, Yusoff asks Povinelli if she considers the Anthropocene a "monstrous geography," meaning "a kind of suicidal exhausting of earth materials" (Povinelli et al., 2014, paras. 20–1). Povinelli responds that she reserves "the idea of the monster for that which decisively disrupts the current organization of the actual—the current distribution of sense," and, given the current state of the Anthropocene discussion, something paradigmatically otherwise has not yet emerged (para. 21). If the Anthropocene is to be monstrous, Povinelli suggests, it will be because it "forces us to experience the threshold of a coming impossibility—namely, the impossibility of distinguishing arrangements of life from arrangements of nonlife" (para. 22). Broken Earth makes this (im)possibility possible, at least in the speculative realm. Speculative figures, like the orogenes, both uphold and call into question arrangements of life and nonlife. They "intensify the contrasting components of nonlife (*geos*) and being (*ontology*) currently at play" in the wider Anthropocene discussion in ways that also interrupt bionormative, innocent, and future-oriented childhoods and suggest otherwise worlds (Povinelli, 2016, p. 4).

Another strategy for interrupting "the current distribution of sense" with geontological figures of Anthropocene Child is to call into question the naming of the Anthropocene as a recentering of biocentric human. Instead, the Broken Earth finds a kindred spirit in Donna Haraway's (2015, 2016) offering of the Chthulucene, perhaps the most speculative oriented addition to the alternative Anthropocene nomenclature. The Chthulucene is a name for "for an elsewhere and elsewhen that was, still is, and might yet be" (p. 31). Chthonic figures are earthy existents—literally the salt of the earth. They spring from the Greek chthonios, which mean "of, in, or under the Earth and the seas" (Haraway, 2015, "Chthulucene"). They "are monsters in the best sense; they demonstrate and perform the material meaningfulness of earth processes and critters. They also demonstrate and perform consequences" (Haraway, 2016, p. 2). They are not innocent; they are not self-sufficient; they are "sympioetic, not autopoietic" (p. 33). The Broken Earth is an elsewhere and elsewhen of the Chthulucene: it is a multispecies world and worlding of the earthbound. Its speculative figures—orogenes, stone-eaters, obelisks, and Father Earth—are made of earth, minerals, and energy.

The Ends of Worlds

The first book of the Broken Earth series opens, "Let's start with the end of the world, why don't we?" (Jemisin, 2015, p. 1), whereas the third book begins, "Let's end with the beginning of the world, shall we?" (Jemisin, 2017, p. 1). Jemisin states that she wanted to trouble the singularity of the end of the world with her invention of the Seasons:

> What I wanted to play with was the concept of "When do we consider an apocalypse to have begun and ended?" Because in a lot of cases, what's considered an apocalypse for some people is what other people have been living every day. It's not the apocalypse, it's just, it's an apocalypse for you.
>
> (Shapiro & Jemisin, 2018, para. 3)

This is not intended in a relative sense, but in a grounded and situated one. For many in this world, the apocalypse is not some grand revelation but everyday efforts to survive the slow violence and environmental racism of the climate crisis (Nixon, 2011). In Jemisin's speculative world, every so often the Stillness experiences a Fifth Season, a particularly severe apocalypse where death overtakes life for a sustained duration. One of the lessons expressed in Broken Earth, however, is that "the ending of one story is just the beginning of another.... When we say 'the world has ended,' it's usually a lie, because *the planet* is just fine" (Jemisin, 2015, p. 14).

In their work on the end of the world, Déborah Danowski and Eduardo Viveiros de Castro (2015, 2016) set up a framework of a "world without us" and an "us without the world" to capture some ontological and cosmological differences between Euro-Western traditions and Amerindian cosmologies. The "world without us" is an end of the world formulated "as a separation or divergence, a divorce or orphaning resulting from the disappearance of one pole in the duality of world and inhabitant—the beings whose world it is" (Danowski & Viveiros de Castro, 2015, para. 1). In other words, a "world without us" is the end of the human species as earthly inhabitants but the continuation of other forms of existents including the planet. On the other hand, "us without a world" is a "humanity bereft of world or environment, a persistence of some form of humanity or subjectivity after the end of the world" (para. 1). An "us without the world" is the living on of humans without anything left to allow themselves to know themselves as human—humanity without a referent, humanity without an Other, humanity without a monster. In a complementary way, Claire Colebrook (2019) adds to this idea:

> There is very little sense, however, that—despite the common recognition that the Anthropocene has a violent, destructive, and barbarous human history as its cause—other (less robustly global and relational) forms of existence might be viable, desirable, or recognisable. Those other forms of human existence, which were erased in order to achieve the state-centred history of humanity that recognises itself as "Anthropos," are deemed to be the "end of the world."
>
> (p. 179)

A world continuing on "without us"—after the Anthropos, after Man, and after whiteness—seems much harder to imagine than the end of the world altogether. As the torrent of post-apocalyptic film of late entertains, however, even a "world without us" usually still leaves a few humans behind to get the whole thing started again. Both the Broken Earth series and *Gifts* put that trope under pressure.

As outlined in the first chapter, the typical storyline of apocalyptic stories involves a white, cis-gendered male, able-bodied hero narrowly averting disaster. The apocalypse in such stories becomes an opportunity to build a new world, only the new world is usually the same world "centered on white male power fantasies in some way" (Hurley & Jemisin, 2018, p. 470). Jemisin presses on this in ways that bring together perspectives foregrounded by Indigenous and Black scholars. A point of connection is that apocalypse in Broken Earth is a recurrent phenomenon and not a one-off event. Jemisin says, "This is what the world is for some people. It is the apocalypse again and again and again" (p. 472). Many Indigenous theorists clearly make the point that they are currently living in the post-apocalypse—Indigenous peoples have already "endured one or many more apocalypses" (Whyte, 2018, p. 236). Anishinaabe scholar Lawrence Gross (2016) coins the term "post-apocalyptic stress syndrome" to capture how living through real apocalypse(s) has multidimensional harmful effects for Indigenous peoples. Indigenous peoples have "seen the end of their respective worlds," and this trauma is inherited intergenerationally (p. 31). While I am not wanting to collapse speculative fiction with histories of Indigenous genocide, Essun and Nassun do live out post-apocalyptic intergenerational trauma on the page. Nevertheless, for Gross (2016), he also notes that Indigenous peoples are actively engaging a "process of building new worlds, worlds that are true to their past history, but cognizant of present realties" (p. 33). There is a parallel here as well: in setting off a series of events to end one world and begin another, Nassun first learns the history of earth and attempts to honor what orogenes before her have sacrificed.

Jemisin has noted on multiple occasions that the trilogy was a way for her to respond to Ferguson and the #BlackLivesMatter movement. For Jemisin, writing the series meant processing the systemic racism that defines

America for Black people. It is no accident that many of the oppressive tactics employed by the Fulcrum and the general fear and hatred of orogenes reflect anti-Black racism in the United States. What the series does though is provide speculative space for Jemisin to say enough is enough and then change things: "sometimes a revolution is necessary; sometimes you do have to burn it all down" (p. 473). Jemisin does not leave it there with a *not this*, however, she shows the aftermath of destruction in great detail. Jemisin insists that we consider "what is at stake in defending a world built on cruelty and oppression—and what is at stake in ending it" (p. 469). Povinelli (2013) insists that potentiation and extinguishment go hand-in-hand, so what gets extinguished if the orogenes become free? Broken Earth details what the end of the world might look and feel like. The Seasons, particularly the Fifth Season underway, show that "if you burn it all down, a whole lot of people get hurt …. It's a giant red rip across the center of the planet, millions of people dead, more people starving to death" (Hurley & Jemisin, 2018, p. 473). Those humans who were not immediately killed by the earth's eruption are left to suffer. There are poisoned rivers and acidic rains; there is limited infrastructure, limited food, and limited hope. For inhumans like the orogenes there is a slower violence, death is not guaranteed as their geos-powers offer some protection, but survival will be difficult. Its potentiation and extinguishment together; it is also a speculative depiction of how "decolonization is always a violent phenomenon" (Fanon, 1963, p. 35).

When the end of the world happens again at the conclusion to *The Stone Sky* what happens next is not shared with readers. There is a chance for sustained orogene freedom, for less hate, for stronger comms, for a more stable climate, but this will not happen right away. The climate catastrophe does not just end overnight and survival will be difficult for a long time. Nassun's final action is no a guarantee of a less cruel world. Jemisin makes the end of the world a temporal, situated, and complicated event with no guarantees. In many ways, how you interpret the end of Broken Earth is contingent upon what you consider to constitute the end of the world: apocalypse for whom—whose world ends? Like we saw with the child-hungries, one existent's apocalypse might be another's regeneration. But the apocalypse can also threaten ways of life, murder many relations, and alter systems of kinship in traumatic intergeneration cycles.

To repeat myself, the end of the world is not a concept or occurrence I take lightly. What counts as the end of the world is put up for serious discussion in Broken Earth. In connection with other texts and figures in this book, the world that needs to go for Nassun and Melanie is not the same world as the #BrightFuture Child inhabits. It is not the same world that provides me so many comforts, but it is also not the kind of world or humanity that I accept as either desirable or inevitable. Ohkay Owingeh writer Rebecca Roanhorse (2018) posits: "We stand with one foot always in the darkness that ended our world, and the other in a hope for our future as Indigenous people. It is from this apocalyptic in-between that the Indigenous voices in speculative fiction speak" (para. 3). From the in-between are new imaginings, re-visioned futurities, and forceful assertions of multispecies relations. I better be listening.

Child-Figures as Geos-Existents

Yusoff (2016) coins the term "anthropogenesis" to signify a new origin and ending story for the human ushered in by the Anthropocene. Despite the genesis in its composition, anthropogenesis can be read as a story about endings as much as beginnings. In one sense, the Anthropos is the Holocene subject's end—the nearly 12,000-year period of relative climate stability after the last ice age. In another, the Anthropocene foreshadows the future event of species nonexistence—humans of all epochs will be gone. What can be born(e) in/of such endings? Anthropogenesis proffers a rebirth, but not necessarily a biological one, as "definitions of being must now acknowledge an eternal but shifting mineralogical root" (Yusoff, 2016, p. 9). This becoming-geos is different than what might be typically assumed by statements referring to the human as a geologic force, a common refrain in Anthropocene discourse. The assumption seems to be that humans exert force on the earth in ways where they stay the main agent in charge. According to Yusoff, "anthropogenesis does not acknowledge the human power to *force* geologic forces," rather it opens humans up to "geologic forces that far exceed any human capacity per se" (p. 13). In other words, this is not a force waged unidirectionally against the rocks by a solitary individual, but a collective becoming-with rocks in different "geosocial formations" with differential geos-sociomaterial effects (Clark & Yusoff, 2017).

One of the reasons I am so drawn to Broken Earth is because the orogenes embody and enact this complex understanding of geosocial formations. Orogenes are geologic forces but only *with* and *in relation* to the earth; earth and orogene are in a symbiotic geosocial relation. They are speculative "comminglings of the geologic and the biologic ... entangled relations of the earth and biologic beings" (Palsson & Swanson, 2016, p. 150). Orogenes intra-act with earthly energies in ways in which neither existent is what they are outside the relation. To be an orogene is to become-with earth. Broken Earth depicts how humans, earth, and inhuman existents rearrange around each other to form and reform worlds.

The world of Broken Earth also challenges a binary of bios/geos understood as alive/inert. Rocks, steams, clouds, mountains, seafloors, and crystals all have lively energies in the Stillness. Dividing existents into life and nonlife does not make sense in this world—everything is connected by threads of sliver, by Nassun's magic. Allied to this line of thought is Yusoff's (2016) proposal of the figure of "humanity-as-strata" as capable of epistemologically and ontologically rupturing the humanism of a humanity that realizes itself solely in social, cultural, and biological terms. Transposed as an Anthropocene geos-subjectivity, the human-as-species and human-as-social are recognized as intimate with strata. As such, geos-subjectivities do not end at the skin, but they mark flesh and move with flesh into and with the earth (Yusoff, 2018). Orogenes are a speculative figure of what Yusoff's humanity-as-strata and Povinelli's geontology might look and feel like. In sharing seismic powers with the earth, Nassun, for example, makes problematic animacy hierarchies that rank order adult/child, nature/culture, biology/geology, and sentient/insentient as dominant and preferred ways of knowing and being.

For me, orogene child-figures invite a grappling with "otherwise forms of existence that do not rely on the reproduction of bio/geo binaries" (Nxumalo, 2017, p. 564). It is not that bios no longer matters but that it matters differently: it is not *the* defining feature of childhood. Nassun is biosgeos; she is engaged in "geontological world-making" (p. 563). If the Anthropocene can be a "provocation to begin to understand ourselves ... as beings who have something *in common* with the geologic forces" (Yusoff, 2013, p. 781), then Nassun offers an invitation to think-with her so we can better live-with the inhuman existents of this world. She allows me to imagine in a speculative form what might be otherwise on this broken earth. From the speculative to the enactive, the early childhood educators, researchers, and children working with Common Worlds' pedagogies are researching these geos-possibilities with children and more-than-human existents in daily early childhood practices and encounters (Common Worlds, n.d.). My hope is that my work enters into conversation with their research. For example, this chapter shares with Fikile Nxumalo's (2017) work on "geotheorizing mountain-child relations" a desire that "geos might be a refusal of the child development perspectives that shape" understandings of children's worlds (p. 559). In storying children's relations with Burnaby mountain in British Columbia, Canada, through the figure of child-mountain-rock, Nxumalo manages to "decentre children as the central actors in these relations by situating the mountain itself as a figure that reveals extractive settler colonial relations, yet also *exceeds* and *refuses* these relations" (p. 560; emphasis added).

Yusoff (2016) argues that the dominant subject emerging from the Anthropocene discussion is "a mythic Anthropos as geologic world-maker/ destroyer of worlds" (p. 5). I am drawn to how mythic alludes to the Anthropos as a genre of Man rather than the human itself (Wynter, 2003). The speculative child-figures in this book also put a shudder into my singular condemnation of the idea of destroyer and draw my attention to how the slash in Yusoff's formulation puts making and destroying into relation. Both Melanie and Nassun destroy their worlds and set about re-making them in ways in which human and planetary extinction do not parallel each other. How might the end of one world instigate the beginning of an otherwise world? Can the monstrous, the viral, and the geos gesture toward less extractive, less disposable, and less oppressive worldly relations? How might the inhuman monstrosities of the child-figures provide "potential exit strategies from the world of Man" (Weheliye, 2014, p. 28)?

In Broken Earth, Jemisin probes possible responses to difference by storying how Stills and the Fulcrum treat orogenes. Her provocation is that there are many possible responses to living with difference: "you could accommodate that difference, you could find a way to wrap your society around that difference and make it healthier and safer for everybody instead of shoving some into a horrible place or genociding them" (Wei & Jemisin, 2016, para. 21). Her point is that living with difference does not have to result in oppression, fear, discrimination, and death. While I prefer to push beyond the terms of acceptance understood as inclusion, recognition, and accommodation, I take Jemisin's point. I have come to appreciate Melanie's and Nassun's difference as too much to subsume under current configurations of the bionormative child. Their active potentiality is too threatening to the current order of things. The child-figures are familiar enough to be recognized (i.e., birth, growth, development), but strange enough in their viral and geos-powers to be excluded and killed. If Melanie is recognized as fully human then the scientists and soldiers could not have rationalized as efficiently the experiments they attempted on the hungries. If orogenes were accepted by the Stills then Damaya's and Nassun's childhoods would not have been lived in fear and shame. My gesture does not quite work—this is not about absorbing these child-figures into the dominant framework but about changing the arrangement, which is why I am so drawn to figurations of the end of the world. Inclusion is not the gift these child-figures desire or deserve. Melanie and the scientific-militaristic-Man complex were never going to coexist; Nassun and the orogenes were never going to be handed their freedom. They needed new worlds.

The next chapter continues my engagement with Anthropocene Child. Figures of child-cyborgs are the main players and they continue the questioning of whether the inclusion of difference is possible in a world designed to absorb it. Made of machine parts and lost lives, the child-cyborg figures upset both biopolitical divisions of life and death and geontological separations of life and nonlife. They regenerate as "human—*but not only*" (de la Cadena, 2014, p. 256), as these child-figures respond to another ongoing crisis: anti-black violence. Along with Melanie and Nassun, these child-cyborg figures insist upon grappling with this speculative question: Is it possible to create a world without racism, capitalism, sexism, ableism, militarism, and whiteness if this world is not extinguished first (Imarisha & Maree, 2015)?

5

Monstrous Love for Regenerative Cyborgs

In "Love Your Monsters: Why We Must Care for Our Technologies as We Do Our Children," Bruno Latour (2011) brings together classic gothic literature, technoscience ethics, nature-culture attachments, and child-centered metaphors to think through the Anthropocene predicament. As a starting point, Latour remarks that Mary Shelly's (1818) *Frankenstein* endures in the contemporary world as a "cautionary tale against technology" (p. 11). This reading, Latour argues, is sorely mistaken. Not only is the doctor commonly confused with the monster, but the figure of Frankenstein has become an "all-purpose modifier to denote technological crimes against nature" (p. 19). For example, Frankenfood and Frankenfish are popular expressions for genetically modified foods. According to Latour, despite these misappropriations, the actual transgression is not that Dr. Frankenstein patched together a creature in a lab but that he deserted the monster. The creature was "not *born* a monster, but ... became a criminal only after being left alone by his horrified creator" (p. 19). The extension Latour then makes of *Frankenstein* is that "our iniquity is not that we created our technologies, but that we have failed to love and care for them. It is as if we decided that we were unable to follow through with the education of our children" (p. 20).[1] Love could have saved the day and shown the monster the right way.

Given my scholarly affiliation with Childhood Studies, I am particularly attuned to invocations of the child. So, while there is much in Latour's article to support, I am left wondering just what he is doing evoking the figure of the child in such a way. After situating Latour's offering within a wider context of ecomodernism, I turn to Ruha Benjamin's (2016) speculative short story called "Ferguson is the Future" to further think through the technologicalization of care. Benjamin's alter-tale of racialized regeneration troubles an ecomodernist narrative of techno-fixes, and, ultimately, points toward a different future for Anthropocene imaginaries of the child at end of the world. I then bring Benjamin's and Latour's provocations together by thinking-with María Puig de la Bellacasa's (2011, 2012, 2017) work on matters of speculative care and Naomi Klein's (2014) proposal for a "kinship of the infertile."

Frankencene Technologies

Across multiple versions of Latour's "Love Your Monsters" is a love-technology-child relation that needs unpacking, particularly as it is formed by equivocating technology "as if" children.[2] In an early iteration, Latour (2007) connects *Frankenstein* to contemporary technoscience by asking readers to "finally atone for: not technology itself, but the absence of *love* for the technology we have created" (p. 11). What comes across is a call for unconditional love that creates a metaphorical ellipsis picked up and revised by the Breakthrough Institute (hereafter BTI) co-founders Michael Shellenberger and Ted Nordhaus (2011) as: "Our technologies, like our children, will go wrong. They will create new problems. We cannot create perfectly formed new technologies, only flawed ones. We must, thus, continually care for and improve them, just as we do our children" (para. 11). What work do child-figures do here? How is care composed? "Who cares? What for? Why do we care?" (Puig de la Bellacasa, 2017, p. 61). What commensurabilities are drawn between children, technology, and improvement? How does the relational equation make accumulation and productionism acceptable? Before discussing "Love Your Monsters" in detail, I situate Latour's work within the BTI. The BTI is a global think-tank that pushes technological and technocratic solutions to environmental problems. Latour was a senior fellow for the BTI when "Love your Monsters" was simultaneously published in their journal and e-book (Latour, 2011; Shellenberger & Nordhaus, 2011).

The BTI advances a vision of continued growth, consumption, economic development, and technological innovation under the auspice of a "good Anthropocene" (Asafu-Adjaye et al., 2015). This is a future where "humans use their growing social, economic, and technological powers to make life better for people, stabilize the climate, and protect the natural world" (p. 6). Instead of a cautionary diagnosis of the present, the Anthropocene is received as an occasion for intensified technoscience development and centralized management. The BTI are successful because there is enough in their writing that appeals to good sense and a #BrightFuture—that is, if the inconsistencies are ignored. For example, they disavow environmental politics grounded in ideas of a pristine nature, which is an important principle shared by critical environmentalists. However, they also argue that the ultimate goal of ecomodernism is to "decouple" nature from humanity. Furthermore, they confront individualized acts of stewardship, for example, backyard gardens and home composting, as inconsequential on a planetary scale, while also positing that "the move toward greater individuation, is universal and largely positive" (Shellenberger & Nordhaus, 2009, para. 8). There is a seductive hopefulness to the BTI's writings that is attributable to their rejection of a "politics of limits" for a "politics of possibility" (Asafu-Adjaye et al., 2015). For the BTI there is no climate emergency, there are no tipping points, and solving climate change is not only possible but plausible because of human ingenuity and exceptionalism. For societies that love to consume this comes as great news. T. J. Demos (2018) counters this rhetoric, "It's not surprising, then, that its 'politics of possibility' fails to mention the terms 'race,' 'equality,' or 'justice,' which would help connect to the actual antagonisms of current social experience" (para. 6). The most well-known expression of the BTI's ideas comes by way of the "An Ecomodernist Manifesto," which is co-written by eighteen authors (Asafu-Adjaye et al., 2015).

"An Ecomodernist Manifesto" paints a picture of a world getting better, fairer, safer, and healthier. In the image the authors create, consumption and well-being go hand-in-hand. In many ways, the Manifesto provides textual accompaniment to Unilever's "Why Bring a Child into the World" campaign that opened this book. Both propagandize the fact that people today have a longer life-expectancy, less lethal disease, increased access to clean water, and more participatory governance. Presented in aggregate form the numbers may well tell this story, but the distributed version is quite different. Coated in the guise of liberal economic policy and development for the few, the BTI figures a future world of "vastly improved material well-being, public health, resource productivity, economic integration, shared infrastructure, and personal freedom" (Asafu-Adjaye et al., 2015, p. 28). According to the think-tank, all these feats are achievable through human imagination, innovative techno-fixes, and economic modernization. Modernization is their watchword and yet its contours are never fully described, unraveled, or interrogated. For the BTI, modernization is an assumed good.

While seemingly strange bedfellows given the premise of Latour's (1993) *We Have Never Been Modern*, Latour was initially attracted to the BTI because of their rejection of an imaginary of an unspoiled nature and their anti-technophobic standpoint. For the BTI, the environmental movement's most significant mistake was rejecting "technology and modernization" in the guise of a leave-nature-alone rationale (Shellenberger & Nordhaus, 2011, para. 8). However, Latour (2015) has come to rethink, if not withdraw completely, his support. Nevertheless, Latour's view of "we must learn to love our technologies as we do our children" is translated by the BTI as, "we must understand technology as natural and sacred, not alien and profane" (Shellenberger & Nordhaus, 2011, para. 7). For me, the figure of the child within this articulation allows for this transition to the naturalization of technology and an accompanying attribution of innocence and goodness (i.e., sacredness). Who could argue against care and love for the child (Edelman, 2004)? Who could argue against "technology and modernization" that will bring "improved health or cleaner air" (Shellenberger & Nordhaus, 2011, para. 8)? To meet the challenges of the Anthropocene, Latour warns that humans cannot "stop innovating, inventing, creating, and intervening" (p. 20). However, what I find more interesting is not re-equating child-nature with technology-good but speculating about child-figures and technologies as "alien and profane." What might be possible in this otherwise embrace?

Latour's "Love Your Monsters"

Latour enacts a rereading of *Frankenstein* writ large with consequence. With "Love Your Monsters," Latour (2011) offers *Frankenstein* as an allegory with wide-ranging explanatory effects. Latour posits: "Let Dr. Frankenstein's sin serve as a parable for political ecology" (p. 20). By invoking political ecology, Latour continues his push for a reconceptualization of the relationship between nature, science, ethics, religion, culture, technology, education, law, and politics from supposedly divisible domains to a mixed-up scene of entanglement and attachment (p. 21). In evoking the figure of the child and care relations, Latour also makes any border between the personal/political and public/private spheres blurry. If someone believes these things can be separated "thanks to Science (capital S), you are modernist," Latour argues, when what the Anthropocene needs are "compositionists" (p. 21). This message, however, is inconsistent in "Love Your Monsters," and especially so when considered in relation to the BTI.

In a sense, Latour's article posits the monster as a child-figure resulting from bad parenting. The monster is not nature gone wrong—the non-bionormative birth is not an issue Latour engages—but the creature only becomes monstrous because he is abandoned by his maker.[3] This has echoes of the child development debate around nature versus nurture. Latour appears to be on the nurture side with this parable, at least on the surface level. He offers quasi-parenting lessons with a theological bend: "The real goal must be to have the same type of patience and commitment to our creations as God the Creator, Himself" (p. 20). In reflecting on the piece years later, Latour (2015) does not seem to change his tune much in this regard. "As you know, if the creature became wicked, it is because it had been abandoned by its maker," Latour laments, "The total hypocrisy of Dr. Frankenstein's fleeing the creature instead of coming back and nurturing it to make it socially acceptable to its fellow organism" (pp. 219–20). Making socially acceptable seems to assign an awful lot of deliberate power to the creator-paternal figure. It seems to ignore the fact that the world is particularly cruel to those who are different. Not only was the monster cast aside by Dr. Frankenstein, but by all the humans he encountered while making efforts to belong, including learning how to speak and read English. This nurture heavy reading is entirely possible given the text of "Love Your Monsters," however, nature versus nurture (i.e., nature versus culture) is the sort of division that Latour otherwise opposes. His early hyphenation of nature-culture conveys a joined rather than separated domains of practice (Latour, 1993). With his larger body of work as reference, Latour (1993) understands the nature versus nurture antagonism as a myth of Modernity writ large—the falsity of an emancipation from nature through Science where the human is in charge rather than intimately attached. In "Love Your Monsters," Latour's larger point is that we must care for that which we are always already entangled, including what is commonly divided as nature and technology, or, in this framing, nature and nurture. This more nuanced point however has been disregarded by both supporters (e.g., the BTI) and critics alike (e.g., Klein, 2014).

Another of the odder readings possible with "Love Your Monsters" is a depiction of technology as somehow an isolated human creation rather than as the entangled distribution of agencies mentioned above—the monster as an object of human creation. While much of Latour's other work interrupts such an individualist-humanist configuration, the main actors in this text are human and the nonhumans are acted upon. Nonhumans are not considered on the same creative level as the godlike Dr. Frankenstein, including any mention of the monster. The way Latour's polemic takes off in places allows for a reading that attributes intentionality to the human scientist alone and the BTI has seized onto this interpretation. In his later rejoinder to the BTI, Latour (2015) is strong on this point: "the ecomodernists are also uchronists, as if they were living a time where they alone were in command" (p. 223). Understandably, what gets overlooked in "Love Your Monsters" is Latour's insistence on a "compositionist" story, as in the "process of becoming ever-more attached to, and intimate with, a panoply of nonhuman natures" with whom "we" owe a great duty of care (Latour, 2011, p. 20). I should note, however, that a compositionist responsibility does not erase all differentiations between monster and maker, for example, the cut between GMOs and Monsanto or oil and Deepwater Horizon.

Klein (2014) offers a harsh criticism of BTI and Latour's essay in *This Changes Everything: Capitalism vs the Climate*. For Klein, the BTI fellows and supporters exemplify the mind-set of "we'll fix it later" (p. 239), which finds its bearings in a conception of humans as "The God Species" (Lynas, 2011), both ideologies she accuses Latour of promoting. In response to Latour's "whole of Creation on our shoulders" statement cited above, Klein (2014) responds: "The earth is not our prisoner, our patient, our machine, or, indeed, our monster. It is our entire world. And the solution to global warming is not to fix the world, it is to fix ourselves" (p. 279). While I could make the case that Klein slips into a similar formulation where humans can save the world by saving themselves—for Klein by ending capitalism and for the BTI by developing techno-fixes—her warnings are important nonetheless.

For Klein (2014) the monster requiring love "is not some mutant creature of the laboratory but the earth itself. We did not create it; it created—and sustains—us" (p. 241). Again, while the easy out might be to accuse Klein of reversing Gaia for God that would be to gloss over the ethical and political import of her argument. If love takes form as an uncritical relation to geo-engineering, then the earth and all existents will be transformed in ways hardly imaginable now. The unintended consequences that Latour otherwise asks us to love will be multi-layered, cumulative, and, likely, destructive. And they will be all the more deadly for those already vulnerable. Techno-fixes are no assurance of "nonexploitative forms of togetherness," which make up an integral part of Puig de la Bellacasa's (2017) theorizing of care for "antiecological times" (p. 24). Perhaps the climate crisis and its Anthropocene relations are not monstrous because we do not care for technologies, but because we have loved the logic of productionism too much.

Speculative Frankenfigures

Benjamin's "Ferguson Is the Future"

While Latour (2011) goes way back in time with *Frankenstein*, Benjamin (2016) journeys to the future with "Ferguson is the Future." The speculative sketch is set in the year 2064 in Oakland, California, yet this futuristic world remains deeply engaged with issues of the present. Much technological advancement has taken place, for example, there are hover cars and inventions of that sort all around. The most impressive innovations however are the medical-scientific breakthroughs of the People's Science Council. Their front piece is the Reparations Movement and its key initiative of stem cell organ regeneration that serves to re-enliven child-victims of police violence. The story's main character is Aiyana whose job it is to protect the Trayvon Martin Biobank from Raiders looking to steal stem cells for resale on the "white market" (p. 4). Aiyana and her team of Risers—which includes Reika, Tamir, and Freddie—keep the biobanks and cryotanks safe and secure.[4] This is especially important as the Council's newest and biggest scientific achievement is about to be revealed at the Revival Ceremony in commemoration of the fiftieth anniversary of the Ferguson uprising. Led by Dr. Lack, the Council has worked tirelessly to regenerate Eric Garner, who has been held in cyrosleep since he gasped his last breath in 2014. Eric will be the first adult to "successfully undergo Doubling—resuscitation and organ renewal. Only children had survived up until that point, and even then not without complication" (p. 9).

The complications of the regenerative surgeries have been debilitating for many of the child recipients, particularly in the early days. Aiyana suffers more than her fair share of "side effects, side affects" (p. 9). Aiyana's new heart, lungs, and spine engender post-operative complications like infections, graft failures, seizures, blackouts, hallucinations, and headaches. This is in addition to the memories which rematerialize as nightmares from the "chronic stress of living [and living again] under siege" (p. 12). Despite the many techno-advances, these somatic traumas still do not have a cure. Given these after-e/affects many children in the reparations-regeneration program find that "being born again was more like purgatory" (p. 9). Nevertheless, Aiyana considers herself one of the lucky ones because with a grant from the Humanity+ Foundation her "transplant team designed the Chairperson™, the first of its kind—an apparatus that maintains internal homeostasis so she no longer experiences the original side effects" (p. 10). Aiyana is cyborg: part human, part technology, part child, part chair, part artificial organs, part machine, and part redress. She is part life and part nonlife. With the publicness of the upcoming Revival Ceremony, it is vital for the Council to prove that the early issues have not only been fixed but that the technological possibilities have been extended to everyone regardless of age, gender, and race—as long as you can afford it, that is.

Overtime the healthcare system in the world of "Ferguson is the Future" transformed. Mandatory gene-testing is required for all citizens for any medical procedure, including something as routine as a blood pressure check. Genome-mapping is now the first stage of healthcare, and it is packaged and sold as the best possible means to offer precision medicine.[5] Healthcare is doubly bankable—both money and genes are currency that can be deposited. But they are not equally valued, as biocapital has bypassed cash. In this world, loved ones open up "tissue accounts" for their children instead of college funds (p. 12). Those who can afford the most cutting-edge techniques bank their own cells because regenerated tissue produced from one's own body has fewer complications than donor cells or generic prophylaxis. The only individuals who receive the regenerative services for free are those who qualify under the Reparations Act. This law mandates coverage of the treatment costs for child-victims of police violence, who—not by accident—are Black.

The day before the Revival Ceremony, Aiyana's friend Sandra ushers her aside to share some stunning information. The break-ins at the biobanks and even the Raiders are all a ruse, an orchestrated "distraction" dreamed up by the Council (p. 16). Rumors of the first attacks coincided with a short-lived pushback to the Reparations Act and the requirement for universal genome-mapping. However, once enshrined in Law, the Council found themselves a pool of experimental bodies unable to resist or consent. Sandra précises: "There is only the People's Science Council honing these techniques on the backs of brutality victims for free. Once they sort out all the kinks, the recipes are going to be patented ... proprietary" (p. 17). But the Reparations Initiative is not all bad, Aiyana thinks in response (and she implicitly asks the story's readers to do the same), the police and prisons have been abolished. There is even a permanent exhibit in the hallowed halls of the Council building which documents the history of decarceration, including the unjust murders of the child-transplant recipients. As Aiyana rewinds everything in her mind however she is stuck on how the museum makes a spectacle of not only her "own murder, but the whole idea of playing and replaying black death, the pornography of genocide. Why, in fact, did we need to *see* to believe?" (p. 12). Sandra further explains that there is a group of elites called the Immortocracy within the top tier of the Council who are obsessed with human finitude and that their regenerated bodies hold the secret to everlasting life. Sandra urges Aiyana to get to Eric before he becomes an unwilling spokesperson and ensures the continuation of the Council and their secret society. The next day, as Eric prepares to address the crowd gathered at the Revival Ceremony, he thinks: "Murdered by the hands of police, born again by the hands of scientists ... both without asking" (p. 18). Next, he stands up and begins off-script, "Who will pay reparations on my soul?" (p. 18).

Do the names Tamir, Sandra, Freddie, Eric, and Reika sound familiar? Does Aiyana Mo'Nay Stanley Jones? Jones was seven years old when she was murdered by police. Shortly after midnight on May 16, 2010, Detroit's version of SWAT charged into the house of Jones's grandmother. Jones was asleep on the living room couch at the time. Accompanying the police was an A&E

television crew shooting an episode of *The First 48*, which is an American true-crime program where detectives have 48 hours to crack a homicide case or face likely failure. The police were looking for a man identified as a suspect in a murder committed the day before. This was not his home. The suspect stayed in the apartment upstairs. The police threw a flash-bang grenade into the house before entering, which is an unusual move according to those well-versed in police tactics: perhaps the explosion was to make better television (LeDuff, 2010)? One of the police officers fired a shot as he charged in and his bullet struck Aiyana and ended her short life. Benjamin's speculative story of a Reparations Movement with experimental biobanks and a People's Science Council with a finitude fixation are an example of how "white life and black death are inextricable" (Benjamin, 2018, para. 12). The real life of Aiyana Mo'Nay Stanley Jones (July 20, 2002–May 16, 2010) is another.

After Jones's autopsy, Dr. Carl Schmidt, Detroit's chief medical examiner, told an investigative reporter: "You might say that the homicide of Aiyana is the natural conclusion to the disease from which she suffered. The psychopathology of growing up in Detroit. Some people are doomed from birth because their environment is so toxic" (LeDuff, 2010, para. 8). What exactly composes this toxic psychopathology? Is it the 50 percent child poverty rate, the fact that only one in three teenagers graduate high school, the lead in the tap water, the high child asthma rates from the smog, or the vacant Ford Motor plants? Life and nonlife form and deform around each other to create these environmental conditions. Or maybe it is the indemnity of gun lobbies, the anti-Black police violence, and the kind of perverse pleasure derived from a reality television genre that confuses violence for entertainment? Detroit began its long precipitous decline during the 1950s, precisely when the Anthropocene's Great Acceleration indicators began to peak.[6] Is Detroit the creator or monster in this scenario? Either way, contrary to Latour's demand, it has been abandoned.

In other work, Benjamin (2018) imagines "afterlives" as "a world of second chances" (para. 3). But what happens in most speculative pop culture productions of the end of the world is that "second chances are the currency of white supremacy" (para. 4). Benjamin's speculative story is particularly affective because it turns something taken-for-granted about this world, at least momentarily, on its head. "Ferguson is the Future" is a world where reparations for anti-Black violence are not only possible but have actually happened. The story plays out a seemingly radical intervention in which Benjamin (2016) tests out the question: "what if the subaltern were positioned as beneficiary?" (p. 19). What if the Black child is the one being given a second chance at life? What if police violence was not the end of Jones's world? However, as soon as readers begin to entertain the possibility of a world that materially follows through on an apology for racialized harms, Benjamin pulls back the proverbial curtain. Benjamin asks us to consider instead: What cover does care provide? What secret does science keep? As the story proceeds, the reparations' gift of regeneration is revealed to be other than it first seems. The Reparations Movement becomes another in a line of second chances for whiteness—this time a forever chance of immortality.

While there is no guarantee of social, reproductive, and technological justice in "Ferguson is the Future"—and I am not so sure that would be a fair request anyway—the story pushes in many probative directions. One of the important moves is that Benjamin does not succumb to a kind of technophobia of manipulating in/organic life, which would immediately exclude her from some important contemporary conversations. The reverse is equally pertinent—techno-fixes and productionist logic without reproductive justice are shown as insufficient for reparative futures. Other provocations include how the Black rebel cyborg might offer an imaginary of the otherwise amidst anti-Black racism and anthropogenic climate crisis.

Figures of the Black Rebel Cyborg

As a regenerative Chairperson™, Aiyana in Benjamin's speculative worlding is cyborg. But what kind of cyborg is she? Marilyn Strathern (1991) describes the cyborg as a figure who brings "together the imaginary and the real ... that is, the connections of circumstances in the world today that make it useful to think with" (p. 36). This is what Benjamin does with her child-figures as she raises questions about technoscience innovation, reproductive justice, anti-Black racism, police, bioethics, and futuristic forms of belonging. The child-figures move from the real to the imaginary and back again; from life to death to non/life; they also move from the end of their respective worlds to a speculative world that cannot fully shake off its past. The spectral presence of the children's real deaths haunts their imaginary futures, and in this spacing blackness and cyborgness become linked. Already denied the humanity conditioned by whiteness in their earthly existence, Benjamin's child-figures become Black rebel cyborgs in their speculative regeneration. The Black rebel cyborg "captures both the nonlinear and postapocalyptic positioning of black subjectivity, as well as the generative and subversive aspects of the black experience, in all of its hybrid, mutant resiliencies" (Maynard, 2018, p. 33). As seen with Aiyana, Black rebel cyborgs are "part divine, part mechanical, part biological" and "capable of movements that inspire flight" (p. 201).

Using Fanon's figure of the rebel intellectual and Haraway's figure of the cyborg as touchstones, Joy James (2013) figures forth a Black rebel cyborg that marks "not just the end of the world but the end of humanity" that is delimited by white supremacy (p. 64). The Black rebel cyborg cannot be "fully tamed and captured, excluded or subjected by the world that denies our humanity" (Maynard, 2018, p. 33). There is a "radical alien-ness to blackness, and to black being" that cannot entirely be contained (p. 29). This excess provides a narrow pathway for a new form of cyborg humanity to emerge that might rewrite the dominant genre of Man (Wynter, 2003). As mentioned with Melanie in Chapter 3, the Black rebel cyborg has the "ability to refuse blackness-as-victimization and reconstitute blackness-as-resistance" (James, 2013, p. 67), and the difficulty of this transition should not be understated.[7] The children who inspired "Ferguson is the Future" reckoned with racism understood as "group differentiated vulnerability to premature death" in the white supremacist state (Gilmore, 2007, p. 237). Their lives were disposable; their lives were not Life. In "Ferguson is the Future," the speculative worlding cannot be entirely hopeful or hopeless because blackness remains a "target of white supremacy" (James, 2013, p. 67). But, then again, how these cyborg child-figures embark on a "flight from the human" (p. 67) offers a kind of "hope against hope, the possibility of politics not simply as hope for a different or better world, but as the ardent refusal of this world" (Bliss, 2015, p. 93).

Evident in the Movement for Black Lives is the confrontation of a harsh truth: Black "lives do not matter under the state of whiteness. They cannot because they are not thought of as lives" (Ziyad, 2017a, p. 145). In the speculative world of "Ferguson is the Future" what resounds is that Black lives matter most in death—in their death lives on potential for whiteness. The real deaths of the child-figures in Benjamin's text haunt her telling. In both speculative and real worlds of Ferguson, Black children are the constitutive exclusion for humanity proper. In Benjamin's worlding, they become the literal key to finally solving human finitude, but only after their (first) death is this possible. Also, take for example, the Council's museum exhibit which both monumentalizes and spectacularizes the death of Black children. In a powerful passage that feels like it was written in direct conversation with Benjamin, Hari Ziyad (2017b) reflects on displays of this sort:

> Black people cannot make those operating within whiteness "feel our pain" because we are not understood to feel pain. Empathy-building projects encourage the incessant streaming and posting of videos and pictures of the bodies of our dead children, desperate to elicit tears that never come, or come only to refresh the liberal do-gooder's spirit. Importantly, whiteness requires dead Black children and that these deaths be unending.
>
> (p. 153)

These words are hard to read and type and repeat; they render the real-world precursor events of Ferguson inseparable from the speculative world of "Ferguson is the Future." Benjamin's story makes clear that the past is not past, and even in speculative worlds the specter of Black childhoods continues to haunt. The point of a museum is to historicize, to commemorate events that have already happened; after all, Benjamin alerts her readers, the police have been abolished so would not that be the end of gratuitous police violence? But the façade of this abolition loses its pretense when the motives of the Immortocracy are revealed. Even before Sandra explicitly tells Aiyana of the plan, readers are subtly alerted to the reiteration of racialized politics in the speculative world. In Benjamin's story, it is only victims of police violence that qualify for free stem cell procedures. Victims of systemic, unspectacular anti-Black racism do not qualify for the state's program for new cyborg lives.

Given the long durée of deathly socio-eco-political anti-Black harm, the Black cyborg cannot automatically be assumed as resistant and rebellious or able to escape systems of domination and oppression. João Costa Vargas and James (2013) therefore propose a range of Black cyborgs, which includes those who reproduce existing structures, those who make modifications from within the system, and those who refuse absolutely. A cyborg continuum is banded by the figure of the "angelic negro/negress" at one end and the Black rebel cyborg at the other (Vargas & James, 2013, p. 194). A particularly exceptional, multifaceted performance of the Black cyborg-child is assigned to Trayvon Martin, a seventeen-year-old youth discriminatorily gunned down in his gated neighborhood while walking home from the corner store. The public outcry engaged both ends of the continuum, which, in contrasting "younger and older Trayvons ... bring[s] us to a space of impossible redemption" (p. 196). Widely circulated on media and protest placards was a picture of Martin at age thirteen in a red Hollister t-shirt. Other popular images showed him carefully cradling a baby, playfully leaning on a snowboard, and smiling ear-to-ear in a cap and preschool graduation gown.[8] In an MSNBC interview, Martin's father shared a story about how his son saved his life by pulling him from a house fire when he was just nine years old. Angelic and heroic: smiling, caring, playing, learning, saving, *childing*. I do not offer this as criticism—this effort of remembering seems a perfectly reasonable response to a life ended prematurely by anti-Black violence.

Vargas and James argue that Martin can only be innocent if he is also "angelic. To be angelical is to be supernatural or infantile; to not grow up, to not have autonomous agency, to not reach puberty, to never rebel against authority" (p. 195). Images of a teenage Martin appeared in the media as the trial of his killer progressed. Much was made of Martin trying on a gold grill for a snap and giving the middle finger to the camera in another. These pictures circulated with a revised narrative of a problematic teen guilty of school suspensions, smoking and drug use, and other inflammatory framings that attempted to paint Martin as somehow responsible for his own death. I see this as the *childing* of the early images being replaced by a *wilding*—a form of disobedient, unlawful, youthful blackness and brownness that emerged into popular discourse with the villainization and animalization of the Central Park Five (i.e., Exonerated Five), who spent their formative years in prison for the brutal rape of a white women they did not commit. In the anti-Black imaginary of wilding, Martin's murderer's actions could be perceived as somehow rational and justifiable: preemptive self-defense. Martin was "a youth worthy of the right to life," but narratives of innocence and guilt both have the effect of delimiting his "right of refusal to wear blackness as victimization; the right to fight back" (p. 194). Both ways of figuring Martin then show the "space of impossible redemption" in the world as currently configured (p. 196).

Vargas and James work with the figure of Martin to bring attention to the sentimental allure of narratives of inclusion into worlds of whiteness. Martin could only be widely mourned if an innocent child; Aiyana could only live as a reborn cyborg. "For a black person to be integrated," Vargas and James confirm, "she/he must either become non-black, or display superhuman and/or infrahuman qualities" (p. 194). Black rebel cyborgs recognize the incommensurability of democracy and freedom under white supremacy and renounce the kind of humanity the system requires. Like Eric, they may even demand "reparations on [their] souls." For Black rebel cyborgs, the great sin is not abandonment to the world as Latour suggests, but inclusion as enclosure in a fundamentally anti-Black world. Black rebel cyborgs refuse what the state offers as care. One way of reading Eric's closing words in "Ferguson is the Future" is as a calling to account *and* as a relinquishing of claims to the nation-state. In asking the impossible of and under whiteness, Eric refuses re-incorporation into the structures that killed him, gesturing instead alongside Aiyana and their cyborg kin-kind "toward new ways of black becoming" (Maynard, 2018, p. 29).

Monstrous Love for Regenerative Cyborgs

"Ferguson is the Future" makes up the middle section of a longer article by Benjamin (2016) titled "Racial Fictions, Biological Facts: Expanding the Sociological Imagination through Speculative Methods." The article opens with the statement: "The facts, alone, will not save us" (p. 2). Benjamin's point is that the facts of racism are all around: consider employment wages, high school graduation, mother and child mortality, child apprehension, arrests, prison sentencings, and poverty. All these facts have numbers, rates, and percentages that do not attest to a problem of population but of anti-Black racism, settler colonialism, and white supremacy. Succinctly put, "we are drowning in 'the facts' of inequality and injustice" (p. 2). Yet scholars and activists of color are repeatedly asked to prove racism exists. At most, facts relay a partial view of the world as is; facts cannot imagine the world as it might be. This is another of the reasons why I think the speculative is so important. Speculative worlds test out "different possibilities for creating more just and equitable societies" (Benjamin, 2018, para. 31), even when, as in the case of "Ferguson is the Future," they are not yet sustainable.

Positioned by a different set of concerns, Latour (2004) also challenges the standing of matters of fact. Latour argues that social constructionism and its accompanying critique have gone too far. In showing the constructedness of all facts, neither knowledge nor politics has any stability anymore. "The mistake we made, the mistake I made," Latour (2004) laments, "was to believe that there was no efficient way to criticize matters of fact except by moving away from them and directing one's attention toward the conditions that made them possible" (p. 231). In pointing out the subjective relations of compositional practices, facts were labelled by detractors as made-up fictions. As an effect of this, for example, climate change deniers are able to claim that global warming is one interpretation of the evidence rather than a materialized truth. Nevertheless, Latour (2004) argues for a move away from the "very partial ... very polemical, very political" refutation of matters of fact toward matters of concern (p. 232). As critical academics, Latour argues, our goal should be no "longer debunk but to protect and care" (p. 232). Both Latour and Benjamin problematize facts, but where and how else they move when it comes to care is quite different.

With reference to Latour's (2004) critique of critique, Puig de la Bellacasa (2011) suggests a framework of matters of care as an additive to Latour's matters of fact and matters of concern. Puig de la Bellacasa (2017) is not looking to cancel out these other matters but supplement their limits with a more robust notion of relationality. Latour's move to matters of concern was important because it recognized the liveliness of things and how researchers are affectively entangled with technologies and the knowledges produced within relations. Matters of concern could not be as easily dismissed as matters of fact as attachment was already embedded into the figuration. However, Puig de la Bellacasa (2011) hesitates when it comes to Latour's dismissal of critique for an alternative of a "balanced articulation of the involved *concerns*" (p. 91; emphasis added). Martin was walking home from the store; his murderer claims he was scared. Aiyana was sleeping on the couch; her murderer claims he was startled. There is no balance here. I am in agreement with Puig de la Bellacasa that "in a deeply troubled and strongly stratified world ... we still need approaches that reveal power and oppressive relations in the assembling of concerns" (p. 39). These matters of care and concern can be applied in analysis of Latour's (2011) appeal to love monsters as if they are children/technology.

How to Care

Puig de la Bellacasa builds her understanding of care from the work of feminist theorists.[9] In particular, she grounds her work in a "generic" conception of care offered by Joan Tronto and Berenice Fisher: care is "everything that we do to maintain, continue and repair our world so that we can live in it as well as possible" (Tronto, 1993, p. 103). Extricable from this definition is the importance of maintenance and repair work. This is significant because it values the everydayness of women's and often racialized women's labor. However, it can also be misused. In "Ferguson is the Future," technoscience innovations of stem cell regeneration "repaired" the child victims and made their cyborg second lives possible. The scientific advancements appeared to overhaul police violence but also created a new form of surveillance. In this way, promises of a #BrightFuture through improved health, safety, and well-being can cover over innovative forms of control. Similarly, global and individual well-being are strategic tenants of the ecomodernist platform. In their take-up of Latour's article, Shellenberger and Nordhaus (2011) argue that technologies "will go wrong" and that "we must ... care for and improve them" with even more technologies (para. 11). This sort of maintenance and repair work seeks to rationalize continued consumption because new technologies will be invented to fix any future harm. This is a vision of the future as a promissory of techno-progress. However, the BTI message ignores the lesson advanced by feminist materialisms that humans are not fully in charge.

For me, I fail to see how Latour's demand not to abandon necessarily translates into practices of care. Physical presence—the sort of non-leaving, non-abandonment Latour invokes—does not necessarily equate to care in any affective sense. Latour tells us to stick with our monsters-children-technologies *as if* proximity is enough. A more generous take recognizes Latour's demand for love as obliging that "we must take care of things in order to remain responsible for their becomings" (Puig de la Bellacasa, 2017, p. 43). I have no qualms with this interpretation so much as responsibility and response-ability is carefully outlined and practiced (Haraway, 2016). This is why the question of "How to care?" must be addressed in each situated encounter (p. 67). Care work is not easy or innocent; it is messy and complex. Care work must involve reciprocity and consent.

In "Love Your Monsters," care and love are a one-sided relation extended from creator to technology; they are not reciprocal practices in Latour's worlding. The actual qualities of care are not much discussed by Latour, we are only told that love must be unconditional. However, practices of love and care "are always shot through with asymmetrical power relations: who has the power to care. Who has the power to define what counts as care and how it should be administered" (Martin et al., 2015, p. 3)? Who can refuse care? The child-cyborgs of Ferguson never consented to a second life—to receiving state-based technoscience care. Remember Eric's thoughts: "Murdered by the hands of police, born again by the hands of scientists … both without asking" (Benjamin, 2016, p. 18). Though unremarked upon by Latour, consent was refused to Dr. Frankenstein's monster also.[10] Without their agreement, Aiyana and her team become a modified form of what prematurely ended their lives in the first place. I think we are meant to be uncomfortable affiliating the names of children murdered by police with an innovative figuration of enforcement called Risers in the story. Technologies in Benjamin's speculative world are not strictly machines, tools, computers, and other forms of nonlife either, but include tactics, strategies, and procedures for not only governing others but caring for selves.

With respect to imbalances of power in the Anthropocene, Puig de la Bellacasa (2017) advises that an ethics of care be "capable of challenging dominant technoscientific productionist ways of thinking and acting" (p. 42). The most quoted phrase from Latour's (2011) article is that we must not "stop innovating, inventing, creating, and intervening" (p. 21). So long as care is attached in principle, Latour is taken-up as advocating for innovation as a good in and of itself. In a sense, this is repair work without political and ethical obligation. Latour and the BTI fail to seriously consider how "emerging technologies reinforce interlocking forms of discrimination," whether intentional or not (Benjamin, 2019a, p. 3). Benjamin's story reveals how technoscience innovation in the name of reparations (arguably a form of care) is not an end in itself but a means to an end of securing finitude—of defeating geontology—life wins ... forever. I read Puig de la Bellacasa's (2017) matters of care as challenging both the Immortocracy and ecomodernist standpoints. Much of what Puig de la Bellacasa's (2017) writes about productionism problematizes the BTI's modernization doctrine.

Ecomodernists tout a form of productionism that promises to solve environmental problems through a "commercial logic of intensification and accumulation characteristic of capitalist economies" (p. 184). It is more, more, more. Productionism overdetermines and "colonizes all other relations: everyday life, relations with other species, and politics (e.g., farmers' subjection to the industry-agribusiness complex)," including care (p. 184). Ecomodernists emphasize quantitatively measurable crop yields, for example, and promote the efficiency of GMOs and monocrops. The livelihoods and desires of small-scale farmers or Indigenous peoples reclaiming traditional cultivating practices are not respectable alternatives according to the BTI, but instead are representative of people left behind by modernization. Technoscience innovation is good, their argument goes, because it makes possible agricultural amplification and maximizes resource extraction. The simplistic conclusion they draw is that if there was just more food than less people would be hungry; however, this way of thinking assumes an equal distribution that has never happened. This rhetoric also perpetuates the historical devaluation of care labors that are not quantifiable—such as childcare. In these ways, ecomodernism and the logic of productionism "not only reduces what counts as care ... but also inhibits the possibility of developing other relations of care that fall out of its constricted targets" (p. 186). The ability to imagine an outside of this targeted constriction, however, is another attribute of the speculative.

As taken up by ecomodernists, the circulation of care through the figure of the child in "Love Your Monsters" becomes a means to suture technological development to productionism. Instead of racing full force ahead with Latour's "innovating, inventing, creating, and intervening," however, perhaps it is best to consider Benjamin's (2019a) advice, perfectly suitable for the Anthropocene moment:

> It starts with questioning breathless claims of techno-utopianism, rethinking what counts as innovation, remaining alert to the ways that race and other

hierarchies of difference get embedded in the creation of new designs, and ultimately refashioning the relationship between technology and society by prioritizing justice and equity.

(p. 11)

Furthermore, in noting the impossibility of non-innocent caring, Puig de la Bellacasa (2017) supposes that an ethics of care resides in the entanglement of critical and speculative becomings. The critical side of care comprises questions like Benjamin's and also includes concerns about who cares, who receives care, and what forms of care are available. The speculative dimension of care marks a "commitment to seek what other worlds could be in the making through caring while staying with the trouble of our own complicities and implications" (p. 204). Speculative care has deep connections with speculative fiction. Speculative care in Puig de la Bellacasa's (2017) theorizing also extends to more-than-human relations, which could include cyborg-figures. The final sections of this chapter bring cyborgs back into the racialized, technoscience fold to consider how forms of care justice in the Anthropocene might be devised.

Care for Regenerative Cyborgs

The most famous cyborg in the scholarly world is Donna Haraway's creation. This cyborg is a mix of machine and organism that hyphenates—instead of slashes (/) apart—constructed dualisms like reality-fiction, life-death, flesh-matter, human-animal, technoscience-science fiction (Haraway, 2004, p. 8). The connective dash acts as a contact zone, which is a non-innocent relational spacing. In Haraway's "Cyborg Manifesto," like in my own writing, not all contact zones are given equal analytical weight. Ziyad (2017a) reads Haraway's cyborg as an important feminist intervention in thinking beyond the human, but that by not engaging anti-blackness directly her worlding ultimately falls short of its liberatory potential. Ziyad does not entirely discount the cyborg figure and appreciates the Black rebel cyborg as "a truer challenge to the human and its essential violence against blackness under whiteness" (p. 157). This is to suggest that the futurity Haraway's cyborg puts into motion is not necessarily commensurable with Black lives, although they are not always mutually exclusive either. The speculative figures of Aiyana and her cyborg-kin carry the scars not just of regeneration but of anti-Black racism. They are doubly birthed and doubly monstrous: they are attached to blackness in divisions of humanness that make them monsters anyway, and they wear regenerated parts in their re- and co-composition as hybrid (non)beings.

An area where these cyborg worldings come together is in a move away from bionormative birth toward regeneration. With the cyborg, Haraway (1991) interrupts how political imaginaries depend on metaphors of birth, growth, and natural development (which calls to mind Povinelli's geontologies also). Haraway writes that "unlike the hopes of Frankenstein's monster, the cyborg does not expect its father to save it through a restoration of the garden" (p. 151). This is particularly interesting in light of Benjamin's and Latour's texts. Although Haraway's cyborg does not have "an origin story in the Western sense," they are "the illegitimate offspring of militarism and patriarchal capitalism, not to mention state socialism" (p. 151). Aiyana's cyborg emergence is tied to similar structures, and, with perhaps less of a socialist bend, the rebranding of *Frankenstein* fits this template also. I see the coming together of Black rebel cyborgs at the end of "Ferguson is the Future" as hinting toward resistance and rebellion—I imagine this as "illegitimate offspring" becoming "exceedingly unfaithful to their origins" (p. 151). This is the gesture emboldened by Eric's impossible closing question. Dr. Frankenstein's monster, on the other hand, builds himself a funeral pyre upon which to float out to sea and die alone, which is an act almost too faithful to the wishes of his father-figure.

The Out of the Woods Collective (Collective, 2015b) proposes the figure of the regenerative cyborg as a provocation for grappling with the Anthropocene. Against dominant discourses of reproductive futurism that think climate futures through invocations of the innocent child, the Collective argues that reproduction is too tethered to "heteronormative and survival-based notions of human life" (para. 18). The Collective reads the figure of the child in climate discourse as a tactic to disguise conservative, neoliberal, and settler colonial practices through "upholding the naturalness and desirability of birthing and reproduction as a beacon" of hope amidst ecological destruction (Collective, 2015b, para. 4). A politics of regeneration, on the other hand, marks out an effort "to go beyond the political limits, both of centering reproduction, and of thinking futurity through reproduction" (para. 12). It is a challenge to biocentricity; it is a challenge to life as only human. A regenerative cyborg ethics does not disavow reproduction in ways that are anti-child or anti-natal but refigures it to include "a complex network composed of machines and organisms, an entanglement of the living and the non-living, a cyborg Earth" (para. 16). A regenerative politics must act in solidarity with reproductive justice movements that intertwine critiques of anti-blackness, settler colonialism, and environmental racism. Perhaps it should not be beholden to divisions of life from nonlife and enact a "kinship of the infertile" (Klein, 2014).

Near the conclusion of Klein's (2014) bestseller is a chapter titled "The Right to Regenerate." In it, Klein parallels her difficultly conceiving a child with the damage being done to the earth and other more-than-human creatures. "If the Earth is indeed our mother," Klein expresses, "then she is a mother facing a great many fertility challenges of her own" (p. 424). To tease out the analogy, Klein takes readers back in time to the deck of a chartered boat where she and some colleagues witnessed and documented evidence of the 2010 Deepwater Horizon oil spill off the coast of Louisiana. Their boat guide explained that what troubled him most "was not what we were all seeing—fish jumping in fouled water, Roseau cane coated in oil—but something much harder to detect without a microscope and sample jars" (p. 426). He was referring to the tiny zooplankton attempting to attach to "the marsh grass [that] acts as an aquatic incubator, providing nutrients and protection from predators" (p. 426). The grass was coated in oil which meant that the newly hatched shrimp, oysters, and crabs who normally merge with the plankton in their first days of life for protection would die, if they had not already. Remember Aiyana's words when confronting the monumentalization of her death: "Why, in fact, did we need to *see* to believe?" (Benjamin, 2016, p. 12). Human eyes cannot see the minutiae of life (and its loss) described by the boat captain without technological assistance and local knowledge. Unbeknownst to Klein at the time, her body was in the early stages of a miscarriage—her third in five years. When she finds out, and despite what the doctors told her about their non-relation, she cannot help wondering if the contaminated water she waded in or the toxic air she inhaled contributed to her ectopic pregnancy. Remembering rocking on the deck of the boat, Klein renders a haunting image of being suspended "not in water but amniotic fluid, immersed in a massive multi-species miscarriage" which turned out to be her "miscarriage inside a miscarriage" (p. 427). Amidst this doubling of double death (Rose, 2012), Klein (2014) "began to feel what [she] can only describe as a kinship of the infertile" (p. 427).

This provocation for an Anthropocene ethical and political praxis of care does not get much follow-up in Klein's text, nor in the academic literature and popular press that follows it. I think part of the fear of taking-up something like a kinship of the infertile is that it can be swallowed up by a logic of extinction that has been heightened by the Anthropocene. However, I receive the kinship of the infertile as a call to enact a regenerative-cyborg praxis. A kinship of the infertile invites a "solidarity with non-reproductive lifeforms" (Collective, 2015a, para. 20), with nonlife, that requires acts of speculation to bring it into being. Another reason for the dangling kinship provocation is that Klein's story moves on to the happy birth of her son—again, not something I am faulting her for by any means. I do however wonder if perhaps a kinship of the infertile is the sort of trouble we should stay with (Haraway, 2016). I agree with the Collective that a regenerative cyborg care is needed for these times. The question then becomes about the conditions required to capacitate such a praxis. These necessary conditions are in large part material but also are imaginative. I believe one requisite is speculative fiction, in order "to expand our own visions of what is *possible*" (Benjamin, 2018, para. 8).

In the next chapter, the ideas of "Love Your Monsters" reappear in the context of parental love in order to further grapple with the possibility that non-abandonment might not be enough in the Anthropocene. Furthermore, intimate and planetary relations are brought together in supportive and divergent ways in order to think though how care for the planet and care for the child are linked through a fear of the infertile. The racial politics of care and complicity are also given more page space in asking what care might look like on a broken earth.

6

Parental Stewardship

Bionormative Care as Environmental Surrogate

It is not unusual for a post-apocalyptic text to end with a child-figure as ultimate survivor. Their weathered, cherub face fills the screen as the fade out begins, the music surges, and the credits roll. Or there is an epilogue of sorts which does not quite manage to tie up all the loose ends, but in a few extra lines of print sets up the child-figure to experience a #BrightFuture. Instead of attributing the child-figure's survival to a bildungsromanish move of innocence to experience, I wonder if it is because they have proven themselves capable of loving our monsters. But have the adults of Anthropocene-related speculative stories loved their creations? How have they cared for their worlds? As outlined in the last chapter, Bruno Latour (2011) demands that we "care for our technologies as we do our children," and, through parabolizing *Frankenstein*, introduces abandonment and attachment into the discussion as well (p. 19). The parental figures in Hulu's television adaptation of *The Handmaid's Tale* (Miller, 2017-ongoing) refuse to abandon their offspring and this insistence comes at a price. They make all else secondary.

It may seem that this kind of intense parental love is a refusal of Rebekah Sheldon's (2016) swing from the child in need of saving to the one who does the protecting, but, while these texts put this relation in tension, I do not think they void the movement. In *The Handmaid's Tale*, the endurance of the child-figures becomes a metonym for species survival and parental love becomes analogue to "planetary stewardship" (Steffen et al., 2011). What happens to care when planetary stewardship takes the form of what I am calling parental stewardship? How does a "heteronormative family romance" demarcate post-apocalyptic stories of the end of the world (Sturgeon, 2010, p. 126)? In this chapter I analyze some "profound drawbacks to reading parental love as the antithesis and antidote to environmental destruction" (Johns-Putra, 2016, p. 521). How does survival of the child become surrogate for the "anxieties surrounding the demise of white supremacy" at the end of the world (Joo, 2018, p. 4)? These are the guiding questions I grapple with in this chapter.

Adapted from Margaret Atwood's (1986) novel of the same name, *The Handmaid's Tale* television series stories the dystopic world of a small group of fertile women called Handmaids who are forced into reproductive servitude by the totalitarian, puritanical, patriarchal, and theocratic government of Gilead. The world of *The Handmaid's Tale* experiences an unknown environmental catastrophe whose effects have made lands and bodies toxic. With post-apocalyptic ecologies like this as background, Alexis Lothian (2018) traces how the end of the world stands as a conventional plot device that can be overcome "through the resolution of a heterosexual family plot" where "children, and the possibility of children, allow a future for humanity in its *current form* to be salvaged from the world's end" (p. 182; emphasis added). Where I depart slightly from Lothian (2018), and align with Claire Colebrook (2017), is that I do not believe it is humanity in its present form that is the object of redemption but humanity as it "should be": an eco-attuned humanity not "guilty of the Anthropocene scar" (p. 84). *The Handmaid's Tale* allows for a case study of these workings.

Anthropocene Stewardship

Planetary Stewardship

Will Steffen and colleagues (2007) sort the Anthropocene into three stages: the Industrial Era (1800–1945) evidenced by fossil fuel expansion; the Great Acceleration (1945–2015) marked by economic globalization; and "Stewards of the Earth System?" (2015–onwards), a speculative period differentiated from the others both by human's awareness of their destructive impact on the environment and that the end date is unknown. The scientists point out that people today are the "first generation with the knowledge of how our activities influence the Earth System, and thus the first generation with the power and the responsibility to change our relationship with the planet" (Steffen et al., 2011, p. 748). There are a multitude of ways that change might take place, but most proposals center on technological innovation; for example, mitigating practices of biofuels or geo-engineering feats of atmospheric aerosol injections. However, these scientists also recognize that technology, no matter how inventive, will "not be enough on its own .... Changes in societal values and individual behaviour will likely be necessary" (p. 619). In short, they argue that humans need to become planetary stewards and fast.

Steffen et al. (2011) confirm that "the need to achieve effective planetary stewardship is urgent .... we risk driving the Earth System onto a trajectory toward more hostile states from which we cannot easily return" (p. 739). I see this perspective as a counterpoint to the ecomodernists' growth and development vision of the last chapter. For these Earth system scientists, planetary stewardship is the necessary relation humans must have to the earth and to the future. Without such caretaking, "the Anthropocene threatens to become for humanity a one-way trip to an uncertain future," and this journey is all but certain to be increasingly "hostile" (p. 739). These promotors of planetary stewardship do not always appear to be tuned in to the antagonisms already waged against lives made disposable in the here and now, let alone the past or future.

My main hesitation with the concept of planetary stewardship is its apparent human exceptionalism. As summarized thus far planetary stewardship is primarily a matter of care, concern, and agency for humans. Stewardship originates in the individual and directs outwards from there. For example, Steffen et al. (2011) write: "Responsible stewardship entails *emulating* nature in terms of resource use and waste transformation and recycling" (p. 756; emphasis added). I interpret this as a call for humans to copy nature or at least match it in hopes of returning to a Holocene-like equilibrium. Emulate also has more antagonistic connotations, especially when considered in the context of other statements to the effect of, in the Anthropocene, "human activities now *rival* global geophysical processes" (Steffen et al., 2011, p. 739; emphasis added). It is hard not to read this figuration of planetary stewardship as divisive. Such sentiments "unwittingly rehearse the division of cultural and natural worlds, not their inseparability" (Taylor, 2017, p. 1453).

Affrica Taylor (2017) notes that what often happens in the field of environmental education is that the interdependence of social, political, and environmental systems is mentioned before moving on to a reconfirmation of "humanist understandings of agency" that "position learners as potential environmental stewards" (p. 1449). In addition to environmental education, Taylor's noticing is visible in Steffen and colleagues' work. The scientists evoke the planetary to get at the interactivity of social and ecological systems, but ultimately make planetary stewardship a human endeavor alone. Who can be a planetary steward? For Steffen et al. (2007) this falls in part to those humans whose behaviors will have to change. Moreover, the real human power to be planetary agents comes via technoscience development and human "creative invention through discovery" (Steffen et al., 2011, p. 755). Planetary stewardship, despite what might be its proponents' best multi-system intentions, "reiterates human-exceptionalism through its renewed emphasis upon the transformative powers of collective (and individual) human agency" and ingenuity (Taylor, 2017, p. 1451).

There is an important difference between the "human inclusive Earth System" of scientists and the multispecies "collective ecology" that Taylor spotlights in her challenge to the anthropocentrism of stewardship pedagogies. The first type "assumes that humans need to band together to take collective action on behalf of the environment" (Taylor, 2017, p. 1451), whereas the second, which Taylor attributes to childhood ethnographer Karen Malone (2017), is an ongoing ethical praxis of human and nonhuman relational encounter and entanglement. This is collective action *with* the environment rather than solely on behalf of it. Collective ecologies strive to build common worlds, which include grappling with environmental, settler colonial, multispecies, and anti-Black inheritances on a damaged planet (Common Worlds Research Collective, n.d.; Nxumalo, 2019; Taylor & Pacini-Ketchabaw, 2018). Common worlds are neither innocent nor conflict free in this framework and are deeply engaged in supporting ethical relations with more-than-human existents. Part of my argument in this chapter is that the humanist stewardship pedagogy that Taylor challenges with her reconstructive model of common worlds finds form in the idealized parental figure of the next section. Figures of the planetary steward and parental steward both operate "from the premise that humans have exceptional capacities, not only to alter, damage or destroy, but also to manage, protect and save" (Taylor, 2017, p. 1453), whether it be saving the child and/or saving the planet.

Parental Stewardship

The challenge of planetary stewardship, as described mainly by Steffen at al. (2011), is for "humanity to become active stewards of our own life support system" (p. 748). I want to propose that what counts as a life support system in speculative texts are intimacies of parental care that come to stand in for humanity facing ecological peril. The climate crisis becomes about "whether we have cared enough, not just about and for each other and the planet but about and for the future" (Johns-Putra, 2016, p. 520). The Anthropocene predicament provides one answer—humans have not cared nearly enough, or, at least, the kind of care provided has been fundamentally of the wrong sort. An important figure that emerges in care discussions, in both planetary and familial ones, is the child. This is at least partly because of the twinning of the child-figure with/as/to the future, and how the child has long been in metonymic relation with the planet. As Haraway (1997) expresses, the planet and child are "sibling seed worlds" that "concentrate the elixir of life as a complex system" (p. 174). Within this relation, the child's "figuration ... stands in the place of the complex systems at work in ecological materiality" (Sheldon, 2016, p. 5). In this way, the child-figure is "a kind of torsion" between planetary systems and intimate relations (p. 5).

Thinking-with the child-figure in the Anthropocene means that in addition to the normal unknowns of childhood a host of hyperobject concerns are added to the mix (e.g. climate change, geological temporality, deep time). In other words, the child-figure "can be a flashpoint of what are otherwise more abstract, and deferrable, concerns" (Clark, 2017, p. 4). Earth system functioning is perceived as complex while the child is assumed as something simpler. By distilling intricacies of planetary change into a smaller, manageable, and more familiar entity, "the figure of the child embodies climate-change concerns" (Johns-Putra, 2016, p. 523). As such, the child-figure captures "contemporary anxieties about whether we are doing enough to protect, shelter, and safeguard that for which we are responsible" (Johns-Petra, 2016, p. 520). I think that in the space of responsibility is the back-and-forth slippage of the figures of the child and planetary. What does it do to implicate childhood "in the geological formations and dynamics of our planet" and of the future (Clark, 2017, p. 4)?

The affective resonances of climate change are one reason for the growing popularity of cli-fi and other post-apocalyptic speculative genres (Colebrook, 2018). Hee-Jung Joo (2018) reads blockbuster disaster films of this type as disclosing a race-futurity bind that mirrors the problematics of much wider Anthropocene discourse. These overlays find shared form in an anxiety and concern for the future of humanity, which are made more accessible and affectable through cinematic plot lines of the bionormative family. After an ecological disaster threatens mass extinction—films like *The Day After Tomorrow* and *2012* are but two examples—the absent fathers-scientists-patriarchs-Man heroically redeem themselves and protect the planet by saving their sons and re-romancing their wives. A trope of many disaster films is that "the unpredictability of climate change" is averted by recomposing "the white, biological, nuclear family" (Joo, 2018, p. 4). Nuclear families are not observed intact in *The Handmaid's Tale*, but the desire for the heteronormative family structure is an active absent-presence. Its loss is felt, mourned, and motivating in such a pronounced way that alternative kin assemblages are what is leftover rather than what might be a valued formation of care relations. In these texts, regaining the heteronormative bio-family is the potential means of rendering stable an ecologically insecure future.

Often in speculative post-apocalyptic texts, planetary precarity takes shape as a failure to maintain the hegemonic family form and is rectified by a fierce commitment to bio-kin survival. The parental bond—focused on care from the adult toward the child—acts as a concentrated unit to think climate change. Care for the planet and care for the future are performed by way of care for the child. Familial relations serve as "a psychological and emotional touchstone" where planetary stewardship is reframed "as a question of one's responsibility for one's children" (Johns-Putra, 2016, p. 524). This cherished relationship allows for a more familiar and "manageable sphere in which to contemplate the uncontemplatable"—the end of the world (p. 525). *The Handmaid's Tale* lends itself to a reading where if the bio-bond is strong enough, care-full (full of care) enough, ardent enough, and durable enough then just maybe there is a possibility of survival among the Anthropocene-induced ruins of climate catastrophe. There might even be some form of hope possible through the heteronormative promise of a new generation and thus a sustained human species (Sheldon, 2016). My argument is that when care for the child becomes a proxy for care for the environment then planetary stewardship becomes a form of paternal stewardship. This raises important questions: what might be the "profound drawbacks to reading parental love as the antithesis and antidote to environmental destruction" (Johns-Putra, 2016, p. 521)? What is the relation of parental love to ecological care? What if care in one domain means destruction for the other? What if abandoning one means saving the other?

Re-Reading *The Handmaid's Tale* in the Anthropocene

My fascination with Hulu's adaptation of *The Handmaid's Tale* relates mainly to the coexistence of repressive reproductive politics with progressive policies of climate action. It terrifies me that the televised world of Gilead appears to be less polluted, less racist, and less consumptive than this one. In this section, I want to grapple with how care and desire for the child-figure smooths over the coming together of violent governance with environmental stewardship. *The Handmaid's Tale* largely accomplishes this connexion by elevating the child-figure to a position of indisputable good. To paraphrase Edelman (2004) again, what would it mean not to fight for children—is there even another side? What if both sides think they are protecting children? Everyone and everything in Gilead turns on the child—both totalitarian and resistance movements. *The Handmaid's Tale* showrunner Bruce Miller characterizes Gilead in this manner: "in a world where birth rates have fallen so precipitously, fertility would trump everything" (Dockterman, 2017, para. 14). In a world dominated by a fertility crisis, where one in four babies are born with serious birth defects as a direct consequence of environmental toxins, how could the healthy child not be precious, protected, and desired? What does privileging the figure of the child in this way do? What gets displaced? Sheldon (2013) offers a complex provocation:

> Although never foregrounded in the novel, the conjunction of toxic pollution, infertility, and mutation suggests that Gilead's militarized reproductive futurism responds as much to the uncontainable liveliness of

biological and ecological forces—including those extra-diegetic reproductive technologies whose absence the novel so conspicuously underscores—as to the threatening break up of hetero-patriarchy in pre-coup America.

(para. 17)

How does the uncontainable liveliness of ecology get embedded in and embodied by the child-figure? How does the child provide justification for what Sheldon calls militarized reproductive futurism? It is also within these complexities that *The Handmaid's Tale* is able to smuggle in a compassionate, conservative sanctioning of naturalized parenthood, specifically bionormative motherhood. While not fronted in the television adaptation either, which post-dates Sheldon's (2013) observations of the novel, there are a few pivotal scenes that allow for a grappling with the intersections of ecological toxicity, post-racial futurism, and bionormative care.

Atwood wrote *The Handmaid's Tale* the midst of the 1980s pro-choice/pro-life abortion debates in the United States and before the fall of the Berlin Wall. The Hulu adaption began airing in 2017 in the midst of renewed political efforts to restrict abortion rights, the global rise of right-wing populism, and just before the nightmare election of Trump and the child border separation polices that the series so aptly foreshadows.¹ The speculative world of Gilead occupies a large part of the eastern United States, and its temporality is presented as a near dystopic future. Given the political context of both the novel's and television series' emergence, the world of Gilead does not feel especially futuristic or fictitious. As a popular hashtag captures: #MakeMargaretAtwoodFictionAgain. The television series largely follows Atwood's plotline for its first season, but currently in production for its fifth season, the series has moved well beyond its source material.

The Handmaid's Tale is a work of speculative fiction, described as such by Atwood (2012) in an article in *The Guardian*. She also describes, "a rule for myself: I would not include anything that human beings had not already done in some other place or time, or for which the *technology did not already exist*" (para. 11; emphasis added). I am particularly interested in Atwood's take on speculative fiction because of its connections with Latour's and Benjamin's thoughts on technology explored in Chapter 4. Technology does not sit still; a future with the technology of today is anachronic. As such, Benjamin's (2019b) work on "race as a technology" seems to offer a rejoinder to Atwood. Race as a technology captures how technology modifies its form to shapeshift social divisions into the future; race is a technology "designed to separate, stratify, and sanctify the many forms of ... social injustice in the architecture of everyday life" (p. 17). As a technology, race is "innovative and future-oriented," so speculative fiction has an essential function to play in "anticipat[ing] and interven[ing] in new racial formations" (Benjamin, 2016, p. 1). If it can be imagined then maybe it can be prevented, or, in other cases, created. Unlike Benjamin's "Ferguson is the Future," *The Handmaid's Tale* uses science and technology very sparingly. It is not only that there are no new technological inventions, it is that there is almost no technology at all. Both the novel and the television show build a world where technology is one of humanity's most corruptive sins. In Gilead it is not about innovating and developing new technologies, as Latour (2011) suggests, but about getting rid of old ones.

Gilead's technophobia is evident in how its representatives explain the fertility crises. The Handmaid's custodial-figure at the re-education Red Center, Aunt Lydia, lectures in an indoctrination class: "They filled the air with chemicals and radiation and poison, so God whipped up a special plague: the plague of infertility.... As birthrates fell, they made things worse—birth control pills, morning after pills ... their Tinder" (Miller & Morano, 2017, 16:25). While the referent of the "they" bounces between women and all humans, technology also seems a fair substitute—in this case, technologies of reproductive health, sexuality, and environmental destruction. In other words, fossil fuels and Plan B are simultaneously culpable. Additionally, despite Gilead's fertility crises, all assisted reproductive technologies are banned. There is no in-vitro fertilization, cryopreservation, or intracytoplasmic sperm injections. The only baby-making allowed is a forced heterosexual transaction between man and Handmaid. Television, computers, money, smartphones, and books all seem to be banned too. Exiled from Gilead to the Colonies, Unwomen work with broken spades to dig up polluted earth. Trucks and machines that could do the work more efficiently (but with more environmental pollution) are nowhere to be found. The Handmaids have even been stripped of their names, which is a different sort of technology. For example, June, who is never named as such the novel, is known as Offred (i.e., Of Fred) to mark her as property to her master Commander Fred Waterford.

According to Gilead doctrine, in the world before the crises—this world—technologies were loved too much. They promoted immorality and contributed to the environmental disaster. The only kind of love allowed in Gilead is for the child and God—almost interchangeable entities. "Think of yourselves as seeds," Aunt Lydia eerily tells the Handmaids, "the future is in your hands" (Atwood, 1986, p. 19). "It is not her hands," Sheldon (2013) retorts, "that bear the future" (para. 14). A lone technology still cherished in Gilead therefore is the fertile women's womb. Handmaids are "two-legged wombs, that's all: sacred vessels *ambulatory chalices*" (Atwood, 1986, p. 176). Handmaids are a technology of childbirth. After one of the Handmaids, Janine, has her eye gouged out as a punishment for disobedience, June's best friend Moira reflects: "We're breeding stock, you don't need eyes for that" (Miller & Morano, 2017, 22:10). *The Handmaid's Tale* is Lauren Berlant's (1997) infantile citizenship to an nth degree: the fetus trumps the Handmaid—the child trumps everything else.

Born Pre-Polluted[2]

As mentioned above, the world of Gilead experiences an unspecified ecological catastrophe which induces a fertility crisis. The crisis provides the pretext for a puritanical, elitist male covenant to usurp governmental power. Women's rights are quickly curtailed, and women's bodies are strictly governed, monitored, used, and regulated by the state. Gilead stands as a totalitarian-theocratic regime maintained by threat, surveillance, indoctrination, and violence. Fertile women are rounded up, re-educated, and re-distributed to high-ranking men and their wives to reproduce. A monthly procreation ceremony is held in the family house—the ritualized theatrics of which would be comical if they did not center on rape. The Handmaids have the opportunity to reproduce with three different families before they are exiled to the toxic wastelands of the Colonies. Given this, Heather Latimer (2009) reads the novel as "a picture of what the world might look like if a woman's only reproductive 'choice' is pregnancy or death" (p. 213). While this has much truth to it, Sheldon (2013) extends a third possibility "that splits open the opposition of pregnancy and death" (para. 16). This possibility is the "unbabies and the mutagens responsible for their deformities" (para. 16), which shakes the geontological boundary of life and nonlife. Unbabies, or Shredders as they are also called, are babies born with severe birth deformities and a small chance at survival.

In her work on natality, Arendt (1958) notes that the "the force of life is fertility" (p. 108). Sheldon (2013) performs an Anthropocene twist on natality to consider how radiation, chemical spills, toxic soils, and other mutagens make it so "biological reproduction is hardly the only source of liveliness" anymore (para. 18). Perhaps Arendt (1958) gestures toward such an awareness with her idea of the "surplus" of life in "its potential multiplication" (p. 108), but, for the most part, natality remains within a biopolitical frame. However, in the Anthropocene, the "force of life" is not only or mainly fertility but toxic liveliness. Gilead's babies are born pre-polluted (MacKendrick & Cairns, 2019), and so are babies in this world. How does mutational liveliness challenge a concept of reproductive futurism that relies on an idealized and bionormative figure of the child? What futurity does a toxic-child figure forth?

I am most drawn to speculative texts of climate catastrophe that put the promise and premise of bionormative reproductive futurism under pressure. The challenge these texts must engage entails how "to consolidate the explosion of other-than-human liveliness under the figure of the child at the same time that it suggests an accelerating horizon of unrecuperable vitality" (Sheldon, 2013, para. 18). In other words, the "other-than-human-liveliness" in *The Handmaid's Tale* consists of all the toxic pollutants and toxic bodies linked to the environmental disaster but for which each new child offers a chance at overcoming and therefore shifting the course of the future. However, what each Unbaby does is reconfirm an inability to fully contain and control toxicity, or, as Sheldon (2013) names it above, the horizon of unrecuperable vitality. Unbabies are figures of Anthropocene Child.

The Unbabies and the Unwomen of the Colonies—those who do not die even though their liveliness and lifetimes are severely reduced—are a form of existence as toxic ongoingness. Toxicity in Gilead is not distributed equally nor entirely controllable, and its unrestrained appearance interrupts the purity narrative of the totalitarian regime. With the figure of the Shredder baby, "*The Handmaid's Tale* shows us the reproductive future behind the sacred child of reproductive futurism" (para. 19). Unlike Edelman's (2004) conceptualization, the reproductive futures of Anthropocene Child are pre-polluted in both their symbolic and material existences. As pointed out by Sheldon (2013), the only baby born in the space of Atwood's novel is an Unbaby, and, as such, represents a failure of militarized reproductive futurism and totalitarian patriarchy to control the environment. Related to the last chapter, the Unbabies of Gilead could have been a lesson in "loving our monsters" or a "kinship of the infertile," yet, in the revisioning of *The Handmaid's Tale* for television, the Shredder-child is not for a visualized world. The novel's baby is reborn onscreen as a healthy, white, perfectly able-bodied baby. And the maternal relation—the baby and her mother Janine—leads into a pivotal scene from which to consider the idolizing of bionormative care, but first a closer look at the text's primary maternal protagonist Offred/June.

Bionormative Motherhood

In the novel, Offred is a passive protagonist. As the book's narrator, readers are privy to her inner thoughts and they are not those of a rebel feminist hero. Nevertheless, we are given enough insight to develop some empathy. In the pre-Gilead world of the novel, Offred has trouble accepting her mother's feminist activism, hesitates to embrace her best friend's queer sexuality, and only notices the world changing when it is too late. As a captive Handmaid, she never really desires to join the resistance and seems to give up and accept her position in the latter half of the novel. The book ends with Offred pregnant and presented with a possible escape. When a black van arrives to transport her, readers are not sure if an ally has arranged her getaway or if she is being arrested. As the star of a television series, this ambiguousness and passiveness will not do. Audiences are much less-likely to rally behind a woman who does not stand up against Gilead and fight. Television series need heroes; patriarchal worlds need feminist de(con)structors. I desire June, not Offred.

Compassion for television's June is immediately built as the audience bears witness to the monthly rape ritual in the first episode (and in the second episode and again and again after that). Support is fully secured with a flashback of her family's failed escape attempt to Canada. Near the border, June and her daughter, Hannah, separate from her husband and run through the woods. A mother gripping her child tight and running, hiding, stumbling, and falling before having her child ripped from her arms by ICE lookalikes plays out like a *Law & Order* ripped from the headlines' episode. Despite the trauma of having her child stolen away, June is witty, smart, and always plotting her escape. Escape, though, might not be the right word because the moment June is assured safe passage to Canada late in season two, she turns it down, turns around, and heads back to Gilead. Why? Hannah is still there. June's goal is reunion not escape (or reunion AND escape). June's entire motivation is to get her child back, and any thoughts of ending Gilead's oppressive policies and practices are secondary. Especially in the second season of Hulu's adaptation, *The Handmaid's Tale* plays into the post-apocalyptic trope that places "the reunification of the heteronormative white family at the center of the drama" (Fojas, 2017, p. 11). The identification of white here does not quite fit, as June's daughter and husband are identified as Black. However, as will be examined, the bionormative whiteness of the hegemonic maternal bond persists nonetheless.

The Handmaid's Tale television series has been a huge critical and popular success. Women dressed in the Handmaid's crimson robes and white bonnets fill state legislature buildings to protest against laws that will further discipline their bodies; tattoos of "Nolite te bastardes carborundorum" [Don't let the bastards grind you down] imprint on bodies and get lots of likes on Instagram; countless posts warning #HandmaidsTaleIsNotAnInstructionManual follow each episode and/or problematic government policy announcement. Amidst this popularity, Jennifer Maher (2018) troubles how the series assembles its critical response, and I would like to extend her provocation to consider how it affectively shifts planetary stewardship toward parental stewardship. Maher (2018) asks:

> In order to most effectively "warn" us against repressive reproductive futurity, does *The Handmaid's Tale* marshal its own kind of neoliberal reproductive fantasies of the substance (if not the sanctity) of the nuclear family, with its roots in romantic love and melodramatic maternity? According the narrative's emotional logic, Gilead is the *most* horrifying of places not only for its cruel gender tyranny but for its distortion of the most "primary" of human relationships: heterosexual love that produces biological children.
>
> (p. 209)

I would add, as Maher entertains later in her article, that the main relationship *The Handmaid's Tale* uplifts is not the heterosexual couple but the maternal bond. The emotional horror of June and Hannah's separation happens not once but multiple times. On one occasion, Commander Waterford's wife, Serena Joy, arranges for her and June to go on a long drive outside the city. After a few hours, Serena gets out of the car, locks June inside, and knocks on the front door of a house. Hannah emerges and Serena puts her arm around the child as they engage in a brief conversation. June is left screaming and trashing around in the car. This glimpse of her child is not given out of kindness but as an assertion of Serena's control and a threat to June to stay in line. Serena knows the power of the bio-bond is more effective than any physical punishment she could inflict. It is not ultimately the sexual violence or queer killings but the separation of mother and child that hits home most affectively in *The Handmaid's Tale*. A powerful example of this involves Janine and her newborn baby in an episode called "The Bridge" (Tuchman & Dennis, 2017).

Handmaids typically remain in their Commander's household for a few months after the birth of their child to breastfeed. After their babies are weaned, they are relocated to another home so they can get to work reproducing again. Janine was moved earlier than usual, and viewers find out the reason why before "The Bridge" concludes. In the pivotal scene, June is awakened by a panicked Serena who tells her Janine is threatening to jump of a bridge with her baby. Earlier that night, Janine had abducted her baby from the Putman's house. When June arrives at the blocked-off bridge there are guards, guns, Aunt Lydia, and the Waterford and Putman families. Commander Putman attempts to talk Janine off the ledge which prompts her to scream out details of their illegal sexual affair and his broken promises for them to form their own happy nuclear family. The Putman wife tries to appease Janine by inviting her back into the household, but Janine does not believe her. As Janine gets closer to the edge, June comes forward to appeal to her maternal side: does she really want to hurt her baby? Is this how to best protect and care for her innocent child? June convinces Janine to hand her the baby, and, as soon as she does, Janine leaps off the bridge before the guards can reach her. Janine's rebellion ends with her in a coma from which she later physically recovers enough to be banished to the Colonies, only to return again when her maternal savourism is desperately needed.[3] Maher (2018) writes about how she watched with bated breath as Janine crept closer to the edge, and that she was relieved when Janine handed her baby over before she jumped. But then Maher catches herself and offers a description that equally captures my reaction:

> I was relieved *when it was just her*. The emotional stakes of *The Handmaid's Tale* are amped up to such an extreme degree that the attempted suicide of an innocent woman who has already had her eye gouged out for disobedience elicits relief from its (feminist) audience because *at least the baby didn't die* ... in siding ourselves against Gilead, we can also find ourselves, albeit unconsciously, emotionally complicit with it .... It wasn't so long ago that feminism insisted on a deconstruction of biological essentialism in the face of such calls via a rigorous analysis of the repression inherent in heterosexist assumptions of the meaning of mothers, fathers, romantic love, and family.
>
> (p. 210)

It is important to be clear that this is not about criticizing those who live and love within this family form, but about the heterosexism implicit in prioritizing a naturalized form of sacrificial love to be waged at the "shrine of the sacred Child" (Edelman, 2004, p. 24). Maher's (2018) concern, one that I share, is if *The Handmaid Tale's* "dramatization of woman-as-womb might reinforce a neoliberal version of the very same claim" (p. 210). Remember June's transition from the passive Offred of the book (who never saw her child again after their initial separation) to the brave resister whose primary motivation is to get Hannah back. The figure of "June will rebel not because she has been forced *into* maternity but because it has been *denied* her" (p. 210).

The undertones of sacrificial love and bionormative motherhood are important to flesh out. *The Handmaid Tale* promotes a maternal form of sacrificial love which justifies rather than juxtaposes violence and survival as moral values. Povinelli (2009) asks how "discourses of sacrifice and sacrificial love coordinate violence and redemption in such a way that suffering and dying, the mortification of bodies, are read from the perspective of the redeemed end of a horizontal time" (p. 77). Janine has one functioning eye, long-term psychological damage from abuse pre- and current Gilead, has her child ripped from her arms, and is condemned to die a slow death in the Colonies—but at least her child is "safe." Safe to be raised by the leaders of a repressive regime? Safe to be subservient? Safe to never learn to read or write or think for herself? Safe to grow up in a privileged household before being forced to become a Handmaid herself? Furthermore, Janine's redemption passes in a moment—it begins at the same time as it ends—when she hands June her baby and jumps. Through June, though, the potential for redemption is kept alive. June has transformed from passive (Offred) to active (June), victim to hero, ignorant to knowing, and so she will be rewarded by getting Hannah back. All the violence June suffers will ultimately be worth it, or so the sacrificial story goes; violent oppression does not deter her from her goal but makes her stronger and more focused, a dangerous lesson in real life. I feel confident wagering almost anything that June and Hannah will be together again before the series ends. That is what happens when you act the hero and when bionormative motherhood is the superpower. And it is not only the speculative world of Gilead that is supporting a narrowed valuation of what counts as maternal care.

Stepping outside speculative texts for a moment, I turn to Kate Cairns, Josée Johnston, and Norah MacKendrick's (2013) work on the organic child and how this idealized figure embodies "expectations about childhood and maternal social and environmental responsibility by emphasizing mothers' individual responsibility for securing children's futures" (p. 97). Behind the figure of the organic child lies a hegemonic understanding of motherhood delimited by care and protection narrowly and traditionally defined. How does this link with *The Handmaid's Tale*? These care-efforts are lived out at an emotional level that can be both empowering and guilt producing. Taking care of the organic child entails "practices and ideals [that] rest upon maternal values of love, care, and responsibility" that are intensified in and by the toxic potential of the Anthropocene (p. 113). Like Puig de la Bellacasa's (2017) three-layered care formulation, the organic child receives care that is labor intensive, affective, and reflective of an eco-sensitive ethics, yet it stays at the level of the individual as a false synecdoche for the planetary. This is a form planetary stewardship individually enacted by buying and feeding the right foods from the right places to the right kind of child from the right sort of mother. Planetary stewardship slips into parental stewardship as the primary maternal responsibility becomes "producing a healthy child and a healthy planet" (p. 98), as if they are one and the same. The figure of the organic child updates the trope of the child as the future. To have a future—to save the future—to be the future—the organic child must be a "pure child," kept away from "harmful impurities of an industrialized food system" (p. 98).

The Handmaid's Tale makes clear that impurities are not limited to agriculture and/or consumerism but are cumulative and co-occurring over many infrastructures. To make a bad pass at a cliché: purity is not only food deep. What Gilead promises is religious purity, sexual purity, racial purity, and environmental purity. While Cairns and colleagues critically link the organic child to neoliberalized, individualized consumption practices, this same kind of connection is not exactly transferable to the speculative economies of Gilead. In Gilead there is no money and all food is organic. In the next section, I look at how organic food is mandated for the Handmaids, especially expectant mothers, in order to safely feed the child/future. My guiding matter of care and concern is how *The Handmaid's Tale* performs the environmentalization of care.

The Environmentalization of Care

The environmental aspects of *The Handmaid's Tale* have not received much attention in scholarly or popular circles. Most critical work has focused on a feminist critique of gendered violence. Such work is important, and my intent is not to diminish it, but to suggest that a feminist plus ecological lens might add something significant to the discussion. The most detailed depiction of Gilead's environmental stewardship occurs in an episode midway through season one titled "A Women's Place" (Hauser & Sigismondi, 2017). In this episode a Mexican trade delegation visits Gilead and the proverbial red carpet is rolled out including a formal banquet. Up until this point, by reading between the lines, viewers assume that chemical pollution and radioactive waste are at least partial causes of the fertility crises. We learn in this episode that Gilead's corrective environmental measures have resulted in fertility rates for its Handmaids well above the global average. For their part, Mexico has not had baby born alive in more than six years.

In the world of Gilead, environmental stewardship is a key component of what Serena, once a successful "domestic feminist" activist and author herself, calls a "healthy and moral way to life" (15:10). In a flashback reveal, we learn that it was Serena who first suggested the doctrine of "fertility as a national resource, reproduction as a moral imperative" (18:30). Stewardship tactics of reducing carbon emissions, restoring healthy soils, limiting fossil fuel usage, and making sure the Handmaids only eat organic foods are all steps toward achieving this goal. In this way, a clean environment goes hand-in-hand with what counts as morality in Gilead, and it is a by-all-means-necessary kind of go(o)dliness. "Gilead's leaders would have people believe that it's the marriage of moral righteousness and a clean environment," Corey Plante (2017) points out, "that inspires fertility in its Handmaids .... By their logic, God blesses Handmaids with fertility because of their green initiatives" (para. 3). It is this equivocation I want to dig into more.

Some key moments of dialogue in the episode are worth repeating. "We've transitioned to a completely organic agricultural model," Commander Waterford tells the Mexican Ambassador (13:40). Serena follows-up later with a statement that Gilead has "reduced its carbon emissions by seventy-eight percent in three years" (15:45). Overhead in passing is how the citrus orchards are progressing "really well," even enduring the "new weather patterns" (14:03). At the evening banquet, Serena brags of Gilead's "great strides cleaning the environment and restoring a healthy and moral way of life" (34:30). Again, the environment, morality, and fertility are interwoven. Serena insists that oranges feature in the banquet presentation, but the true highlight of the evening festivities is the parade of healthy young children born to the Handmaids. The episode makes clear that fertility has replaced money as valuable commodity, and, as it turns out, it is the Handmaids that are up for trade with the Mexican government. Demonstrating naiveté more expected of the novel's Offred, June assumes the delegation is after oranges: "Gilead only has one thing that anyone wants," another Handmaid whispers in a corrective fashion to June at the dinner (37:25). The next morning, June summons her courage and dangerously steals away a private moment of time with the Ambassador. June tells her of the horrors for women in Gilead, but the potential ally turns her back—the procreation potential is too much.

Outside the urban center of Gilead are the Colonies, which are vast radioactive wastelands. This is where those who break with Gilead's rigid theocratic code are expelled. They are wastelands because the soils are full of chemical pollutants but also because this is where disposable bodies are sent to labor and die. The inhabitants are mainly Unwomen—women who are too old, too infertile, too rebellious, and too queer. In a season two episode called "Unwomen" (Miller & Barker, 2018), viewers are transported to the Colonies for the first time. All previous mentions were verbal hints only. Unwomen are shown toiling all day in the fields where they shovel toxic soil into bags for removal to who knows where. They are performing a version of "soil care" that appears trapped within a productionist logic: their labor "is aimed at increasing soil's efficiency to produce for [some] humans at the expense of all other relations" (Puig de la Bellacasa, 2015, p. 700), including their own health. Their nails fall out along with their teeth; their skin is raw and broken; their bones protrude from lack of food. The Aunts that guard the workers have breathing masks, but I wager these are more of a status reminder than any real protection from the radioactivity.

Despite the dreariness and deathliness of the Colonies, what comes through the darkness of this episode is the Unwomen's relational, reciprocal care for each other. They are shown practicing love for each other's monstrous degradations. The Unwomen find moments of kindness, friendship, and love within the monotony of enforced labor and gradual poisoning. They create "care time" that is "irreducible to productionist time" (Puig de la Bellacasa, 2015, p. 707). They bandage each other's cracking hands; exchange gentle looks, words, and touches; share what little medicine has been smuggled in; and brew mint tea for one another. In the episode, there is even a low-key commitment ceremony and celebration. The Unwomen form a "kinship of the infertile" on multiple scales (Klein, 2014). Reproductively, they are infertile; agriculturally, they labor in toxic fields; futuristically, they die a gendered, slow violence together. I am not trying to romanticize their queer-kin care: this care is an ephemeral means of survival against the backdrop of inevitable death. Nevertheless, there is a sort of inarticulable beauty in their refusal to abandon one another and practice a toxic common worlding.

On the one hand, Gilead's extreme misogynistic reproductive policies are violent and should be condemned. FULL STOP. On the other, their environmental policies and practices appear to be quite advanced—progressive even—though not many details are ever revealed. But can Gilead's regenerative stewardship practices, such as organic farming and the curtailing of emissions, be recognized as some form of environmental justice? Can environmental stewardship be separated out from the political, physical, and religious violence of the regime? I argue that it cannot, or, at least, I desire that such a separation is not possible. I also think that this concurrence (evil political regime plus good environmental policy) is where speculative texts are especially valuable. I mean this in the sense that Benjamin (2016) refers to as speculative stories providing anticipatory assistance for imagining and intervening in futures. What political programs will be introduced as this world becomes warmer and more toxic?

My refusal to unlink violent practices from environmental stewardship in *The Handmaid's Tale* connects to what Anna Reser and Leila McNeill (2017) have named the text's "logic of cultivation" (para. 1). This logic revolves around the primacy of reproduction and its intra-affectivity with the sacredness of the child. For example, Reser and McNeil summarize Gilead's governmental rationale as: "A clean environment promotes health and decreases infant mortality. Organic farming reduces concentrations of pesticides that are believed to be a contributing factor in the fertility crisis" (para. 3). The common devotional refrain among members of Gilead is "Blessed be the fruit." This reminds the Handmaids of the child-bodies they must bear, the organic food they must eat, and also that their bodies are a valuable commodity to be traded like produce. In this way, "the Handmaids are transformed into the image of nature itself, the ultimate erasure of their humanity" (para. 7). In work on planetary stewardship outlined earlier, Steffen et al. (2011) approach the Anthropocene as a call "to fundamentally alter our relationship with the planet we inhabit" (p. 739). Despite the organic food, reduced CO_2 emissions, and regenerating soils, *The Handmaid's Tale* is definitely not the kind of alteration needed. A conversation between June and Commander Waterford catches some of this dilemma: "We only wanted to make the world better," says the Commander. "Better?" June questions. He continues, "Better never means better for everyone. It always means worse for some" (Fortenberry & Barker, 2017, 34:08). This is a massive impasse that planetary stewardship must grapple with. Another is how planetary and parental stewardship can perpetuate racialized oppressions.

Post-Racial Parenthood

The Handmaid's Tale allows for a serious problematizing of misogynistic totalitarianism and religious fundamentalism, but how this censure is achieved matters. Does critique lose some of its force when racialization is not taken into account? Ben Merriman (2009) points out that Atwood's novel offers "an archetypal account of female exploitation, but the stand-in for this universal experience is Offred, a White, college-educated American" (p. 43). I do not know the statistics but I wager this same demographic makes up the largest share of the show's viewing audience. In this way, the novel's affective horror is "basically a nightmare vision in which white, college-educated women like Atwood [and June and myself] are forced to undergo the experiences of women of color" (Berlastsky, 2015, para. 4). Noah Berlastsky (2017) notices that fiction developed in, by, and for the Global North has a horrible habit of framing "dystopic stories" as a thought-experiment about "what if this atrocity had happened to white people instead?" (para. 1). It is hard not to read Atwood's novel in this light, especially with the recognition that one of the "terrible things about being a handmaid is that you cease to be white" (para. 6). By this Berlastsky is referring to the privileges granted by whiteness—freedom of movement, freedom to read, freedom to work, freedom to leisure, freedom to travel, freedom to not conceive—that blur lines between the institutional and the personal and the fictional and the real. As a middle-class, educated, attractive, employed, white-settler married women, June is a figure of the least-likely victim given the way power is typically distributed in this world. More generously, perhaps this is Atwood's point: it could happen to anyone; your privilege will not protect you forever; pay attention. Where *The Handmaid's Tale* hits a big limit is that there is little indication that oppression is intersectional, particularly when fertility is threatened.

Rather than engage how violence works across sociopolitical categories, Atwood's (1986) novel worlds an all-white world. So, while Gilead is both sexist, homophobic, and racist, Atwood spends no time explicitly acknowledging their connection. In the novel, white Handmaids are forced to breed for elite white men in what can reasonably be assumed as a technique not only to propagate the human species but the white race. Everyone else, including those who identify as queer, are exiled to the Colonies. In *Wayward Reproductions*, Alys Eve Weinbaum (2004) proposes a "race/reproduction bind" to capture the "inextricability of the connection ... the fact that these phenomena ought not to be thought of as distinct" (p. 5). As noted, the novelized Gilead is an all-white enclave. Black people are erased in just two lines, cloaked in an Old Testament euphemism: "Resettlement of the Children of Ham is continuing on schedule ... Three thousand have arrived this week in National Homeland One, with another two thousand in transit" (Atwood, 1986, p. 83). The point

I am getting at is that the oppression depicted in *The Handmaid's Tale* is most recognizable to audiences as that inflicted on Black women during slavery and its afterlife.[4] With a quick act of literary banishment, however, Atwood "didn't have to interact with characters of color while capitalizing from implementing systems of oppression that about were first used in the U.S. on enslaved Africans" (Abraham, 2017, para. 6). Angelica Jade Bastién (2017) finds that the expulsion "feels like the mark of a writer unable to reckon with how race would compound the horrors of a hyper-Evangelical-ruled culture" (para. 5). In the novel, readers never learn what happens in National Homeland One let alone in Homeland Two or Three or Ten.

Recall Atwood's speculative fiction mantra cited earlier that she does not put anything in her stories that has not happened somewhere at some time before. This deserves a second look because of the important critiques raised about *The Handmaid's Tale*'s treatment of blackness. Much of this critical scholarship is produced on blogs, social media, and magazine websites rather than academic journals, including the sources cited above (e.g., Abraham, 2017; Bastién, 2017; Berlatsky, 2017; Phoenix, 2018; Priya, 2017). Atwood, along with many who study her in more traditional scholarly circles, have traced many historical precedents for Gilead's oppressive regime.[5] However, I join with the pop culture critics in arguing that anti-Black slavery is the strongest historical context for the story's horrors. The list is long: stolen children, enforced labor, banned literacy, master's names, involuntary procreation, people as property, public hangings, restricted movement, and constant surveillance. Atwood (1986) even names the escape route to Canada the "Underground Femaleroad" (pp. 303, 309), an all too obvious referent. While not necessarily intentional, Atwood may have relied heavily on these historical practices "to bring realism to the speculative. The suffering of the Black people in her world is, however, rendered invisible" (Phoenix, 2018, p. 206). Atwood has admitted, when pressed hard about her reliance on tropes of anti-Black slavery, that "it's not just African Americans; it's slavery in general. Or, say, oppression in general" (Dodson, 1997, p. 101). Priya's (2017) critique, however, drives the point home: "By taking the specific oppression of enslaved Black women and applying them uncritically to white women, *The Handmaid's Tale* ignores the historical realities of an American dystopia founded on anti-Black violence" (para. 2). As such, *The Handmaid's Tale* "remains silent on the central feature of American history: anti-Blackness" (para. 2).

Fast forward thirty-years from the novel's publication and Hulu showrunner Miller flips the script on racial exclusion for a racially diverse cast. Miller positions Black actors in the major supporting roles of June's best friend, husband, and child. Nothing in my discussion is meant to discount the talent of these actors—particularly the brilliant Samira Wiley who plays Moira—or to repudiate the good intentions behind Miller's wish to diversify Gilead. In an interview, Miller mentions long conversations he has had with Atwood about the differently racialized Gilead. The point he pushes is that there is a big difference between reading that "there are no people of color in this world," and seeing it visually on screen. He asks, "What's the difference between making a TV show about racists and making a racist TV show where you don't hire any actors of color?" (para. 11). What *is* the difference? This is a really important question. I am not sure exactly how to respond. At first, Atwood was hesitant about the multicultural update. Miller recalls her saying, "Well that would change everything" (para. 12). Thinking of Klein's (2014) work in the last chapter: what is the *everything* that is changed? Did adding actors of color actually alter anything? What is happening to the people of Gilead is not new, as Atwood herself confirms in many interviews, but because it is happening to a white, middle-class, educated, affluent, working-mother June, there remains an air of natalistic invention.

This is all to say that the inclusion of Black actors in key roles does not mean *The Handmaid's Tale* has moved beyond its source text's racial shortcomings. Instead, it has transitioned from expulsion to multiculturalism. The result of Miller's update is a colorblind sort of equality of risk "that ultimately supports white erasure" of the violence experienced by Black, Indigenous, and other people of color (Abraham, 2017, para. 8). Both the novel and series, in my opinion, are still valuable given the political present, including that both versions allow for serious questions about fetishizing the child, governing women's bodies, unjust family separation practices, bionormative parenthood, nationalistic pride and populism (e.g., Make American Great Again could be a Gilead slogan), and, even, environmental destruction. Like much of this world, however, Gilead is a white supremacist state, and even in June's moments of resistance and in her fierce color-blind maternal love it is still that. In an awful, regrettable, needs-to-be-changed-now kind of way, Atwood's worlding is almost more believable than Miller's world where racialized difference no longer matters. Soraya Nadia McDonald (2017) caricatures my point and brings an Anthropocene-related concept of extinction into play: "So Gilead is post-racial because the human race is facing extinction, and that prompted Americans to get over several hundred years' worth of racist education and social conditioning that depicted Black people as inferior and less than human?" (para. 19). This ecoanxiety over extinction knots the whiteness of Gilead's puritanism, environmentalism, and reproductive futurism together.

The Handmaid's Tale encourages me to reconsider the environmental a/effects of being in non-bionormative relations on a broken earth and also the dangers of elevating parental bonds above other forms of relation. How do planetary stewardship and parental stewardship offer care for some forms of existence (i.e., human) while outcasting and abandoning others (i.e., Shredders)? Unbabies are not the kind of life that warrants care in Gilead—that world requires organic existence (Sheldon, 2016). Nevertheless, the Shredder-child challenges the habit of seeing birth, growth, and survival as holding the promise of futurity for bionormative babies alone. The Shredder-child shows how toxicity is not something that can be easily exiled to National Homeland One. It underlies everything and is in everyone. Meanwhile, the Unwomen demonstrate care for the polluted—for the infertile. More than the parental figures in *The Handmaid's Tale*, the Unwomen put into existence the kind of care necessary in the Anthropocene.

7

Educational Imaginaries for Child-Climate Futures

In the conclusion, I consider the relationship of child-figures in speculative texts and children in this world. Lee Edelman (2004) is adamant that the figure of the child not "be confused with the lived experiences of any actual ... children" (p. 11). I do not think the lines of separation are so clear cut. Instead, they are entangled. It is not a 1:1 correspondence, but it is a relationship. Another way to frame this concern are the (im)commensurabilities between figures of Anthropocene Child and Children of the Anthropocene that were briefly mentioned in Chapter 1. The latter is used by both Karen Malone (2017) and Margaret Somerville (2017) to collectively name their young co-researchers who are making their way amidst the climate crisis in relation with others—human and more-than-human. The geostories in this book largely depict an eventalization of crisis (e.g., zombie apocalypse, planetary earthquake, torrential flood), and the child-figures emerge from creative adult endeavors, whereas Children of the Anthropocene live and remark upon the mundane, everyday small moments that nevertheless scale up to big questions of "planetary ethics posed by the Anthropocene" (Taylor & Pacini-Ketchabaw, 2015, p. 508). What I take from this is the necessity of keeping Elizabeth Povinelli's (2013) cautionary words in mind when working with child-figures: "Why don't we ever ask what it is like to be this figure?" Some related questions that move between worlds include: What is it to be a toxic-child? What is it to be "born pre-polluted" (MacKendrick & Cairns, 2019)? What is it to be the one who is supposed to save? Can thinking-with child-figures at the end of the world actually grapple with the kinds of conditions, resources, and institutions required to capacitate lives capable of flourishing? With these concerns in mind, I bring figures of Anthropocene Child from previous chapters together with provocations for educational futures.

Gatherings of Anthropocene Child

In her book, *Willful Subjects,* Sara Ahmed (2014) describes her methodological strategy as following a figure around to see what collects. Applied in this way, Anthropocene Child instigates a kind of archive that is composed of literary works, multidisciplinary theory, newspaper headlines, commercial advertisements, blockbuster and indie films, critically acclaimed television shows, and photographs.[1] Spotlighted in this book have been speculative works (of theory, of fiction, of fact) that act as a catalyst for analytical grapplings with the Anthropocene through geos-imaginaries of the end of the world. I have aimed to show that not all ends are equal. For example, Aiyana in "Ferguson is the Future" has her life literally ended by racialized police violence to then regenerate and protect an imaginary cyborg-world; Melanie in *The Girl with All the Gifts* ends the human exceptional world in order to begin a multispecies-oriented one; and the young people in *The Marrow Thieves* rebuild in the ongoing post-apocalypse through community, ceremony, and language. Because the end of the world entails multiple arrangements it allows for child-figures to stay on the move, as was evidenced by the continuum of Black cyborgs in Chapter 5 (James, 2013; Vargas & James, 2013).

A danger in following particular child-figures around is that the field of vision is narrowed. Focusing intently on specific figures can cut them off "*from the histories of [their] determination* ... the social and material relations which overdetermine their existence, and the consequent perception that such figures have a 'life of their own'" (Ahmed, 2000, p. 5). The slippage into a fetishism of figures is easy and it is something I am learning (and failing and trying again) to pay attention to and not enact. This is why the connection of the zombie and slavery was important to draw out in a discussion of Melanie, and why the doubling inhuman geography of the Anthropocene—the inhuman as matter and the inhuman as race (Yusoff, 2018)—was necessary to the geostorying of Nassun. This is also why symbiotic entanglement is important to foreground. Nassun does not exhibit autonomous agency because she intra-acts with the earth: together they are a geos-force. Melanie seems to commit a solitary act of heroism when she sets the seed pod tower ablaze but each movement and thought depends on an intradependent relation with the fungal pathogen. These child-figures help me appreciate "that no one stands or acts alone" (Taylor, 2013, p. 117). Brought together under the broad category Anthropocene Child, speculative child-figures are able to embody distinct histories and enact conflicting ideas and imaginaries. The goal is cumulative—a gathering, a collecting—rather than comparative; it is an additive rather than subtractive practice. Bringing figures together is an act of assemblage that is never innocent. With the collection of child-figures here, I have aimed to show the asymmetrical slide in the image of the child from protected and protector along racialized lines (Sheldon, 2016). It is a punitive position for some and transformative for others, even as they share challenges of surviving the climate crisis.

"Following the child" is frequently invoked in early childhood education and other child-studies related fields as a catchphrase for child-centered pedagogy. It supposes an intentional process on behalf of both educator and child in that the teacher steps back and the student leads (perhaps another indicator of Sheldon's shift?). This pedagogical instructive has been challenged for positioning the child as individualistic and anthropocentrically elevated in a hierarchical and non-dependent relationship to others, including existents of more-than-human worlds (Common Worlds Research Collective, n.d.; Nxumalo, 2019; Taylor & Pacini-Ketchabaw, 2018). Similar dangers haunt my analytic practices. In focusing intently on child-figures, even in trying to highlight their geos-entanglements, what is missed? Instead of turning "*away from dominant discourses that reproduce grand narratives of transcendent heroic solutions . . . and, that represent children as the 'solution' for the future*" (Nxumalo, 2018, p. 2), how might turning *toward* child-figures reaffirm those same discourses and positionalities? The researchers I cite above engage with children and more-than-human worlds in situated encounters and places. Their work aims to "eschew the heroic tales of major individuals on the big stage and seek out alternative, minor, but powerful polyphonic stories of multiple small players, quietly changing worlds together on the margins"

(Taylor & Pacini-Ketchabaw, 2018, p. 7). I cannot claim the same.[2] Nevertheless, I share with these scholars a concern about children inhabiting and inheriting ecologically and colonially damaged worlds.

Ontological Demands

Povinelli (2013) questions how much contemporary critical theory has thought about what happens when figure meets ground—when theories of potentiality go live. Given that many of the speculative child-figures I think-with are Black and Indigenous characters, I refuse to stay solely within Edelman's symbolic realm and instead connect issues of speculative worlds to pressing problems in this one. That said, I do not intend a seamless correspondence of child-figures with children in this world. This is not to deny connections, but to insist that some differences are incommensurable. For example, thinking-with the generativity of Unbabies and the Colonies in *The Handmaid's Tale* is not the same thing as living-with Aamjiwnaang First Nation children who experience the everyday chemical exposures of survival in sacrifice zones (Wiebe, 2017). As Malone (2017) insists, "We are not all in the Anthropocene together—the poor and the dispossessed, the children are far more in it than others" (p. 249). Yet, toxicity brings these worlds into conversation: these child-figures and children are born(e) pre-polluted. At times I have not articulated the lines of difference because it can be useful to think them together. However, I do not want to discount that it matters where analytic cuts are made (Barad, 2007). This leads me into another unresolved question: why do why theorists, myself included, keep turning to child-figures to think through and with/in worlds under threat? By distilling intricacies of the climate crisis into a supposed smaller, manageable, and more familiar entity, "the figure of the child embodies climate-change concerns" (Johns-Putra, 2016, p. 523). As such, the child-figure becomes a concentrated unit to locate contemporary eco-anxieties about the future. This is not something I am uncritically endorsing. The slippage between the figures of the child and planetary can be dangerous—they are not the same in terms of scale, temporality, or ontology—but they can bring into view shared concerns about response-ability, history, desire, and futurity.

I want to bring one last figure of Anthropocene Child into the fold as they bring to the fore these concerns. They are on this book's cover and I affectionately call them Elephant Annie. They are named Annie because their red hair and dress resembles orphan Annie from the movie-musical of the same name (Huston, 1982). At first glance though, it is probably not the musical allusion that captures your attention but the gas mask. They are wearing a vintage GP-5 gas mask, a Soviet era relic from the Cold War. The mask is nicknamed elephant because of the crinkled hose that joins the face piece to the filter—Elephant Annie's mask is missing this latter life-saving component. I understand Elephant Annie as a geontological figure of Anthropocene Child: they are both Virus and Animist (Povinelli, 2016). Their mask signals chemical radiation and pollution that long outlasts human lifespans; it also hints at a sort of becoming-animal at the end of the world (Deleuze & Guattari, 1987). The Desert is also evoked in the cover image, as there are signs of struggling vegetation. The layered planters that frame the scene indicate that maybe plant life is ongoing, although the overwhelming brown hues put that reading in question. A stronger sign of life is far in the background: green tree tops. It is in the horizon, much like the future the figure of the child typically symbolizes. Still, much in the frame seems at risk, even with Elephant Annie's defiant power stance, so my takeaway is that this is a dying earth. When I think of the figure of the Desert in connection with this picture, however, I keep coming back to the masks.

The elephant masks are the iconography of life abandoned after the Chernobyl disaster. The Exclusion Zone was set up after the 1986 nuclear meltdown and covers a thousand-mile square radius around the Chernobyl Nuclear Power Plant. Humans were evacuated following the disaster, but many not quickly enough. Those who lived in its vicinity or that worked for the Plant have faced an assortment of health problems: around 4000 people who worked at the Plant have died from "Chernobyl-related cancers" (Nolan, 2019). Additionally, in the days following the explosion, cows ate contaminated grass and passed radiated iodine to children who drank their milk. Since 2011, tourists, artists, and photographers have been allowed back into areas of the Exclusion Zone under strict conditions. One thing emerging from these visitations are thousands of photographs, and the dominant image has been the elephant gas masks. Many photos depict rooms inside Middle School Number 3 in Pripyat, Ukraine, a city of 50,000 people before the explosion. The school had boxes of gas masks stored in the basement pre-explosion, protective leftovers from the Cold War scare of potential chemical and biological warfare (Chernobyl Gallery, n.d.). These masks have since been scattered about the classrooms—some think by looters who snuck into the Exclusion Zone to remove tiny amounts of sliver from the masks' filters (Chernobyl Gallery, n.d.). Redditt users who have visited the site share that their guides told them the masks were strewn about for tourists in order to make the scene even more eerie and unnerving. Regardless of how they got there, they are the focal point of thousands of photos about the ongoingness of nuclear disaster. Particularly haunting are the photos of abandoned dolls wearing the same gas masks as Elephant Annie (see Figure 5): the gas masks as iconography of nuclear disaster and the doll as iconography of childhood meet to generate geos-imaginaries of the end of the world in which toxic liveliness outlasts human occupation and abandonment.

Pripyat was mentioned in passing in Chapter 3 as the real location of the overhead drone shots that close out *The Girl with All the Gifts*. These images challenge the idea of the end of the world in toto and cause me to restate it as the end of the human world. My takeaway is without humans—

Figure 5 Iconography of Abandonment. Photo by Cristian Fischer/EyeEm @ Getty Images.

and even after nuclear disaster—forms of life and nonlife continue: grass will poke up through pavement, vines will cover skyscrapers, isotopes will remain radioactive, fungus will flourish, forests will replenish, and plastic dolls will survive. In *Alliances in the Anthropocene*, Christine Eriksen and Susan Ballard (2020) map interrelations of people, plants, and fire in the Red Forest in the Exclusion Zone. The Red Forest is one of the world's most contaminated areas and humans have long abandoned the place. The bulk of radioactivity is concentrated in the soil and pine forests have been planted to absorb the nuclear chemicals. The thirty-kilometer square area is now over 70 percent forest (Wendle, 2016). Radiation contamination has made adaptation and mutation normal course for the plants and animals that still live there: certain plants grow differently, some birds grow tumors, and several species of small animals no longer grow babies. However, many larger animals have found refuge in the Exclusion Zone, including moose, deer, beavers, and wolves. Without humans around to hunt, build, or clear-cut, the Przewalski horse has come back from near extinction and much flora and fauna has flourished (Wendle, 2016). Humans have little place in this radioactive wasteland and the result has been booming density rates for many nonhuman species.

Life and nonlife are all mixed up in Chernobyl and its afterlife, and engaging with Elephant Annie's entanglements allow me to unearth these connections. As a figure of Anthropocene Child, Elephant Annie is a projection, a symptom, an indication, and an opening into discussions of nuclear power as a solution to fossil fuel extraction in the Anthropocene. Elephant Annie points me toward a concern for children who drank the poison cow milk after the disaster, and for those who still ingest it today. Up to 140 miles from the disaster site are radioactivity readings in cow milk twelve times the recommended limit for children (Pérez-Peña, 2018). Recounting interviews with the families, researchers from the University of Exeter recall: "These people know that the milk is unsafe, but they tell us, 'We don't have a choice, we have to feed our families.' These are rural communities and the people are poor" (para. 5). Elephant Annie can open up a critique of the unequal distribution of wealth and healthcare access in the world. They also want me to care about the cows that produce the milk and graze the contaminated grass, in what I receive as a gesture toward more-than-human kin making and caretaking. These various "matters of care and concern" co-emerge from thinking-with figures of Anthropocene Child (Puig de la Bellacasa, 2017).

One last connection Elephant Annie brings up for me is to Edelman's (2004) *No Future*. Specifically, a passage in which Edelman polemically fumes:

> Fuck the social order and the Child in whose name we're collectively terrorized; fuck Annie; fuck the waif from *Les Mis*; fuck the poor, innocent kid on the Net; fuck Laws both with capital ls and small; fuck the whole network of Symbolic relations and the future that serves as its prop.
>
> (p. 29)

I understand the theoretical move: Edelman is calling for queer jouissance and the death drive to topple the heteronormative reproductive futurism embodied by the figure of the Child, including Annie. The rage is directed against Annie's assurance that "the sun'll come out tomorrow," a form of optimism as futural promise secured by a spunky red-headed child. However, while orphan Annie seems to embody a brighter tomorrow, her "hard knock life" was not a sentimental form of childhood. Her tomorrow may be brighter but it might also be childhood's end. Another line from the song goes: "Tomorrow, tomorrow, I love ya tomorrow/You're always a day away." There is a sense of hope conveyed that attests to reproductive futurism as perpetual horizon. But there is also something at risk and ungraspable—it is always a day away—I interpret Annie's mantra not so much as a taken-for-granted assurance of futurity but as a survival statement of cruel optimism.

Cruel Optimism of Speculative Futures

As proposed by Lauren Berlant (2011), "a relation of cruel optimism exists when something you desire is actually an obstacle to your flourishing" (p. 1). An attachment to tomorrow, for example, becomes cruel when its potential impedes you from living fully today. Or, when tomorrow marks a future that under severe conditions of climate change is no longer guaranteed. As Berlant asks, "What happens to optimism when futurity splinters as a prop for getting through life?" (p. 18). What happens when the figure of the child is no longer futurity's guarantee? Reproductive futurism is cruel optimism if the unremitting deferment embodied by the child-figure justifies a lack of pro-climate and pro-family policies now for pledges of techno-fixes and living wages someday. If Melanie, Aiyana, Nassun, Unbabies, and Frenchie were to desire inclusion in this world as is—a white supremist world that does not recognize them as human—that would be a relation of cruel optimism. Cruel optimism often emerges under conditions of "extended crisis, with one happening piling on another" where "extensive threats to survival are said to dominate the reproduction of life" (p. 7). As we saw with Hushpuppy, anti-blackness piles on poverty piles on abandonment piles on climate change. It is exhausting. Yet, simultaneously, "the genre of crisis can distort something structural and ongoing within ordinariness into something that seems shocking and exceptional" (p. 7). Here we can see the limits of both resignation to the climate crisis and the eventfulness of disaster in speculative texts of the end of the world.

There seems to be a widespread rule to not overstate the seriousness of the climate crisis, or at least to follow up severe predictions with declarations of hope. Alarmist is a designation thrown about for having gone too far too fast too severely, even when scientific modelling is the source of concern. Leading climate scientists have warned that there are only twelve years left for steps to be taken to keep global warming below a 1.5C rise compared with pre-Industrial levels (IPCC, 2018). If that goal is missed then existing inequalities will continue to amplify: more fire, more floods, more pandemics, more poverty, more climate refugees. There is even an emergent vocabulary to capture extreme weather novelties: heat domes, atmospheric rivers, thundersnows, and bomb cyclones. A new report by Save the Children International (2021) compares the frequency of extreme weather events for a child born in 2020 with a person born in 1960 *if* the Paris Agreement targets are met. The projections reveal that children "born into the climate crisis" will experience 2 times as many wildfires, 2.8 times the number of crop failures, 2.6 times as many droughts, 2.8 times as many floods, and 6.8 times more heatwaves across their lifetimes, and that children in low-income counties will continue bear the worst of this. This kind of scientific modelling is speculative, but not in the way I am drawn to it. The report is about *not this* and a kind of *not yet* but the *what if* of otherwise speculation is missing. The authors are also careful to balance dire predictions with positivity. They ask us to "recognise that this crisis is an opportunity for hope and positive change" (p. 40). This is cruel optimism at work.

As much as I can recognize these limits, I also get the desire. It would be easy to accede defeat given the momentous challenges. Changing personal habits are not enough to shift anything substantially so why bother—why care? Knowing the entanglements of greenhouse gas emissions and racial capitalism does not generate much confidence in system change either. Dreams of geo-engineering techno-fixes also seem futile and dangerous: "hoping that science will provide a solution is its own kind of surrender, relieving the pressure of confronting the ways of life that have given rise to climate change in the first place" (Lynch, 2017, para. 5). Still, while I find it difficult to articulate the logic, it is important to not give in or give up. I am comforted that "resignation and hope aren't our only options" though, and perhaps "global warming discussions need apocalyptic thinking" (para. 5). I find this statement provocative and would add the caveat: apocalyptic thinking needs speculative fiction.

Speculative fiction that engages with the climate crisis is often critiqued because it is future-orientated so it encourages passiveness now. It can be escapist instead of realist—entertainment rather than activism. Other noted issues revolve around the prototypical heroics and endings: the world is saved by a solitary hero, and/or the apocalypse is diverted by a techno-fix invented by heroic genius. These tropes tie in again to cruel optimism wherein the "something you desire"—heroes, techno-fixes, and happy endings—are "actually an obstacle to your flourishing" (p. 1), as in real systemic transformation. These tropes and hopes pass over the sorts of multispecies alliances that are necessary for future survival. Author Kim Stanley Robinson waivers on whether he has contributed to the cruel optimism of speculative fiction: "Maybe my positive science-fiction stories are part of a cruel optimism, and we're heading towards a disaster so black, so bad, that I'm just part of a false consciousness, part of the zombies walking to the edge of the cliff type of thing" (Robinson & de Vicente, 2017, para. 56). Robinson then reverses and marks out a difference between "cruel optimism and angry optimism," because "after the disaster comes the next world" (para. 56). I believe this sort of speculative fiction and affective response is necessary and urgent; it acknowledges that only transformative change will do, change akin to the end of the world as we know it. Speculative fiction can "produce meaning and material with which to build (and destroy) what we call 'the real world'" (Benjamin, 2018, para. 21).

Amidst the turmoil of these times, speculative fiction apportions "windows into alternative realities, even if it is just a glimpse, to challenge ever-present narratives of inevitability" (Benjamin, 2016, p. 19). Inevitability is different than cruel optimism. It demands action. It demands change. Speculative formations of Black and Indigenous futurities are particularly important as they refuse to accede the inevitability of anti-blackness, settler colonialism, white supremacy, and climate devastation. For the most part, speculative stories are not about the end of the planet or even the end of life but the refiguration of the world as it is currently constituted: "whenever we envision a world without war, without prisons, without capitalism, we are producing speculative fiction" (Imarisha, 2015, p. 10). Daniel Heath Justice (Cherokee) advises: "Indigenous peoples know what it is to face the end of the world many, many times. And I think our stories give us a lot of guidance, and also speak to a life beyond the despair of the now.... *Imagine otherwise*" (Tennant, 2020, paras. 9–10). To play on a refrain from queer feminist poet Adrienne Rich (1993), the speculative addresses "the first revolutionary question—*what if*?" (p. 242).

In the conceptualization forwarded in this book, the speculative extends from the realm of fiction to contemporary scholarship in Childhood Studies. Recent work by the Common Worlds Research Collective (2020) demonstrates how the speculative can be used to fashion visionary declarations for a pluriversal, multispecies education for ecological justice in the year 2050. Fikile Nxumalo and kihana miraya ross (2019) challenge the white supremacy of mainstream environmental education and offer their own speculative revisioning of early childhood education for Black children and communities (p. 502). Brought together, these scholars enact what Ruha Benjamin (2018) finds most generative about speculative fiction: a capacity to "experiment with different scenarios, trajectories, and reversals, elaborating new values and testing different possibilities for creating more just and equitable societies" (para. 31). These are recuperative pedagogies for educational futures. They generatively enact the *not this, not yet*, and *what if* of speculative otherwises.

Educational Futures for the Anthropocene

Nxumalo (2019) forwards a call to "unsettle whiteness: toward a Black Anthropocene" in her ethnographic work with children, waterways, bees, worms, tree stumps, and mountains (p. 117). Another practice of worlding Black Anthropocenes entails speculative stories and pedagogies (Nxumalo & ross, 2019). Collectively, they offer necessary experiments in developing "a decolonizing, anti-racist, and situated ethics in environmental and place-attuned early childhood studies" that resists the romanticization of nature and refuses deficit constructions of Black children in nature (Nxumalo & Cedillo, 2019, p. 108). In particular, the critical and creative work by Nxumalo and ross (2019) exemplifies this sort of experimentation. They enact "Black speculative fiction as a creative and generative mode of imagining fugitive educational spaces for young Black children" (p. 502). Not only do the authors highlight important works by Black feminist writers like Octavia Butler, they make a speculative offering themselves. They geostory what Black childhoods in environmental education might look and feel like once blackness and nature are unhinged from "assumed natural couplings of pure and innocent children with pure, romantic nature" (p. 502).

Nxumalo and ross begin with *not this*. This includes how Western ways of knowing and relating to place, plants, people, and animals are insufficient given ongoing ecological destruction. They also refuse police presence in schools and curriculum that continues the erasure of Black people from history and thus the future. They reject forms of nature schooling that have "been reserved for 'innocent' white children whose parents could afford to provide them with a 'proper' education," or that only admitted Black children as "a way to rescue them from their culture of poverty" and improve their grades (p. 513). Nxumalo and ross next perform a *not yet* in a near-future mass movement walk-out of Black people from traditional schooling where their children were always perceived as a risk and put at risk of violence. In playing out the collective de-institutionalization of school, they conceive of what will come in its place: Yoruba cadres where students focus "on spiritual studies" and learn "other subjects through a Yoruba lens" (p. 514). Nxumalo and ross end with a series of *what ifs* fleshed out in story form. What if education was about children building "on what they intuitively know about the significance of their relationship to the more than human world" (p. 514)? What if the hyperempathy of Lauren in the *Parable of the Sower* was passed to a teacher named Nyawela who then shared her gift with the children of the Wild Seed cadre? These children can then viscerally experience past-present-futures of both harm, resistance, and revolution "through the environment" (p. 515). What if environmental education for children unsettled racialized child-nature innocence through pedagogies of "play, embodied encounters with the outdoors, humor, activism, environmental science, environmental racism, history, Black and Indigenous geographies, and more" (p. 520)? Nxumalo and ross write into possibility educational futures for ecological justice by "imagining what kinds of early childhood pedagogy might be possible within an ethics of radical relationality" (p. 509). They give it texture, feeling, and force.

The Common Worlds Research Collective (2020) co-authored a background paper for UNESCO's Futures of Education initiative that also moves the speculative and the geontological into educational worlds. The co-authors insist that education needs "to be reimagined and reconfigured around the future survival of the planet," and propose seven speculative declarations of what education might look like in 2050 if we make a paradigm shift from "learning about the world in order to act upon it, to learning to become *with* the world around us" (p. 2). Immediately, I am struck by the timeframe of their address. Without stating it explicitly, a program of this sort for 2050 assumes that any climate targets currently proposed were not only met but exceeded. The ominous headline that opened this book and evokes the IPCC timeline discussed earlier—"Climate Change: 12 Years to Save the Planet? Make that 18 Months" (McGrath, 2019)—has been proven wrong. There is time and space for flourishing in the futuristic temporality of the Collective's proposals. The authors credit the children and youth climate activists for the actualization of climate pledges. It was them who demanded action from governments on climate and capitalism. These students fulfilled Sheldon's (2016) proposition of a shift in the image of the child from protected to protector that co-emerged with the Anthropocene.

Due to the students' resolve for change and the intersectional planetary ethics that guided them, what counts as education also transformed. The Cartesian divides—"for example, mind/body, nature/culture, subject/

object"—that structure education's "established humanist knowledge traditions and pedagogies" were dissolved into a *not this* (p. 10). I think the bios/geos divide also fits into the dualistic listings. In this speculative future perhaps the adversarial boundaries between life and nonlife have been recomposed into geontological relations of respect and reciprocity. The Collective further marks out a *not yet* move of social justice to ecological justice as one of their "visionary declarations," which I also receive in geontological terms: a shift from bio-social justice for humans alone to geos-justice that exceeds the human and recognizes entanglements of life and nonlife existents.

By 2050, education for human exceptionalism has been completely refigured to recognize the intradependence of humans and more-than-humans. Human exceptionalism has been brought back down to earth and agency is appreciated as "relational, collectively distributed, and more-than-human" (p. 5). This makes room for pedagogies that "no longer position the world 'out-there' as the object we are learning about. Learning to become with the world is a situated practice and a more-than-human pedagogical collaboration" (p. 7). This can also be framed as a kind of geontological learning. Geontological learning is a very different kind of learning than the sort of learning-about that many of us in early childhood education and Childhood Studies know so well (Ashton, 2015). Learning-about is the kind of learning that happens when we go to a book or website to learn about the animals, plants, places, and other inhuman existents that already exist in our communities. Learning-about consists of those existing truths out there in nature that children set out to discover. Learning-about questions are those we ask children when we already know the answer. There is little that is speculative in learning-about; there are not many *what ifs*. As captured by Affrica Taylor (2013), what is needed is "a pedagogical shift—away from knowing *about* nature, or even *in* nature and towards learning with those others with whom we are already entangled" (p. 120). As the Collective (2020) asserts repeatedly in their speculative visioning of educational futures for 2050, our very survival depends on making this shift. While this may come across as hyperbolic, I do not think it is an exaggeration. It is the urgency the climate crisis requires.

The *with* in "learning to become *with* the world" asserts a different kind of relationship to the world than the extractive and accumulative one that brought the Anthropocene into being. It is one that I have tried to highlight with the speculative child-figures in this book who are intimately attached to bones, pathogens, earth, machines, and masks in ways that are not cruel but sustaining. The Collective's emphasis on survival also brings me back around to one of the main figurations in this book: the end of the world. To play on a refrain from Ashon Crawley (2015), the end of the world can be otherwise than apocalypse and otherwise than extinction—worlds can be "otherwise than this." The Collective (2020) proposes a form of otherwise survival that requires "the mutual flourishing of all—human and more than human—and on recuperating our damaged common words together, even if only partial recuperation is possible" (p. 9). Recuperation has much in common with rebuilding. Anishinaabe writer Waubgeshig Rice (2020) advises something similar:

> Many communities around the world have already endured apocalypse and they've rebuilt. They've found ways to start over and I think it's comforting as well, and maybe a little hopeful, to think about what is possible on the other side .... So it is possible to rebuild. That's why we need to look to Indigenous people and their stories about the end of the world.
> (Yohannes, 2020, paras. 21 & 27)

To rebuild is to move beyond mere survival. To rebuild is to generate otherwises in the ruins of anti-blackness, settler colonialism, and climate crisis. I think that speculative fiction and speculative figures can offer a glimpse of what otherwise might feel, look, and be like. To think-with Aiyana, Unbabies, the Boy with the Bones, #BrightFuture Child, Melanie, Nassun, Frenchie and friends, and the Wild Seed cadre is to be attuned to *not this* but also to imagine *not yet* and *what if*. Donna Haraway (2016) repeats that "It matters what stories we tell to tell other stories with" (p. 4). Telling a story of the Anthropocene with speculative child-figures gestures toward geos-futurities. It is a speculative praxis of the otherwise.

Notes

Chapter 1

1. I first became aware of this advertising campaign in Clark (2017).
2. In this book, I occasionally use the pronoun "we." I recognize that power relations, positional privilege, and constitutive exclusions can be obscured in this performance. For the most part, I use "we" in follow-up to a theorist and quotation that sets the terms for belonging. Other times, I employ "we" in the sense of making space for a shared readership and viewership of speculative texts. While "we" may interpret these texts differently, I want to gesture toward collaborative meaning making that nonetheless maintains space for refusal. I understand "we" as an ephemeral invitation to think-with contemporary problems that gather us together—not in sameness—but as differently situated beings inhabiting this ecologically damaged planet. As much as I do attempt to qualify my "we" in the pages that follow, I acknowledge that there are slippages that reflect my privileged position as a white settler scholar.
3. For example, on not one but two occasions in recent years, Ugandan activist Vanessa Nakate has been cropped out—virtually, figuratively, and literally erased—from internationally circulated photographs that feature her with other white youth climate activists. The first was an Associated Press photo from Davos, Switzerland, after a youth climate science event in January 2000. Nakate was together with Luisa Neubauer, Greta Thunberg, Isabelle Axelsson, and Loukina Tille, but in the published photo only her jacket arm was visible. The second occasion was a meeting between Thunberg, Nakate, and Nicola Sturgeon at COP26 in November 2021. Many news headlines named Thunberg and left out Nakate, and Nakate was cropped out of a photo, published by Sky News on their social media account, where all three sat together at a socially distanced table. Both photos were reformatted after social media uproar.
4. Some of the more critically attuned alternative names are: Anglocene (Bonneuil & Fressoz, 2016), Anthrobscene (Parikka, 2015), Anthropo-not-seen (de la Cadena, 2015), Anthropo-scene (Lorimer, 2017), a/Anthropocene (Revkin,

2016), Anthropomeme (Macfarlane, 2016), Capitalocene (Moore, 2016), Chthulucene (Haraway, 2016), Ecocene (Armstrong, 2015), Manthropocene (Raworth, 2014), Planthropocene (Myers, 2016), Plantationocene (Haraway, 2015; Haraway et al., 2015; Haraway & Tsing, 2019), and white-supremacy-scene (Mirzoeff, 2018). Much of this alter-terminology foregrounds power relations and localized inequalities in questions of global change and climate justice, often centering more-than-human relations as well.

5   At a conference outside Mexico City on Earth system science in late 1999, Nobel-prize winning atmospheric chemist Paul Crutzen announced in a session, "We're not in the Holocene anymore. We're in the ... the Anthropocene!" The exactly wording varies depending on who is telling the tale, but the story is most remarkable, in my opinion, for how much it is retold, especially as the narrative hook into writings about the Anthropocene (e.g., Davies, 2016; Kolbert, 2011; Macfarlane, 2016; Revkin, 2016). Why is there such widespread interest in this moment? What is it about the birth of a concept—and the Anthropocene idea in particular—that invites so many retellings? Other noted moments for the birth of the Anthropocene idea include, firstly, a two-page newsletter submission by Crutzen and freshwater biologist Eugene Stoermer in 2000 (Crutzen & Stoermer, 2000). Stoermer had been using the term informally for almost twenty years but had never published it until Crutzen contacted him (Kolbert, 2011). Secondly, two years later, Crutzen (2002) repurposed the earlier co-authored piece in the more widely read *Nature* journal, therein marking "the emergence of the concept into widespread scientific awareness" (Davies, 2018, p. 44).

6   To this suggestion I take the position, regardless of where the italics are put, that "rather than touting togetherness, we fight best by embracing our not-togetherness. The fact that there are sides .... So we start with the non-totality of the 'we'" (Miéville, 2015, para. 39). It is to those who theorize the non-totality of "we" that I turn to in order to build my understanding of the Anthropocene, which includes important works by Métis/otipemisiw scholar Zoe Todd (2015; Davis & Todd, 2017; Mitchell & Todd, 2016) and Potawatomi scholar Kyle Whyte (2017, 2018).

7   For theoretical overviews of Indigenous Futurisms see Anishinaabe scholar Grace Dillon (2012), Cherokee scholar Sean Teuton (2018), and Anishinaabe-Nehiyaw scholar Lindsay Nixon (2016). For creative arts approaches see Elizabeth LePensee (Anishinaabe, Métis), Rebecca Roanhorse (Ohkay Owingeh/Black), Christi Belcourt (Métis), Sonny Assu (Ligwilda'xw Kwakwaka'wakw), Daniel Heath Justice (Cherokee), and so, so many others. For Afro-futurism

see the founding work of Alondra Nelson (2002) and Ytahsa Womack (2013), the critique of the African American centrism in much Afrofuturism (Mashigo, 2018; Okorafor, 2017; Ryman, 2017), and creative works by Octavia Butler, Wangechi Mutu, Janelle Monae, Wanuri Kahiu, and N. K. Jemisin. These few names and citations do not do justice to the vast amount of critical and creative works by Indigenous and Black artists and scholars, but it is a start.

8   While not commonly cited in Childhood Studies, Giorgio Agamben's bios offers an alternative framework for expanding the scope of the biological. For Agamben (1998), zoe is akin to the biological facts of life (much like what I reference as the first wave of Childhood Studies' mantra) and bios is a way of life—life as it is lived. In this way, bios (political life) gives meaning to zoe (biological substance). While a full discussion of Agamben's work is outside my scope here, this brief mention signals that biological and bios are not fixed substances or meanings, but are used creatively by many—including critiques of Agamben, whether that be his deracialization of bare life (Weheliye, 2014) or a celebration and complication of zoe as posthuman, vital force (Braidotti, 2013).

9   Elizabeth Ellsworth and Jamie Kruse (2011) explain how it is becoming "increasing difficult for geologists and biologists to hold to categorical distinctions between the brute materiality of geology's external world (rocks, minerals, mountains) and the soft, inner worlds of biology's living things" ("Zuihitsu 2"). They propose "geo-bio-socio assemblages" as an indication of how "the geologic passes through our time as the materials and forces that compose us, and that we take up and transform to compose our world." I think their material-discursive assemblage (Deleuze & Guattari, 1987) has much to offer a refiguring of childhoods in the Anthropocene.

10 Karen Barad (2007) proposes intra-action, rather than the usual interaction, to get at "the mutual constitution of entangled agencies" (p. 33). What the "intra" foregrounds is that figures do not preexist their relating but "emerge through their intra-action" (p. 33). When I use the prefix "intra" in this dissertation, I am gesturing toward this understanding of relationality.

Chapter 2

1   I want to be careful to not gather all biology under the same rubric. I am taken by Puig de la Bellacasa's (2012) description of the varied meanings biology takes, for example as "a knot of relationships between living matters and social modes

of existence, crafts, practices and love stories; a range of situated 'epistemological, semiotic, technical, political and material' connections; an omnipresent discourse ... a metaphor too, but also much 'more than a metaphor'" (p. 199). This is to say that when I write of the figure of the bionormative child, this sort of expansive field of biology is not my reference point, but instead the narrow and reductive conceptualizations of positivistic child developmentalism that maintain a large influence on early childhood education today. Additionally, Povinelli's (2016) "biocentric subject of late liberalism," a figure who shared much with Wynter's (2003) Man2 (aka "colonial man"), inform my (re)figuration.

2   Anishinaabe author Gerald Vizenor (2008) offers the term *survivance*—a combination of survival and endurance—to capture the ongoingness and ongoing resistance of Indigenous peoples in settler colonial states.

3   While this phrase is often attributed to Duncan Campbell Scott, and aptly captures the rationale of the assimilative schools while he was in command, it was actually spoken by an American militantly officer (Abley, 2013, para. 2). Additionally, Dr. Peter Bryce's censored reports documented the maltreatment and alarming death rates in Canadian residential schools as early as 1907.

Chapter 3

1   For Povinelli (2016), the metabolic imaginary and its key biological processes (birth, growth, reproduction) "transpose" onto theoretical concepts of event, conatus, affect, and finitude (p. 16). The meeting place for these biological and ontological concepts is the "Carbon Imaginary," a term most evocative of the Anthropocene. In this book, I show how the eventalization of climate change occurs through the dramatization of world-destructing events (like a zombie pandemic or tsunami wave) instead of the slow violence of environmental racism (Nixon, 2011), for example, the erosion of coastal communities in *Beasts of the Southern Wild* in the last chapter. Finitude is an analytic focus in Chapter 6 with the re-enlivening of child victims of police and a secret society of the Immortocracy (Benjamin, 2016). Conatus and affect, while I do not employ those terms, nevertheless are spectral presences in some of the geostories I feature. In Chapter 4, conatus—as in continued efforts of perseverance via Spinoza—haunts discussions of survival in worlds without end, and, Chapters 5 and 6 look at care as an affective ethics that takes different forms under conditions of climate crisis.

2   There are numerous contemporary examples of this attribution of insensateness, including systemically giving Black children less pain medicine when injured (Cheney-Rice, 2015). The disproportionate composition of prisons, school suspensions, social service removals of children from homes, and the poisoned drinking water in Flint are further examples. Another is the desire to prove Trayvon Martin a "child" in the spectacle surrounding the miscarriage of justice that was his killer's trial where Martin was villainized, animalized, and adultized, which is addressed in Chapter 5 (Vargas & James, 2013). In Canada, the medical atrocities inflicted on Indigenous children at residential schools, specifically the ruse of nutrition research at six schools from 1942 to 1952 (Mosby, 2013), is a potential point of connection among others between Black and Indigenous lives.

3   The zombie traces back to West Africa before developing more fully in Afro-Caribbean communities, most specifically Haiti (Davis, 1988). In Haiti in the seventeenth century, known then as Saint-Domingue under colonial French rule, enslaved Africans were trafficked to perform grueling physical labor on sugar plantations. The original zombie was not the familiar Hollywood figure who eats human brains, bodies, and flesh, but a person robbed of their language, family, community, culture, and continent. In early incarnations, the walking dead were a zombified form of the working dead. Therefore, the zombie's genealogy is undeniably racialized, structured as it is by slavery. It was only in death that the enslaved thought they might obtain some semblance of freedom (Cohen, 1972). For many stolen away from their homelands, death meant a spiritual return to Africa, "a passage to a second life of the soul … finally being set free" (Timofeeva, 2018, para. 3). This is why "the fear in Haiti is not *of* zombies, but rather of *becoming* a zombie," in that enslavement was considered "a fate worse than death" (Davis, 1988, p. 9). The original zombie was a real live physical human reduced to conditions of the living dead.

4   Drawing on Fanon's work, Samira Kawash (1999) complicates the monster-figure as quintessential abject subject. Picking up on the figure of the vampire that haunts one of Fanon's (1963) clinical patients in *The Wretched of the Earth*, Kawash rewrites decolonization as a form of terrorism. Kawash rejects a simplified substitution of the vampire for the colonizer who consumes the oppressed in an excising of otherness. The contagion of colonialism might be threatened by the vampire's bite, "such that to be bitten by a vampire is to become a vampire, [but] the colonized does not unequivocally take up the position of the vampire" (p. 238). Instead, "the vampire is simultaneously the force that

threatens to drain the life from the colonized, and the condition of the colonized as living dead" (p. 249). In Kawash's worlding, the vampire is in-between and in-excess of the opposition between the living (the colonizer as vampire nourished by native blood) and dead (colonized bodies emptied of liveliness) in ways that connect with the Anthropocene-related instability of the geontological division of life versus nonlife (Povinelli, 2016).

5   While the pathogen in *Gifts* is a fungal rather than viral, that detail is not impactful to the analytical import of my argument that follows. What could be called into question is that the fungus is a living organism and the virus is indeterminate in this way of thinking (e.g., need a host to replicate), but that is an argument for another time.

6   Without a cure or scientist hero, the outbreak narrative pulls on racialized and sexualized imaginaries not based on scientific fact. Wald (2008) gives an example from the early days of HIV/AIDS diagnosis when a persistent rumor circulated, with no scientific basis but big anti-Black racist appeal, that the species barrier was broken when African men raped monkeys (p. 260). When scientific success is not forthcoming, the outbreak narrative names and shames particular figures as Patient Zeros or "superspreaders" (p. 4). The history of HIV/AIDS again provides a representative case. Gaëtan Dugas, a Canadian flight attendant, was wrongly assumed to be Patient Zero for many years. In the 1980s the Centers for Disease Control (CDC) in California tracked the sexual partners of gay and bisexual men diagnosed with HIV. Along the way Dugas's medical chart was misread—the letter-O for "Out-of-California" was mistaken for the number zero—Patient Zero was born.

7   A key thinker for Haraway is Lynn Margulis whose multi-layered, multispecies work in and understanding of biology is worlds away from the narrowed notion of child development science I storied in the Chapter 1. Margulis also used the term autopoiesis/autopoietic. Haraway (2016) responds as such: "Perhaps she would have chosen the term sympoietic, but the word and concept had not yet surfaced. As long as autopoiesis does not mean self-sufficient 'self making,' autopoiesis and sympoiesis, foregrounding and backgrounding different aspects of systemic complexity, are in generative friction, or generative enfolding, rather than opposition" (p. 61).

8   When considering Arendt's natality, I always have Orlando Paterson's (1982) formation of natal alienation at the back of my mind. I am, of course, not the first to think natal alienation and natality together. Ewa Ziarek (2012) concludes that the "spectral character of social death ... destroys the principle of natality,

understood in the most broad terms, not only as the biological birth, but also as the claims of genealogy, the principle of a new beginning" (p. 153). For Arendt, the child's entrance into a "web of human relationships" indicates respect for plurality, community belonging, and the possibility of freedom itself (p. 54).

I have much suspicion about natality in that I fear it overlooks the structures, institutions, and histories that insist on the ongoingness of anti-blackness and makes these natal features inaccessible for many. In many ways, natal alienation makes the genealogical inheritance impossible.

9 There are natality-overlaps with how the Anthropocene is being conceptualized. Leading scientists argue that the Anthropocene is "a new and unique phase of our planet's geological history, and one that will inevitably now send history (and geology) on a new trajectory" (Zalasiewicz et al., 2018, p. 177). "A no-analogue state" is perhaps the most succinct and repeated natalistic refrain (e.g., Angus, 2015a; Crutzen & Steffen, 2003; Kammer, 2017; O'Farrell, 2018).

Chapter 5

1 Latour's "we" is unspecified throughout "Love Your Monsters," even as it occupies a pronounced placement in his subtitle: "Why We Must Care for Our Technologies as We Do Our Children." This appears to be a habit of Latour's that is evident in his most cited work titled *We Have Never Been Modern* (1993). In the present case, I am interpreting the "we" as including all those concerned for both technological and child development. However, I also caution that this "we" has exclusions already built in.

2 Latour's (2011) article is an abridged version of ideas developed elsewhere, particularly in *We Have Never Been Modern* (1991), where he refuses a nature-culture split, and *Armamis, or Love of Technology* (1996), where he first rereads *Frankenstein* as a modern environmental parable. The "Love Your Monsters" (2011) article was published in the *Breakthrough Journal* and the quoted text is attributed to the article unless otherwise stated. Latour's piece was also included as a chapter in an edited e-book from Breakthrough Institute called *Love Your Monsters: Postenvironmentalism and the Anthropocene* (Shellenberger & Nordhaus, 2011). Latour's contribution was a shortened version of a piece called "'It's Development, Stupid!' or: 'How to Modernize Modernization'" (Latour, 2007), which is unpublished but archived on his personal website: http://www.bruno-latour.fr/node/153.html.

3   I am not calling for hetero-reproductive purity here either. Mary Shelley's biographer Anne Mellor writes in the preface to a 2017 special edition of *Frankenstein*, which was "annotated for scientists, engineers, and creators of all kinds," that the text "portrays the penalties of violating Nature ... Nature prevents Victor from constructing a normal human being: His unnatural method of reproduction spawns an unnatural being, a freak" (Ball, 2017, paras. 1–2). This assumes both a biologically delimited role for women, undesirability of an atypical child, and romanticizing of an innocent state of nature to be recovered. Inspired by Alexis Shotwell (2016), I am "against purity" of this sort.

4   I use first names when referring to characters in the speculative story (e.g., Aiyana, Reika, Tamir, Freddie, Eric) and last names when recounting events that have already happened in this world (e.g., Jones, Boyd, Rice, Gray, Garner).

5   Relatedly, a University of British Columbia research project recently received more than $10 million in funding to "bridge Canada's gap in medical care for Indigenous communities" through genome sequencing and the development of precision medicine techniques (CBC News, 2018). The benefits of more accurate diagnoses are not my concern here. What raises flags for me is the possibility that DNA maps will become property of a settler state institution via supposedly neutral technologies of science. This gene databank may well become another means in a long, deadly line of claims of ownership over what Kim TallBear (2019) critically problematizes as Canada's other "natural resources"—not only lakes and trees but Indigenous peoples.

6   Originally published in 2004 and revised in 2015, The Great Acceleration graphs plot data from 1750 to 2010 and track twelve features of Earth system functioning and twelve "human enterprise" factors (Steffen et al., 2004, 2015). The Earth system indicators include, for example, measurements of methane concentration, carbon dioxide, nitrous oxide, and surface temperatures. The "human enterprise" indicators include population, GDP, energy use, and urbanization, among other factors. Presently, the graphs are used to establish the Great Acceleration as the top candidate for the Anthropocene start date. Advocates maintain that only "beyond the mid-twentieth century is there clear evidence for fundamental shifts in the state and functioning of the Earth system that are beyond the range of variability of the Holocene and driven by human activities" (Steffen et al., 2015, p. 81).

7   I mean this to invoke Saidiya Hartman's (2006) afterlife of slavery, which captures the ongoing condition of slavery in the present so much as "the critical components of both are fungibility and accumulation, or the ability to be

commodified and treated as an object" (Ziyad, 2017a, p. 145). Fungible bodies make ideal experimental subjects; fungible bodies can also become cyborg bodies. For the People's Science Council, Black child-bodies enact the otherwise abstract "interchangeability and replaceability" of the commodity (Hartman, 1997, p. 21). Their lives as well as their limbs and organs are interchanged and replaced. Tiffany King (2016) describes "Black fungibility [as] the treatment of the Black enslaved body as an open sign that can be arranged and rearranged for infinite kinds of use" (p. 1025). The subjects for cyborg experimentation were not accidentally or innocently chosen but cultivated and procured systematically. "Arranged and rearranged" in a hospital, the commodified, experimental, vulnerable Black child-body is another story of the afterlife of slavery (p. 1025). This theme appears earlier in the discussion of Melanie in Chapter 3.

8   Not all public protests and campaigns invoked the sentimental image of an innocent child to mark their support of Martin and their resistance to anti-Black racism. For example, the Hoodie-movement and #WeAreAllTrayvonMartin made incontrovertible in a different imagery the link of blackness, boyhood, premature death, community, and the impossibility of innocence-redemption for the Black child in the United States (see Dumas & Nelson, 2016).

9   The danger of engaging care at a chapter's end is that the rich feminist histories of care ethics are not given enough space. For introductory genealogies see Martin et al. (2015), Murphy (2015), Sevenhuijsen (1998, Chap. 3), and Puig de la Bellacasa (2017, Chap. 2); foundational works by Held (2006), Mol (2008), Nodding (1984), Ruddick (1989), and Tronto (1993). Care research has been dominated by European and white-settler feminists so texts by Collins (1990), Combahee River Collective (1983), Crenshaw (1991), hooks (1992), and Sharpe (2016) provide necessarily perspectives. In early childhood education, see Dahlberg and Moss (2005), Hodgins (2019), and Langford (2019).

10 The epilogue of *Frankenstein* contains a passage from Milton's *Paradise Lost*. It reads: "Did I request thee, Make, from my clay/ To mould me Man, did I solicit thee/ From darkness to promote me?" While Latour inquires into the failed duty of care of Dr. Frankenstein, he glides past the questions of consent raised here.

Chapter 6

1   Several mentions are made in this chapter to the ongoing child separation policy of political asylum seekers entering the United States. Child-parent

separation has long been a technology of settler colonialism on Turtle Island. Métis artist Christi Belcourt shares, "One Indigenous newborn a day is apprehended from the arms of their mothers in Winnipeg hospitals by the province of Manitoba." A tweet by ndnviewpoint (2018) cites a documentary called "Stolen Childhoods," which points out, "by the 1960s, about 1 in 4 Native children in the US were living apart from their families." Any condemning of American policy without also considering what is happening in Indigenous communities is akin to a "settler move to innocence" (Tuck & Yang, 2012).

2 I first encountered the phrase "born pre-polluted" in a WRISK project guest blog post by Norah MacKendrick and Kate Cairns (2019) entitled, "Born pre-polluted: Mothers and environmental risk," in which they hyperlink to a report by Suzanne Reuben (2010) for the US President's Cancer Panel which used the phrase at an earlier point. A Canadian report by the Environmental Defence (2013) organization also uses the phrase in their title.

3 In Season 2, Episode 5, called "Seeds," the Putnam's baby has fallen ill and no doctors can figure out what is wrong. The baby appears near death when Serena suggests that Janine, the baby's real mother, come see the baby. After more tests fail to reveal the ailment, everyone seems resigned to the fact that the baby will die overnight. June suggests that they let Janine hold the baby before she dies and the day ends with Janine rocking the baby. In the morning, the baby is cooing and has pinked up—saved by a true mother's love.

4 While perhaps most familiar to the history of American slavery, racialized practices of stolen children, enforced labor, banned literacy, restricted movement, constant surveillance, rape, and family refiguration are also dominant practices of settler colonialism. The lack of identifiable Indigenous characters in the television show and the absence of any mention of Indigenous peoples in the novel suggests the "elimination of the Native" has been accomplished in the post-apocalyptic landscape of Gilead (Wolfe, 2006). Gilead and the Colonies still exist on stolen land.

5 There are many historical sources for the violent practices and ideologies of *The Handmaid's Tale*. For example, for the Biblical practice of sexual surrogates and the Nazi's Lebensborn eugenic program to reproduce blonde, blue-eyed children. Atwood has also noted that the "National Homelands" find their correlate in the apartheid practices of South Africa's white governments (Dodson, 1997). For a detailed look at some of these antecedents, minus an emphasis on racialized slavery, see Evans (1994).

Chapter 7

1. Perhaps archive is too conventional and institutional an image, a carrier bag might better express the sort of collecting going on here (Le Guin, 1988; Haraway, 2004; Taylor et al., 2012). A carrier bag would not only include the speculative texts, but the human and non-humans of the stories. Technologies, stem cells, pathogens, bones, minerals, and all sorts of other nonhuman existents that compose the geos-child figures are in and out of this porous receptacle: it is a gathering up and a letting go instead of an archival form of entrapment as permanent inventory and repository.

2. While Taylor (2013) does not dismiss textually based work, she does note differences between discursive analyses and reconstructive methods (pp. 61–6; 87–9). For Taylor, deconstructive methods are effective in exposing how and why particular images of the child are "enduring and seductive idea[s]," but they can be limited in their capacity to create "alternative conceptualizations" (p. 62). In other words, deconstructive methods tend to rehearse and trace arguments while reconstructive methods "neither jettison nor valorize ... but queer" (p. 62). This is not to say that there is something inherently liberating in ethnographic practices but that they can enable an "irreverent and political" playfulness that extends well beyond a text—it is an active practice of co-constituting worlds.

References

Abley, M. (2013, November 8). The man wrongly attributed with uttering "kill the Indian in the child." *Maclean's*. https://www.macleans.ca/culture/books/conversations-with-a-dead-man-the-legacy-of-duncan-campbell-scott/

Abraham, S. (2017, May 2). What's not being said about *The handmaid's tale*. *Ms*. http://msmagazine.com/blog/2017/05/02/whats-not-said-handmaids-tale/

Agamben, G. (1998). *Homo sacer: Sovereign power and bare life* (D. Heller-Roazen, Trans.). Stanford University Press.

Ahmed, S. (2000). *Strange encounters: Embodied others in post-coloniality*. Routledge.

Ahmed, S. (2014). *Willful subjects*. Duke University Press.

Alagraa, B. (2021, January 22). The third event: Bedour Alagraa on Sylvia Wynter and Black radical thought [Podcast]. *Millennials Are Killing Capitalism*. https://millennialsarekillingcapitalism.libsyn.com/the-third-event-bedoura-alagraa-on-sylvia-wynter-and-black-radical-thought

Alibar, L. (2013). *Juicy and delicious* [Play]. https://www.dramatists.com/previews/4739.pdf

Alkebulan, P. (2012). *Survival pending revolution: The history of the Black Panther Party*. University of Alabama Press.

Andreotti, V. de Oliveira (2012). Education, knowledge and the rightings of wrongs. *Other Education: The Journal of Educational Alternatives, 1*(1), 19–31.

Arendt, H. (1958). *The human condition*. University of Chicago Press.

Aries, P. (1962). *Centuries of childhood*. Vintage Books.

Armstrong, R. (2015, June 18). Ecocene [Keynote]. *Urban ecologies*. OCAD.

Asafu-Adjaye, J., Blomqvist, L., Brand, S., Brook, B., DeFries, R., Ellis, E., Foreman, C., Keith, D., Lewis, M., Lynas, M., Nordhaus, T., Pielke, R., Pritzker, R., Roy, J., Sagoff, M., Shellenberger, M., Stone, R., & Teague, P. (2015). *An ecomodernist manifesto*. http://www.ecomodernism.org/manifesto

Ashton, E. (2015). Possibilities for geontological learning in Common Worlds. *Journal of Childhood Studies, 40*(2), 9–21.

Atwood, M. (1986). *The handmaid's tale*. Virago.

Atwood, M. (2012, January 20). Haunted by *The handmaid's tale*. *The Guardian*. https://www.theguardian.com/books/2012/jan/20/handmaids-tale-margaret-atwood

Baker, K. (2008). Bionormativity and the construction of parenthood. *Georgia Law Review, 649*. https://ssrn.com/abstract=996160

Baldwin, A. (2016). Premediation and white affect: Climate change and migration in critical perspective. *Transactions, 41*, 78-90.

Ball, P. (2017, April 20). Frankenstein reflects the hopes and fears of every scientific era. *The Atlantic*. https://www.theatlantic.com/science/archive/2017/04/franken-science/523560

Bandura, A. (1971). *Social learning theory*. General Learning Press.

Barad, K. (2007). *Meeting the universe halfway: Quantum physics and the entanglement of matter and meaning*. Duke University Press.

Barnsley, V. (2010). The child/the future. *Feminist Theory, 11*(3), 323-30.

Bastién, A. J. (2017, June 14). In its first season, *The handmaid's tale's* greatest failing is how it handles race. *Vulture*. http://www.vulture.com/2017/06/the-handmaids-tale-greatest-failing-is-how-it-handles-race.html

BBC. (2020, January 7). Australia fire: Almost 2,000 homes destroyed in marathon crisis. *BBC News*. https://www.bbc.co.uk/news/world-australia-51015536

Benjamin, R. (2016). Racial fictions, biological facts: Expanding the sociological imagination through speculative methods. *Catalyst, 2*(2), 1-28.

Benjamin, R. (2018, July 16). Black afterlives matter: Cultivating kinfulness as reproductive justice. *Boston Review*. http://bostonreview.net/race/ruha-benjamin-black-afterlives-matter

Benjamin, R. (Ed.). (2019a). *Captivating technology: Race, carceral technoscience, and liberatory imagination in everyday life*. Duke University Press.

Benjamin, R. (2019b). *Race after technology: Abolitionist tools for the New Jim Code*. Polity.

Berlant, L. (1997). *The queen of America goes to Washington: Essays on sex and citizenship*. Duke University Press.

Berlant, L. (2011). *Cruel optimism*. Duke University Press.

Berlatsky, N. (2015, January 4). *The handmaid's tale* and bad slavery comparisons. http://www.hoodedutilitarian.com/2015/01/the-handmaids-tale-and-bad-slavery-comparisons/

Berlatsky, N. (2017, June 15). Both versions of *The handmaid's tale* have a problem with racial erasure. *The Verge*. https://www.theverge.com/2017/6/15/15808530/handmaids-tale-hulu-margaret-atwood-black-history-racial-erasure/

Bernstein, R. (2011). *Racial innocence: Performing American childhood from slavery to civil rights*. New York University Press.

Bey, M. (2016). Between blackness and monstrosity: Gendered blackness in the cyborg comics. *Gender Forum, 58*, 41-58.

Bignell, J. (2005). Familiar aliens: Teletubbies and postmodern childhood. *Screen*, *46*(3), 373–88.

Blaise, M. (2005). *Playing it straight*. Routledge.

Bliss, J. (2015). Hope against hope: Queer negativity, black feminist theorizing, and reproduction without futurity. *Mosaic: A Journal for the Interdisciplinary Study of Literature*, *48*(1), 83–98.

BLM. (2016, November 15). Black Lives Matter Global Network's statement of the election of Donald Trump. https://www.mic.com/articles/159496/exclusive-black-lives-matter-issues-a-statement-on-trump-s-election#.5zuNat29p

Bonneuil, C., & Fressoz, J-B. (2016). *Shock of the Anthropocene: The earth, history and us* (D. Fernbach, Trans.). Verso.

Braidotti, R. (2013). *The posthuman*. Polity.

Brown, J. (2013, September 27). Beasts of the southern wild—the romance of precarity II. *Social Text*. https://socialtextjournal.org/beasts-of-the-southern-wild-the-romance-of-precarity-ii/

Brown, S. (2017, July 25). *The girl with all the gifts* is a nightmare for white supremacy. *RaceBaitR*. https://racebaitr.com/2017/07/25/girl-gifts-nightmare-white-supremacy/

Burman, E. (2017). *Deconstructing developmental psychology*. (3rd ed.). Routledge.

Cairns, K., Johnston, J., & MacKendrick, N. (2013). Feeding the "organic child": Mothering through ethical consumption. *Journal of Consumer Culture*, *13*(2), 97–118.

Cannella, G. S. (1997). *Deconstructing early childhood education*. Peter Lang.

Cannella, G., & Radhika, V. (2004). *Childhood and postcolonialism: Power, education, and contemporary practice*. RoutlegeFalmer.

Carey, M. R. (2014). *The girl with all the gifts* [ePUB]. Orbit.

Castañeda, C. (2002). *Figurations: Child, bodies, worlds*. Duke University Press.

Cecire, N. (2015). Environmental innocence and slow violence. *WSQ: Women's Studies Quarterly*, *43*(1&2), 164–80.

Cheney-Rice, Z. (2015, April 24). 7 times we decided people of color don't feel pain like white people do. *The MIC*. https://www.mic.com/articles/116304/7-times-we-decided-people-of-color-don-t-feel-pain-like-white-people-do

Chernobyl Gallery. (n.d.). Middle school number 3. Galleries. http://www.chernobylgallery.com/galleries/pripyat-middle-school-3/

Clark, N. (2017). Anthropocene bodies, geological time and the crisis of natality. *Body & Society*, *23*(3), 156–80.

Clark, N., & Yusoff, K. (2017). Geosocial formations and the Anthropocene. *Theory, Culture & Society*, *34*(2–3), 3–23.

Cohen, D. (1972). *Voodoo, devils, and the invisible world*. Dodd, Mead & Company.

Colebrook, C. (2014). *The death of the posthuman: Essays on extinction, volume one*. Open Humanities Press.

Colebrook, C. (2017). We have always been post-anthropocene. In R. Grusin (Ed.), *Anthropocene feminism* (pp. 1–20). University of Minnesota Press.

Colebrook, C. (2018). The future in the Anthropocene: Extinction and the imagination. In A. Johns-Putra (Ed.), *Climate and literature* (pp. 263–80). Cambridge University Press.

Colebrook, C. (2019). A cut in relationality: Art at the end of the world. *Angelaki, 24*(3), 175–95.

Collins, P. H. (1990). *Black feminist thought: Knowledge, consciousness and the politics of empowerment*. Unwin Hyman.

Combahee River Collective. (2002). A Black feminist statement. In C. Moraga & G. Anzaldúa (Eds.), *This bridge called my back: Writings by radical women of color* (3rd ed., pp. 234–44). Kitchen Table & Women of Color Press.

Common Worlds Research Collective. (n.d.). Common Worlds Research Collective. https://commonworlds.net/

Common Worlds Research Collective. (2020). *Learning to become with the world: Education for future survival*. Background paper for UNESCO Futures of Education initiative. https://unesdoc.unesco.org/ark:/48223/pf0000374032

Crawley, A. (2015). Otherwise, Ferguson. *Interfictions Online: A Journal of Interstitial Arts*. 5. http://interfictions.com/otherwise-fergusonashon-crawley/

Crenshaw, K. (1991). Mapping the margins: Intersectionality, identity politics, and violence against Women of Color. *Stanford Law Review, 43*(6), 1241–99.

Crist, E. (2013). On the poverty of our nomenclature. *Environmental Humanities, 3*, 129–47.

Crutzen, P. (2002). Geology of mankind—the Anthropocene. *Nature, 415*, 23.

Crutzen, P., & Stoermer, E. (2000). The "Anthropocene." *IGBP* Newsletter, *41*, 17–18.

Cunningham, H. (2006). *The invention of childhood*. BBC Books.

Cutter-Mackenzie-Knowles, A., Malone, K., & Hacking, E. B. (2020). *Research handbook of childhoodnature: Assemblages of childhood and nature research*. Springer.

Dahlberg, G., & Moss, P. (2005). *Ethics and politics in early childhood education*. Routledge.

Dahlberg, G., Pence, A., & Moss, P. (2006). *Beyond quality in early childhood education and care: Postmodern perspectives*. (2nd ed.). RoutledgeFalmer.

Dancy, T. E. (2014). The adultification of Black boys. In K. J. Fasching-Varner, R. E. Reynolds, K. A. Albert, & L. Martin (Eds.), *Trayvon Martin, race, and American justice: Teaching race and ethnicity* (pp. 49–55). Sense Publishers.

Danowski, D., & Viveiros de Castro, E. (2015, July 7). Is there any world to come? *e-flux*. http://supercommunity.e-flux.com/texts/is-there-any-world-to-come/

Danowski, D., & Viveiros de Castro, E. (2016). *The ends of the world*. Polity.

Davies, B. (1990). The problem of desire. *Social problems, 37*(4), 501–16.

Davies, J. (2016, October 16). Birth of the Anthropocene: Summary. *Made Ground: Notes of the Anthropocene Epoch*. https://madeground.com/2016/10/16/five-maxims/#more-1506

Davies, J. (2018). *The birth of the Anthropocene*. University of California.

Davis, H., & Todd, Z. (2017). On the importance of a date, or decolonizing the Anthropocene. *ACME: An International Journal for Critical Geographies, 16*(4), 761–80.

Davis, W. (1988). *Passage of darkness: The ethnobiology of the Haitian zombie*. University of North Carolina.

de la Cadena, M. (2014). Runa: Human but not only. *Hau: Journal of Ethnographic Theory, 4*(2), 253–9.

de la Cadena, M. (2015). Uncommoning nature: Stories from the Anthropo-Not-Seen. In P. Harvey, C. Krohn-Hansen & K. Nustad (Eds.), *Anthropos and the material* (pp. 35–58). Duke University Press.

Deleuze, G., & Guattari, F. (1987). *A thousand plateaus: Capitalism and schizophrenia*. University of Minnesota Press.

Demos, T. J. (2018). To save a world: Geoengineering, conflictual futurisms, and the unthinkable. *e-flux, 94*. https://www.e-flux.com/journal/94/221148/to-save-a-world-geoengineering-conflictual-futurisms-and-the-unthinkable/

Diaz-Diaz, C., & Semenec, P. (Eds.). (2020). *Posthumanist and new materialist methodologies: Research after the child*. Springer.

Dillon, G. (Ed.). (2012). *Walking the clouds: An anthology of Indigenous science fiction*. The University of Arizona Press.

Dimaline, C. (2017). *The marrow thieves*. Cormorant Books.

Dockterman, E. (2017, April 25). *The handmaid's tale* showrunner on why he made some major changes from the book. *Time*. http://time.com/4754200/the-handmaids-tale-showrunner-changes-from-book/

Dodson, D. (1997). An interview with Margaret Atwood. *Critique: Studies in Contemporary Fiction, 38*(2), 96–104.

Dowdall, L. (2020). Black futures matter: Afrofuturism and geontology in N. K. Jemisin's Broken Earth trilogy. In I. Lavender & L Yaszek (Eds.), *Literary Afrofuturism in the twenty-first century* (pp. 149–67). Ohio State University Press.

Dumas, M. (2016). Against the dark: Antiblackness in education policy and discourse. *Theory into Practice, 55*(1), 11–19.

Dumas, M., & Nelson, J. (2016). (Re)imagining Black boyhood: Toward a critical framework for educational research. *Harvard Educational Review, 86,* 27–47.

Edelman, L. (1998). The future is kid stuff: Queer theory, disidentification, and the death drive. *Narrative, 6*(1), 18–30.

Edelman, L. (2004). *No future: Queer theory and the death drive.* Duke University Press.

Ellsworth, E., & Kruse, J. (Eds). (2011). *Making the geologic now: Responses to material conditions of contemporary life.* Punctum Books. https://geologicnow.punctumbooks.com/index.php

Environmental Defence. (2013). *Born pre-polluted: A report of the toxic substances in the umbilical cord blood of Canadian newborns.* Environmental Defence Canada. https://d36rd3gki5z3d3.cloudfront.net/wp-content/uploads/2016/01/CordBloodReport_EnglishWEB.pdf?x17002

Erasmus, Z. (2020). Sylvia Wynter's theory of the human: Counter-, not post-humanist. *Theory, Culture & Society, 37*(6), 47–65.

Eriksen, C., & Ballard, S. (2020). *Alliances in the Anthropocene: Fire, plants, and people.* Springer Nature.

Evans, M. (1994). Versions of history: *The handmaid's tale* and its dedicatees. In C. Nicholson (Ed.), *Margaret Atwood: Writing and subjectivity* (pp. 177–88). Palgrave Macmillan.

Falduit, A. (Producer) (2014). *Why bring a child into the world?* [Commercial]. DAVID, Buenos Aires, Argentina. Unilever: Project Sunlight. http://www.welovead.com/en/works/details/eedwntuAk

Fanon, F. (1952 [1967]). *Black skin, white masks* (C. Markmann, Trans.). Pluto Press.

Fanon, F. (1963). *The wretched of the earth* (C. Farrington, Trans.). Grove Press.

Fendler, L. (2001). Educating flexible souls: The construction of subjectivity through developmentality and interaction. In K. Hultqvist & G. Dahlberg (Eds.), *Governing the child in the new millennium* (pp. 119–42). Taylor & Francis.

Ferguson, A. (2001). *Bad boys: Public schools in the making of Black masculinity.* University of Chicago Press.

Fojas, C. (2017). *Zombies, migrants, and queers: Race and crisis capitalism in pop culture.* University of Illinois Press.

Fortenberry, D. (Writer), & Barker, M. (Director). (2017, May 10). Faithful (Season 1, Episode 5) [TV series episode]. In B. Miller (Producer), *The handmaid's tale.* Hulu.

Foucault, M. (2003[1976]). Lecture 11, 17 March 1976. In A. Fontana, & D. Macey (Eds.), *Society must be defended: Lectures at the college de France* (pp. 239–64). Allen Lane.

Gergen, M., Smith, S., & Vasudevan, P. (2018). Earth beyond repair: Race and apocalypse in collective imagination. *Environment and Planning D: Society and Space*, 1–20. Advance online publication. https://doi.org/10.1177/0263775818756079

Gill-Peterson, J., Sheldon, R., & Stockton, K. (2016). Introduction: What is the now, even of then. *GLQ: A Journal of Lesbian and Gay Studies, 22*(4), 495–503.

Gilmore, R. W. (2007). *Golden gulag: Prisons, surplus, crisis, and opposition in globalizing California*. University of California Press.

Ginn, F. (2015). When horses won't eat: Apocalypse and the Anthropocene. *Annals of the Association of American Geographers, 105*(2), 351–9.

Global Coordination Group of the Youth-Led Climate Strikes. (2019, March 1). Climate crisis and a betrayed generation. *The Guardian*. https://www.theguardian.com/environment/2019/mar/01/youth-climate-change-strikers-open-letter-to-world-leaders

Goff, P. A., Eberhardt, J. L., Williams, M. J., & Jackson, M. C. (2008). Not yet human: Implicit knowledge, historical dehumanization, and contemporary consequences. *Journal of Personality and Social Psychology, 94*, 292–306.

Goff, P. A., Jackson, M. C., Di, L., Culotta, C. M., & DiTomasso, N. A. (2014). The essence of innocence: Consequences of dehumanizing black children. *Journal of Personality and Social Psychology, 106*(4), 526–45.

Gordon, L. (2017, 17 June). *The handmaid's tale* contains a chilling environmental warning. https://lwlies.com/articles/the-handmaids-tale-environmental-warning/

Gross, L. (2016). Postapocalypse stress syndrome and rebuilding American Indian communities. *Shifting Borders*. http://www.shiftingborders.ku.edu/presentations/gross.html#paper

Grosz, E., Yusoff, K., & Clark, N. (2017). An interview with Elizabeth Grosz: Geopower, inhumanism and the biopolitical. *Theory, Culture & Society, 34*(2–3), 129–46.

Halberstam, J. (2011). *The queer art of failure*. Duke University Press.

Hamilton, J., & Neimanis, A. (2016, June 30). What was "Hacking the Anthropocene"? (Or, why the Environmental Humanities needs more feminism). *The Seed Box*. https://theseedboxblog.wordpress.com/2016/06/30/what-was-hacking-the-anthropocene-or-why-the-environmental-humanities-needs-more-feminism/

Hanifin, L., & Jemisin, N. K. (2015). Black Lives Matter inspired this chilling fantasy novel. *Wired Magazine*. https://www.wired.com/2015/08/geeks–guide–nk–jemisin/

Haraway, D. (1991). *Simians, cyborgs and women: The reinvention of nature*. Routledge.

Haraway, D. (1997). *modestwitness@second-millennium. Femaleman-meets-oncomouse: Feminism and technoscience*. Routledge.

Haraway, D. (2004). *The Haraway reader*. Routledge.

Haraway, D. (2008). *When species meet*. Routledge.

Haraway, D. (2015). Anthropocene, Capitalocene, Plantationocene, Chthulucene: Making kin. *Environmental Humanities, 6*, 159–65.

Haraway, D. (2016). *Staying with the trouble: Making kin in the Chthulucene*. Duke University Press.

Haraway, D., Ishikawa, N., Gilbert, S. F., Olwig, K., Tsing, A., & Bubandt, N. (2016). Anthropologists are talking—about the Anthropocene. *Ethnos, 81*(3), 535–64.

Haraway, D., & Tsing, A. (2019, June 18). Reflections of the Plantationocene: A conversation with Donna Haraway & Anna Tsing, moderated by Gregg Mitman. *Edge Effects* magazine. https://edgeeffects.net/wp-content/uploads/2019/06/PlantationoceneReflections_Haraway_Tsing.pdf

Hartman, S. (1997). *Scenes of subjection: Terror, slavery and self-making in nineteenth-century America*. Oxford University Press.

Hartman, S. (2006). *Lose your mother: A journey along the Atlantic slave route*. Farrar, Straus & Giroux.

Harvey, F. (2021, August 9). Global climate crisis: Inevitable, unprecedented and irreversible. *The Guardian*. https://www.theguardian.com/science/2021/aug/09/humans-have-caused-unprecedented-and-irreversible-change-to-climate-scientists-warn

Hauser, W. (Writer), & Sigismondi, F. (Director). (2017, May 17). A women's place (Season 1, Episode 6) [TV series episode]. In B. Miller (Producer), *The handmaid's tale*. Hulu.

Held, V. (2006). *The ethics of care: Personal, political, and global*. Oxford University Press.

Hirsi, I [@israhirsi]. (2019, November 5). The climate crisis is everything. It's health care, it's racial justice, it's criminal justice—everything. It's our lives on the line [Tweet]. Twitter. https://twitter.com/justicedems/status/1191738512460173312

Hodgins, B. D. (2019). *Gender and care with young children: A feminist material approach*. Routledge.

hooks, b. (1992). *Black looks: Race and representation*. South End Press.

hooks, b. (2012, September 5). No love in the wild. *New Black Man*. https://www.newblackmaninexile.net/2012/09/bell-hooks-no-love-in-wild.html

Hurley, J., & Jemisin, N. K. (2018). An apocalypse is a relative thing: An interview with N. K. Jemisin. *ASAP/Journal, 3*(3), 467–77.

Huston, J. (Director). (1982). *Annie* [Film]. Columbia Pictures.

Imarisha, W. (2015). Introduction. In W. Imarisha & B. A. Maree (Eds.), *Octavia's brood: Science fiction stories from social justice movements* (pp. 3–7). AK Press.

Imarisha, W., & Maree, B. A. (2015). *Octavia's brood: Science fiction stories from social justice movements*. AK Press.

The Independent. (2021, August 10). Code red for humanity. *The Independent*. https://twitter.com/Independent/status/1424827114809929729?s=20

Intergovernmental Panel on Climate Change (IPCC). (2018). *Global warming of 1.5°C*. Geneva, Switzerland. IPCC https://www.ipcc.ch/sr15/

Internet Movie Database (IMDb). (2016). *The girl with all the gifts*: Did you know? *IMDb*. https://www.imdb.com/title/tt4547056/

James, A., & Prout, A. (1997). *Constructing and reconstructing childhood: Contemporary issues in the sociological study of childhood* (2nd ed.). Polity Press.

James, J. (2013). "Concerning violence": Frantz Fanon's rebel intellectual in search of a black cyborg. *South Atlantic Quarterly, 112*(1), 57–70.

Jemisin, N. K. (2015). *The fifth season*. Orbit.

Jemisin, N. K. (2016). *The obelisk gate*. Orbit.

Jemisin, N. K. (2017). *The stone sky*. Orbit.

Jenkins, H. (Ed.). (1998). *The children's culture reader*. New York University Press.

Johns-Putra, A. (2016). "My job is to take care of you": Climate change, humanity, and Cormac McCarthy's *The road*. *MFS Modern Fiction Studies, 62*(3), 519–40.

Joo, H-J. (2018). Race, disaster, and the waiting room of history. *Environment and Planning D: Society and Space, 38*(1), 72–90.

Justice, D. H. (2018). *Why Indigenous literatures matter*. Wilfrid Laurier University Press.

Katz, C. (2008). Childhood as spectacle: Relays of anxiety and the reconfiguration of the child. *Cultural Geographies, 15*(1), 5–17.

Kawash, S. (1999). Terrorists and vampires: Fanon's spectral violence of decolonization. In A. Alessandrini (Ed.), *Frantz Fanon: Critical perspectives* (pp. 235–57). Routledge.

Kincaid, J. (1998). *Erotic innocence*. Duke University Press.

King, T. L. (2019). *The Black shoals: Offshore formations of Black and Native studies*. Duke University Press.

Klein, N. (2014). *This changes everything: Capitalism vs. the climate*. Simon & Schuster.

Kolbert, E. (2011, March). Enter the Anthropocene—Age of man. *National Geographic*. http://ngm.nationalgeographic.com/2011/03/age-of-man/kolbert-text.

Kolbert, E. (2014). *The sixth extinction: An unnatural history*. Henry Holt.

Kromidas, M. (2019). Towards the human, after the child of Man: Seeing the child differently in teacher education. *Curriculum Inquiry, 49*(1), 65–89.

Kraftl, P. (2020). *After childhood: Re-thinking environment, materiality, and media in children's lives*. Taylor & Francis.

Ladson-Billings, G. (2011). Boyz to men? Teaching to restore Black boys' childhood. *Race, Ethnicity, and Education, 14*, 7–15.

Langford, R. (Ed.). (2019). *Feminist ethics of care in early childhood practice: Possibilities and dangers*. Bloomsbury Academic.

Latimer, H. (2009). Popular culture and reproductive politics: *Juno, Knocked up* and the enduring legacy of. *The handmaid's tale. Feminist Theory, 10*(2), 209–24.

Latour, B. (1993). *We have never been modern* (C. Porter, Trans.). Harvard University Press.

Latour, B. (1996). *Armamis, or love of technology* (C. Porter, Trans.). Harvard University Press.

Latour, B. (2004). Why has critique run out of steam? From matters of fact to matters of concern. *Critical Inquiry, 30*(2), 225–48.

Latour, B. (2007). *It's the development, stupid! Or how can we modernize modernization*. http://www.bruno-latour.fr/node/153

Latour, B. (2011). Love your monsters: Why we must care for our technologies as we do our children. *Breakthrough Journal, 2*, 19–26.

Latour, B. (2014). Agency at the time of the Anthropocene. *New Literary History, 45*(1), 1–18.

Latour, B. (2015). Fifty shades of green. *Environmental Humanities, 7*, 219–25.

LeDuff, C. (2010). What killed Aiyana Stanley-Jones? *Mother Jones*. https://www.motherjones.com/politics/2010/09/aiyana-stanley-jones-detroit/

Le Guin, U. (1988). The carrier bag theory of fiction. In D. DuPont (Ed.), *Women of vision: Essays by women writing science fiction* (pp. 1–9). St. Martin's Press.

Lee, N. (2013). *Childhood and biopolitics: Climate change, life processes and human futures*. Palgrave Macmillan.

Lee, N., & Motzkau, J. (2011). Navigating the bio-politics of childhood. *Childhood: A Global Journal for Childhood Studies, 18*(1), 7–19.

Lemire, C. (2013, January 11). Beautiful *Beasts* is one of the year's best. *SiFy*. https://www.sify.com/movies/beautiful-ibeastsi-is-one-of-years-best-review-hollywood-pcmaFhiaaefaf.html

Lenz Taguchi, H. (2010). *Going beyond the theory/practice divide in early childhood education: Introducing an intra-active pedagogy*. Routledge, Taylor & Francis group.

Leong, D. (2016). The mattering of Black lives: Octavia Butler's hyperempathy and the promise of the new materialisms. *Catalyst: Feminism, Theory, Technoscience, 2*(2), 1–35.

Lewis, T. (2012). King of the wild things: Children and the passionate attachments of the anthropological machine. In P. Costello (Ed.), *Philosophy in children's literature* (pp. 285–300). Lexington Books.

Livingston, J., & Puar, J. (2011). Interspecies. *Social Text, 29*(1), 3–14.

Lorimer, J. (2017). The Anthropo-scene: A guide for the perplexed. *Social Studies of Science, 47*(1), 117–42.

Lothian, A. (2018). *Old futures: Speculative fiction and queer possibility.* NYU Press.

Lury, K. (2010). Children in an open world: Mobility as ontology in New Iranian and Turkish cinema. *Feminist Theory, 11*(3), 283–94.

Lynas, M. (2011). *The god species: How the planet can survive the age of humans.* National Geographic.

Lynch, T. (2017, July 25). Why hope is dangerous when it comes to climate change: Global warming dicussions need apocalyptic thinking. *Slate.* https://slate.com/technology/2017/07/why-climate-change-discussions-need-apocalyptic-thinking.html

Macdonald, S. N. (2017, April 26). In *Handmaid's tale*, a postracial, patriarchal hellscape. *The Undefeated.* https://theundefeated.com/features/hulu-handmaids-tale/

Macfarlane, R. (2016, April 1). Generation Anthropocene: How humans have altered the planet for ever. *The Guardian.* https://www.theguardian.com/books/2016/apr/01/generation-anthropocene-altered-planet-for-ever

MacKendrick, N., & Cairns, K. (2019, February 27). Born pre-polluted: Mothers and environmental risk. *WRISK.* https://www.wrisk.org/uncategorized/born-pre-polluted-mothers-and-environmental-risk/

Maher, J. (2018). Torture born: Babies, bloodshed and the feminist gaze in Hulu's *The handmaid's tale. Communication, Culture & Critique, 11*(1), 209–11.

Malkki, L. (2010). Children, humanity, and the infantilization of peace. In I. Feldman (Ed.), *In the name of humanity* (pp. 58–85). Duke University Press.

Malm, A., & Hornborg, A. (2014). The geology of mankind? A critique of the Anthropocene narrative. *The Anthropocene Review, 1,* 62–9.

Malone, K. (2017). *Children in the Anthropocene: Rethinking sustainability and child friendliness in cities.* Palgrave Macmillan.

Martin, A., Myers, N., & Viseu, A. (2015). The politics of care in technoscience. *Social Studies of Science, 45*(5), 625–41.

Martinez, X [@xiuhtezcatl]. (2019, September 24). There have always been, and will always be indigenous, black and brown youth at the forefront of creating systemic change [Tweet]. Twitter. https://twitter.com/xiuhtezcatl/status/1176642441920811008

Mashigo, M. (2018). *Intruders*. Picador Africa.

Mayall, B. (2013). *A history of the sociology of childhood*. IOE Press.

Maynard, R. (2018). Reading Black resistance through Afrofuturism: Notes on post–apocalyptic blackness and Black rebel cyborgs in Canada. *TOPIA: Canadian Journal of Cultural Studies, 39*, 29–47.

McCarthy, C. (Producer), & Carey, M. (Writer). (2016). *The girl with all the gifts* [Film]. BFI.

McGrath, M. (2019, July 24). Climate change: 12 years to save the planet? Make that 18 months. *BBC*. https://www.bbc.com/news/science-environment-48964736

Merriman, B. (2009). White-washing oppression in Atwood's *The handmaid's tale*. *Notes on Contemporary Literature, 39*(1), 8. http://link.galegroup.com.ezproxy.library.uvic.ca/apps/doc/A206534450/LitRC?u=uvictoria&sid=LitRC&xid=53660ce2

Miéville, C. (2015, August 1). The limits of utopia. *Salvage Zone*. http://salvage.zone/in-print/the-limits-of-utopia

Miller, B. (Executive producer). (2017-ongoing). *The handmaid's tale* [TV series]. Hulu.

Miller, B. (Writer), & Barker, M. (Director). (2018, April 25). Unwomen (Season 2, Episode 2) [TV series episode]. In B. Miller (Producer), *The handmaid's tale*. Hulu.

Miller, B. (Writer), & Morano, R. (Director). (2017, April 26). Offred (Season 1, Episode 1) [TV series episode]. In B. Miller (Producer), *The handmaid's tale*. Hulu.

Mirzoeff, N. (2018). It's not the anthropocene, it's the white supremacy scene; or, the geological color line. In R. Grusin (Ed.), *After extinction* (pp. 123–49). University of Minnesota Press.

Mitchell, A., & Todd, Z. (2016). Earth violence: Indigeneity and the Anthropocene. Presentation at *Landbody: Indigeneity's Radical Commitments*, Center for 21st Century Studies, University of Wisconsin, Milwaukee. https://worldlyir.files.wordpress.com/2016/04/earth-violence-text-mitchell-and-todd.pdf

Mitchell, B. (2018, June 17). Harry Taylor plays with the bones of dead livestock [Photo]. *Getty Images News*. https://www.gettyimages.ca/detail/news-photo/harry-taylor-plays-with-the-bones-of-dead-livestock-on-the-news-photo/1007071402?adppopup=true

Mol, A. (2008). *The logic of care: Health and the problem of patient choice*. Routledge.

Monbiot, G. (2018, November 14). The earth is in a death spiral. *The Guardian*. https://www.theguardian.com/commentisfree/2018/nov/14/earth-death-spiral-radical-action-climate-breakdown

Moore, J. (2016). *Name the system! Anthropocene & the Capitalocene alternative*. https://jasonwmoore.wordpress.com/tag/anthropocene/

Mosby, I. (2013). Administering colonial science: Nutrition research and human biomedical experimentation in Aboriginal communities and residential schools, 1942-1952. *Social History, 46*, 145-72.

Muñoz, J. E. (2009). Cruising the toilet: LeRoi Jones/Amiri Baraka, radical black traditions, and queer futurity. *GLQ: A Journal of Lesbian and Gay Studies, 13*(2-3), 353-67.

Murphy, M. (2015). Unsettling care: Troubling transnational itineraries of care in feminist health practices. *Social Studies of Science, 45*(5), 717-37.

Murris, K. (2016). *The posthuman child: Educational transformation through philosophy with picturebooks*. Routledge.

Myers, N. (2016). Natasha Myers talks plants and the Planthropocene with Cymene Howe & Dominic Boyer. *Cultures of Energy* [Audio podcast]. http://culturesofenergy.com/ep-12-natasha-myers/

Ndnviewpoint. [@mahtowin1]. (2018, February 17). By the 1960s, about 1 in 4 Native children in the US were living apart from their families. [Tweet]. Twitter. https://twitter.com/mahtowin1/status/965017646877069312

Nelson, A. (Ed.). (2002, June 3). *Afrofuturism: A special issue of social text*. Duke University Press.

NIH. (2012). NIH human microbiome project defines normal bacterial makeup of the body. *News Releases*. National Institutes of Health. https://www.nih.gov/news-events/news-releases/nih-human-microbiome-project-defines-normal-bacterial-makeup-body

Nixon, L. (2016, May 20). sâkihito-maskihkiy acâhkosiwikamikohk [Visual Cultures of Indigenous Futurisms]. *GUTS, 6*. http://gutsmagazine.ca/visual-cultures/

Nixon, R. (2011). *Slow violence and the environmentalism of the poor*. Harvard University Press.

Noddings, N. (1984). *Caring: A feminine approach to ethics and moral education*. University of California Press.

Nolan, M. (2019, January 28). An art opening at Chernobyl. *The Outline*. https://theoutline.com/post/7017/an-art-opening-in-chernobyl-artefact?zd=1&zi=n5puxlqd

Nordhaus, T., & Shellenberger, M. (2009). *Break through: From the death of environmentalism to the politics of possibility*. Houghton Mifflin.

Nunn, W. (2018, December 2). *We have 12 years left*. Redbrick. https://www.redbrick.me/we-have-12-years-left/

Nyong'o, T. (2015). Little monsters: Race, sovereignty, and queer inhumanism in *Beasts of the southern wild*. *GLQ: A Journal of Lesbian and Gay Studies, 21*(2-3), 249-72.

Nxumalo, F. (2017). Geotheorizing mountain–child relations within anthropogenic inheritances. *Children's Geographies, 15*(5), 558–69.

Nxumalo, F. (2018). Stories for living on a damaged planet: Environmental education in a preschool classroom. *Journal of Early Childhood Research, 16*(2), 148–59. https://doi.org/10.1177/1476718X17715499

Nxumalo, F. (2019). *Decolonizing place in early childhood education*. Routledge.

Nxumalo, F., & Cedillo, S. (2017). Decolonizing place in early childhood studies: Thinking with Indigenous onto-epistemologies and Black feminist geographies. *Global Studies of Childhood, 7*(2), 99–112.

Nxumalo, F., & ross, kihana miraya (2019). Envisioning Black space in environmental education for young children. *Race, Ethnicity and Education, 22*(4), 502–24.

Okorafor, N. (2017, August). *Sci-fi stories that imagine a future Africa* [Video]. *TEDGlobal*. https://www.ted.com/talks/nnedi_okorafor_sci_fi_stories_that_imagine_a_future_africa?utm_campaign=tedspread&utm_medium=referral&utm_source=tedcomshare

Oler, T. (2018, December 3). Changing the lore: N. K. Jemisin is reimagining other worlds, and ours. *Slate*. https://slate.com/culture/2018/12/nk-jemisin-short-stories-broken-earth-review.html

Out of the Woods Collective. (2015a, January 9). Klein vs Klein. *Out of the Woods*. https://libcom.org/blog/klein-vs-klein-09012015

Out of the Woods Collective. (2015b, May 17). The future is kids' stuff. *Out of the Woods*. https://libcom.org/blog/future-kids-stuff-17052015

Pacini-Ketchabaw, V. (2011). Developmental theories and child and youth care. In A. Pence & J. White (Eds.), *New perspectives in child and youth care* (pp. 19–32). UBC Press.

Palsson, G., & Swanson, H. (2016). Down to earth: Geosocialities and geopolitics. *Environmental Humanities, 8*(2), 149–71.

Palsson, G., Szerszynski, B., Sörlin, S., Marks, J., Avril, B., Crumley, C., Hackmann, H., Holm, P., Ingram, J., Kirman, A., Buendia, M., & Weehuizen, R. (2013). Reconceptualizing the "Anthropos" in the Anthropocene: Integrating the social sciences and humanities in global environmental change research. *Environmental Science & Policy, 28*, 3–13.

Parikka, J. (2015). *The anthrobscene*. University of Minnesota Press.

Penn, H. (2007). *Unequal childhoods: Young children's lives in poor countries*. Routledge.

Peppers, C. (1995). Dialogic origins and alien identities in Butler's Xenogenesis. *Science Fiction Studies, 22*(1), 47–62.

Pérez-Peña, R. (2018, June 8). Decades later and far away, Chernobyl disaster still contaminates milk. *The New York Times*. https://www.nytimes.com/2018/06/08/world/europe/chernobyl-nuclear-disaster-radiation-milk.html

Phoenix, A. (2018). From text to screen: Raising racialized difference in *The handmaid's tale*. *Communication, Culture and Critique, 11*(1), 206-8.

Plante, C. (2017, May 19). What caused infertility in *The handmaid's tale*? https://www.inverse.com/article/31832-what-caused-infertility-in-the-handmaids-tale

Povinelli, E. (1995). Do rocks listen? The cultural politics of apprehending Australian Aboriginal labor. *American Anthropologist, 97*(3), 505-18.

Povinelli, E. (2002). *The cunning of recognition: Indigenous alterities and the making of Australian multiculturalism*. Duke University Press.

Povinelli, E. (2009). Beyond good and evil, whither liberal sacrificial love? *Public Culture, 21*(1), 77-100.

Povinelli, E. (2011). *Economies of abandonment: Social belonging and endurance in late liberalism*. Duke University Press.

Povinelli, E. (2013, January 14). *Potentiation and extinguishment* [Presentation]. London School of Economics and Political Science, London, UK. http://www.lse.ac.uk/newsAndMedia/videoAndAudio/channels/publicLecturesAndEvents/player.aspx?id=1701

Povinelli, E. (2016). *Geontologies: A requiem for late liberalism*. Duke University Press.

Povinelli, E., Coleman, M., & Yusoff, K. (2014, March 6). An interview with Elizabeth Povinelli: On biopolitics and the Anthropocene. *Space & Society*. http://societyandspace.org/2014/03/06/on-biopolitics-the-anthropocene-and-neoliberalism/

Priya. (2017, April 14). *Get out* of Gilead: Anti-blackness in *The handmaid's tale*. *Bitch Media*. https://www.bitchmedia.org/article/anti-blackness-handmaids-tale

Prout, A. (2005). *The future of childhood*. Routledge.

Puig de la Bellacasa, M. (2011). Matters of care in technoscience: Assembling neglected things. *Social Studies of Science, 41*(1), 85-106.

Puig de la Bellacasa, M. (2012). "Nothing comes without its world": Thinking with care. *The Sociological Review, 60*(2), 197-216.

Puig de la Bellacasa, M. (2015). Making time for soil: Technoscientific futurity and the pace of care. *Social Studies of Science, 45*(5), 691-716.

Puig de la Bellacasa, M. (2017). *Matters of care: Speculative ethics in more than human worlds*. University of Minnesota Press.

Qvortrup, J. (2009). *Sociological studies of children and youth, vol. 12: Structural, historical and comparative perspectives*. Emerald.

Racebending.com. (2011, February 23). What is "racebending"? *Racebending.com: Media consumers for entrainment equity*. http://www.racebending.com/v4/about/what-is-racebending/

Raworth, K. (2014, October 24). Must the Anthropocene be a manthropocene? *The Guardian*. https://www.theguardian.com/commentisfree/2014/oct/20/anthropocene-working-group-science-gender-bias

Renner, K. (2016). *Evil children in the popular imagination*. Palgrave Macmillan.

Reser, A., & McNeill, L. (2017, May 23). The logic of cultivation in *The handmaid's tale*. *Lady Science*. https://www.ladyscience.com/commentary/handmaidstalelogicofcultivation?rq=handmaid%27s%20tale

Reuben, S. (2010). *Reducing environmental cancer risk: What we can do now*. US Department of Health and Human Services and the National Cancer Institute, President's Cancer Panel. https://deainfo.nci.nih.gov/advisory/pcp/annualReports/pcp08-09rpt/PCP_Report_08-09_508.pdf

Revkin, A. (2016, October). An Anthropocene journey. *Anthropocene magazine, 1*. A publication *Future Earth*. http://www.anthropocenemagazine.org/anthropocenejourney/

Roanhorse, R. (2018). Postcards from the apocalypse. *Uncanny: A Magazine of Science Fiction and Fantasy, 20*. https://uncannymagazine.com/article/postcards-from-the-apocalypse/

Robinson, K. H. (2008). In the name of "childhood innocence": A discursive exploration of the moral panic associated with childhood and sexuality. *Cultural Studies Review, 14*(2), 113–29.

Robinson, K. S., & Luis de Vicente, J. (2017, October 31). Angry optimism in a drowned world: A conversation with Kim Stanley Robinson. https://lab.cccb.org/en/angry-optimism-in-a-drowned-world-a-conversation-with-kim-stanley-robinson/

Rose, D. B. (2012). Multispecies knots of ethical time. *Environmental Philosophy, 9*(1), 127–40.

Ruddick, S. (1990). *Maternal thinking: Toward a politics of peace*. Ballantine Books.

Ryan, B. (2011). The new wave of childhood studies: Breaking the grip of bio-social dualism? *Childhood, 19*(4), 439–52.

Ryman, G. (2017). Geoff Ryman and 100 African writers of SFF [Audio podcast]. *The Coode Street Podcast, 306*. http://www.jonathanstrahan.com.au/wp/2017/04/29/episode-306-geoff-ryman-and-100-african-writers-of-sff/

Saldanha, A., & Stark, H. (2016). A new earth: Deleuze and Guattari in the Anthropocene. *Deleuze and Guattari Studies, 10*(4), 427–39.

Save the Children International. (2021). *Born into the climate crisis*. https://resourcecentre.savethechildren.net/document/born-climate-crisis-why-we-must-act-now-secure-childrens-rights/

Scott, A. O. (2012, June 26). She's the man of this swamp. *The New York Times*. https://www.nytimes.com/2012/06/27/movies/beasts-of-the-southern-wild-directed-by-benh-zeitlin.html

Sellers, M. (2013). *Young children becoming curriculum: Deleuze, Te Whāriki and curricular understandings*. Routledge.

Sevenhuijsen, S. (1998). *Citizenship and the ethics of care: Feminist considerations on justice, morality, and politics*. Routledge.

Sevenhuijsen, S. (2013). Interview in June 2013. *Ethics of Care*. http://ethicsofcare.org/interviews/selma-sevenhuijsen/

Shapiro, A., & Jemisin, N. K. (2018, December 26). At the end of the year, N.K. Jemisin ponders the end of the world. *All Things Considered. NPR*. https://www.npr.org/2018/12/26/680201486/at-the-end-of-the-year-n-k-jemisin-ponders-the-end-of-the-world

Sharpe, C. (2013, September 27). *Beasts of the southern wild*—the romance of precarity I. *Social Text*. http://socialtextjournal.org/beasts-of-the-southern-wild-theromance-of-precarity-i/

Sharpe, C. (2016). *In the wake: On blackness and being*. Duke University Press.

Sharpe, C. (2018). And to survive. *Small Axe, 22*(3), 171–80.

Sheldon, R. (2013). Somatic capitalism: Reproduction, futurity, and feminist science fiction. *Ada: A Journal of Gender, New Media, and Technology, 3*. https://adanewmedia.org/2013/11/issue3-sheldon/

Sheldon, R. (2016). *The child to come: Life after the human catastrophe*. University of Minnesota.

Shellenberger, M., & Nordhaus, T. (2011). *Love your monsters: Postenvironmentalism and the Anthropocene*. Breakthrough Institute. https://thebreakthrough.org/issues/conservation/love-your-monsters-ebook

Shelly, M. (1818). *Frankenstein; or, the modern Prometheus*. Lackington, Hughes, Harding, Mavor & Jones.

Shotwell, A. (2016). *Against purity: Living ethically in compromised times*. University of Minnesota Press.

Shotwell, A. (2020, March 25). *Survival will always be insufficient but it's a good place to start*. https://alexisshotwell.com/2020/03/25/survival-will-always-be-insufficient-but-its-a-good-place-to-start/

Simpson, L. (2011). *Dancing on our turtle's back: Stories of Nishnaabeg re-creation, resurgence, and a new emergence*. Arbeiter Ring.

Smith, A. (2010). Queer theory and native studies: The heteronormativity of settler colonialism. *GLQ: A Journal of Lesbian and Gay Studies, 16*(1–2), 42–68.

Somerville, M. (2017). Thinking critically with children of the Anthropocene: (Un)learning the subject in qualitative and postqualitative inquiry. *International Review of Qualitative Research, 10*(4), 395–410.

Strathern, M. (1991). *Partial connections*. Rowman & Littlefield Publishers.

Steffen, W., Crutzen, P., & McNeill, J. (2007). The Anthropocene: Are humans now overwhelming the great forces of nature? *Ambio, 36*, 614–21.

Steffen, W., Grinevald, J., Crutzen, P., & McNeill, J. (2011). The Anthropocene: Conceptual and historical perspectives. *Philosophical Transactions of the Royal Society A: Mathematical, Physical and Engineering Sciences, 369*, 842–67.

Steffen, W., et al. (2015). Planetary boundaries: Guiding human development on a changing planet. *Science, 347*(6223). DOI: 10.1126/science.1259855

Stockton, K. B. (2009). *The queer child, or growing sideways in the twentieth century.* Duke University Press.

Sturgeon, N. (2010). Penguin family values: The nature of planetary environmental reproductive justice. In C. Mortimer-Sandilands & B. Erickson (Eds.), *Queer ecologies: Sex, nature, politics, desire* (pp. 102–34). Indiana University Press.

TallBear, K. (2019, February 19). *Molecular death, desire, and redface reincarnation: Indigenous appropriations in the USA and Canada* [Presentation]. Columbia University, New York. https://www.socialdifference.columbia.edu/events-1/2019/2/19/talk-by-dr-kimberly-tallbear

Taylor, A. (2010). Troubling childhood innocence: Reframing the debate over the media sexualisation of children. *Australasian Journal of Early Childhood, 35*(1), 48–57.

Taylor, A. (2013). *Reconfiguring the natures of childhood.* Routledge.

Taylor, A. (2017). Beyond stewardship: Common world pedagogies for the Anthropocene. *Environmental Education Research*, 1–14. Advance online publication. https://doi.org/10.1080/13504622.2017.1325452

Taylor, A., Blaise, M., & Giugni, M. (2013). Haraway's "bag lady story-telling": Relocating childhood and learning within a "post-human landscape." *Discourse: Studies in the Cultural Politics of Education, 34*(1), 48–62.

Taylor, A., & Pacini-Ketchabaw, V. (2015). Learning with children, ants, and worms in the Anthropocene: Towards a common world pedagogy of multispecies vulnerability. *Pedagogy, Culture & Society, 23*(4), 507–29.

Taylor, A., & Pacini-Ketchabaw, V. (2018). *The common worlds of children and animals: Relational ethics for entangled lives.* Routledge.

Tennant, Z. (2020, April 9). "Our stories give us a lot of guidance": Daniel Heath Justice on why Indigenous literatures matter. *Unreserved. CBC.* https://www.cbc.ca/radio/unreserved/why-stories-matter-now-more-than-ever-1.5526331/our-stories-give-us-a-lot-of-guidance-daniel-heath-justice-on-why-indigenous-literatures-matter-1.5527999

Teuton, S. K. (2018). *Native American literature: A very short introduction.* Oxford.

Thomas, E. E. (2018). Toward a theory of the dark fantastic: The role of racial difference in young adult speculative fiction and media. *Journal of Language and Literacy Education, 14*(1), 1–10.

Thomas, M. G., & Thomas, N. S. (2009). *How to survive a zombie apocalypse*. Sword Works.

Thunberg, G. (2019). *Our house if on fire* [Video]. YouTube. World Economic Forum. https://youtu.be/U72xkMz6Pxk

Timofeeva, O. (2018). Zombie. In R. Braidotti & M. Hlavajova (Eds.), *Posthuman glossary*. Bloomsbury. https://monoskop.org/media/text/posthuman_glossary_2018/#p150

Todd, Z. (2015). Indigenizing the Anthropocene. In H. Davis & E. Turpin (Eds.), *Art in the Anthropocene: Encounter among aesthetics, politics, environment and epistemology* (pp. 241–54). Open Humanities Press.

Tronto, J. C. (1993). *Moral boundaries: A political argument for an ethic of care*. Routledge.

Truman, S. (2019). Inhuman literacies and affective refusals: Thinking with Sylvia Wynter and secondary school English. *Curriculum Inquiry*, 1–20. https://doi.org/10.1080/03626784.2018.1549465

Tsing, A. (2015). *The mushroom at the end of the world: On the possibility of life in capitalistic ruins*. Princeton University Press.

Tuchman, E. (Writer), & Dennis, K. (Director). (2017, June 7). The bridge (Season 1, Episode 9) [TV series episode]. In B. Miller (Producer), *The handmaid's tale*. Hulu.

Tuck, E, & Yang, W. (2012). Decolonization is not a metaphor. *Decolonization: Indigeneity, Education & Society, 1*(1), 1–40.

Vargas, J. C., & James, J. (2013). Refusing blackness-as-victimization: Trayvon Martin and the Black cyborgs. In J. Jones & G. Yancy (Eds.), *Pursuing Trayvon Martin: Historical contexts and contemporary manifestations of racial dynamics* (pp. 193–205). Lexington Books.

Vizenor, G. (2008). *Survivance: Narratives of Native presence*. University of Nebraska Press.

Wade, A. G. (2017). "New genres of being human": World making through viral blackness. *The Black Scholar, 47*(3), 33–44.

Wald, P. (2008). *Contagious: Cultures, carriers, and the outbreak narrative*. Duke University Press.

Walkerdine, V. (1997). *Daddy's girl: Young girls and popular culture*. Macmillan.

Watling, E. (2019, August 1). Drought in Australia turns farmland to barren dustbowl: Heartbreaking photos. *Newsweek*. https://www.newsweek.com/drought-australia-turns-farmland-barren-dustbowl-heartbreaking-photos-1052170

Weheliye, A. (2014). *Habeas viscus: Racializing assemblages, biopolitics, and Black feminist theories of the human*. Duke University Press.

Wei, K., & Jemisin, N. K. (2016). Hugo Winner N.K. Jemisin talks *The fifth season* and the *Obelisk gate*. http://www.fantasyliterature.com/author-interviews/n-k-jemisin/

Weinbaum, A. E. (2004). *Wayward reproductions: Genealogies of race and nation in transatlantic modern thought*. Duke University Press.

Weinstein, J., & Colebrook, C. (2017). *Posthumous life: Theorizing beyond the posthuman*. Columbia Press.

Weisberger, M. (2017, March 3). Meet a new kind of zombie in the film *The girl with all the gifts. Live Science*. https://www.livescience.com/58096-zombie-science-girl-with-all-the-gifts-movie.html

Weisman, A. (2007). *The world without us*. St. Martins.

Wendle, J. (2016, April 18). Animals rule Chernobyl three decades after nuclear disaster. *National Geographic*. https://www.nationalgeographic.com/news/2016/04/060418-chernobyl-wildlife-thirty-year-anniversary-science/

Whyte, K. P. (2017). Our ancestors' dystopia now. Indigenous conservation and the Anthropocene. In U. Heise, J. Christensen, & M. Niemann (Eds.), *Routledge companion to the Environmental Humanities* (pp. 206–15). Routledge.

Whyte, K. P. (2018). Indigenous science (fiction) for the Anthropocene: Ancestral dystopias and fantasies of climate change crises. *Environment and Planning E: Nature and Space*, *1*, 224–42.

Wiebe, S. (2016). *Everyday exposure: Indigenous mobilization and environmental justice in Canada's chemical valley*. UBC Press.

Wilderson III, F. B. (2010). *Red, white & Black: Cinema and the structure of U.S. antagonisms*. Duke University Press.

Wilderson III, F. B. (2014). "We're trying to destroy the world": Anti-Blackness and police violence after Ferguson–An interview with Frank B. Wilderson III. Ill Will Editions, 3–23. http://ill-will-editions.tumblr.com/post/103584583009/were-trying-to-destroy-the-world

Wilderson III, F. B. (2015). Afro-Pessimism and the end of redemption. *Humanities Futures*. Franklin Humanities Institute, Duke University, Durham. https://humanitiesfutures.org/papers/afro-pessimism-end-redemption/

Wise, D. (2012, September 24). *Beasts of the southern wild* review. *Empire*. https://www.empireonline.com/movies/reviews/beasts-southern-wild-review/

Wolfe, P. (2006). Settler colonialism and the elimination of the native. *Journal of Genocide Research*, *8*(4), 387–409.

Womack, Y. (2013). *Afrofuturism: The world of Black sci-fi and fantasy culture*. Review Press.

Wood, R. (2020, October 9). From dust bowl to lush green land: Photographer captures farms' recovery from drought. *9News*. National. https://www.9news.com.au/national/drought-hit-farms-transformed-after-winter-rain-weather-news/a8a5ed64-27f7-4759-9c86-2d214d091e99

Wynter, S. (1995a). 1492: A "new world" view. In V. L. Hyatt & R. Nettleford (Eds.), *Race, discourse, and the origin of the Americas: A new world view* (pp. 5–57). Smithsonian Institution.

Wynter, S. (1995b). The Pope must have been drunk, the King of Castile a madman: Culture as actuality and the Caribbean rethinking of modernity. In A. Ruprecht & C. Taiana (Eds.), *Reordering of culture: Latin America, the Caribbean and Canada in the hood* (pp. 17–41). Carleton University Press.

Wynter, S. (2000). The re-enchantment of humanism: An interview with Sylvia Wynter. *Small Axe, 8*, 119–207.

Wynter, S. (2003). Unsettling the coloniality of being/power/truth/freedom: Towards the human, after man, its overrepresentation–An argument. *New Centennial Review, 3*(3), 257–337.

Wynter, S. (2005). Race and our biocentric belief system: An interview with Sylvia Wynter. In J. E. King (Ed.), *Black education: A transformative research and action agenda for the new century* (pp. 361–6). Lawrence Erlbaum Associates.

Wynter, S. (2006). On how we mistook the map for the territory, and reimprisoned ourselves in our unbearable wrongness of being, of desetre: Black studies toward the human project. In J. Gordon & L. Gordon (Eds.), *A companion to African–American studies* (pp. 107–18). Blackwell.

Wynter, S. (2015). The ceremony found: Towards the autopoetic turn/overturn, its autonomy of human agency and extraterritoriality of (self-)cognition. In J. Ambroise & S. Broeck (Eds.), *Black knowledges/Black struggles: Essays in critical epistemology* (pp. 184–252). Liverpool University Press.

Wynter, S., & McKittrick, K. (2015). Unparalled catastrophe for our species? Or, to give humanness a different future: Conversation. In K. McKittrick (Ed.), *Sylvia Wynter: On being human as praxis* (pp. 1–55). Duke University Press.

Yaeger, P. (2013, February 13). *Beasts of the southern wild* and dirty ecology. *Southern Spaces*. https://southernspaces.org/2013/beasts-southern-wild-and-dirty-ecology/

Yohannes, S. (2020, March 19). Margaret Atwood, Waubgeshig Rice and Daniel Kalla share their pandemic reading lists. *CBC: As it happens*. https://www.cbc.ca/radio/asithappens/as-it-happens-thursday-edition-1.5502954/margaret-atwood-waubgeshig-rice-and-daniel-kalla-share-their-pandemic-reading-lists-1.5502962

Yusoff, K. (2013). Geologic life: Prehistory, climate, futures in the Anthropocene. *Environment and Planning D: Society and Space, 31*, 779–95.

Yusoff, K. (2016). Anthropogenesis: Origins and endings in the Anthropocene. *Theory, Culture & Society, 33*(2), 3–28.

Yusoff, K. (2018). *A billion Black Anthropocenes or none*. University of Minnesota Press.

Yusoff, K. (2019, May 2). Kathryn Yusoff with hosts Dominic Boyer and Cymene Howe [Audio podcast]. *Culture of Energy, 175*. http://culturesofenergy.com/175-kathryn-yusoff/

Zeitlin, B. (Director). (2012). *Beasts of the southern wild* [Film]. Twentieth Century Fox.

Ziyad, H. (2017a). Playing "outside" in the dark: Blackness in a postwhite world. *Critical Ethnic Studies, 3*(1), 143–61.

Ziyad, H. (2017b, July 19). *The girl with all the gifts and Black girls destroying the world to save themselves*. Black Youth Project. http://blackyouthproject.com/girl-gifts-black-girls-destroying-world-save/

Index

Locators followed by "n." indicate endnotes

Afro-futurisms/Afrofuturisms 10, 23, 81, 156 n.7
Agamben, G., bios 156 n.8
Ahmed, S., *Willful Subjects* 140
Alabaster (*The Fifth Season*) 79
Alagraa, B. 66
Alibar, L., *Juicy and Delicious* 39
alternative names (global change) 154–5 n.4
Animist (geontology figure) 21, 29–31, 34–42, 143
Anthropocene 1, 5–7, 13, 80, 93, 119, 155 n.5
Anthropomeme 1
Anthropos 6–7, 18, 84–5, 87, 89
anti-Black racism 76, 86, 101, 103, 105, 111, 162 n.8
apocalypse/apocalyptic tropes 7–10, 14, 22, 42, 85–6, 148
  apocalyptic thinking 148
  post-apocalyptic blockbusters 8–9, 30, 42–3, 48, 80, 85, 120, 127
  as product of Anthropocene 8
  as revelation, disclosure 7
  social dreaming 10
Arendt, H.
  force of life 125
  natality 67, 125, 159–60 n.8
Atwood, M.
  The Handmaid's Tale 23, 116, 122, 124, 126, 134–8
  National Homelands 163 n.5
autopoiesis 64, 66–7, 159 n.7
Avatar: The Last Airbender 51
awareness (climate change) 4, 77, 116
  Global Day of Action 5
Axelsson, I. 154 n.3

Baldwin, A. 57
Ballard, S., *Alliances in the Anthropocene* 145
Barad, K., intra-action 156 n.10
Barnsley, V. 14
Bastién, A. J. 136
Beasts of the Southern Wild (Zeitlin) 157 n.1
  Miss Bathsheba 38
  The Bathtub 36–7, 40–1
  characterizations 37
  Hushpuppy 21, 31, 33, 35–42, 147
  Wink 36, 38–9
Belcourt, C. 163 n.1
Benjamin, R. 133, 149
  Ferguson is the Future (*see* Ferguson is the Future (Benjamin))
  race as technology 122–3
  Racial Fictions, Biological Facts: Expanding the Sociological Imagination through Speculative Methods 105
  technoscience innovation 101, 107–9
Berlant, L. 124, 146
Berlastsky, N. 135
Bernstein, R., *Racial Innocence* 15–17, 50
biocentric/biocentrism 19–20, 47, 54, 60, 76, 83, 112, 157 n.1
bionormative care 126
bionormative child 12–13, 22, 26–8, 46, 71, 90, 111, 157 n.1
  and bio-centric human 54
  motherhood 126–31
  parent-child relationship 24
bionormative reproductive futurism 125
biopower 25, 27
bios/geos divide 22, 25, 30, 72, 75, 77, 82, 88, 152

bios-mythoi worlding 65
bio-social dualism 27–8
biosocial waves 11–14, 27–9
    hybrid childhoods 12
    nature-cultures 12–13
    social construction of childhood 11–12
bios (political life) 156 n.8
Black children 15–16, 18, 40, 101, 103, 158 n.2, 162 n.7
    decolonization 54
    early childhood education 149–50
    and Indigenous lives 158 n.2
Black female power fantasy 78
A Black Feminist Statement (Combahee River Collective) 55–6
Black Lives Matter Global Network 56
#BlackLivesMatter movement 10, 18, 23, 57, 85, 102
Black Science Fiction Society 2
Boy with the Bones 2–4, 21, 31–3
    becoming boy-animal-monster 33–4
Breakthrough Institute (BTI) 92–3, 95–6, 107–8, 160 n.2
    An Ecomodernist Manifesto 93
    politics of possibility 93
    technology and modernization 94, 109
#BrightFuture Child 3–4, 17, 87, 93, 107, 115
Broken Earth trilogy (Jemisin) 9, 20, 22, 35, 69, 71–6, 88
    end of the world 69, 74, 83–7
    Father Earth 73–4, 83
    The Fifth Season 74, 84, 86
    Fulcrum 74–5, 77–9, 82, 86, 89
    The Obelisk Gate 75
    Stillness 73–9
    The Stone Sky 76, 86
Brown, M. 57
Brown, S. 54
Bryce, P. 157 n.3
Butler, O. 150
    Dawn 60
    Xenogenesis trilogy (*Lilith's Brood*) 60

Cairns, K. 130–1, 163 n.2
Cannella, G. 17
capitalism, climate and 151
Carbon Imaginary 157 n.1
care 146

collective 42–6
    environmentalization of (*The Handmaid's Tale*) 131–4
    ethics 157 n.1, 162 n.9
    parental 119–20
    for regenerative cyborgs 110–13
    speculative (Puig de la Bellacasa) 92, 97, 106–10
Carey, M. R., *The Girl with All the Gifts* 22, 47, 51–2
cautionary tale against technology 91
Césaire, A., 64
Chernobyl disaster 55, 143–5
child-centered pedagogy 141
child-climate relations 5
child-future entanglements/relation 3, 14–16, 131
childhood innocence 16–17, 50
Childhood Studies 10–13, 20, 27–8, 91, 149, 152
child-parent separation 162–3 n.1
Chivington, J., Sand Creek massacre 15
Clark, N. 28, 67–8
    crisis of natality 3
climate change 3, 17, 33, 46, 146–8, 157 n.1
    affective resonances of 120
    awareness 4–5
    multi-racial 37
climate crisis 4–6, 8, 14, 25, 29, 47, 84, 97, 101, 119, 139, 141–2, 147–8, 157 n.1
    child-future relationship 3
    parental relationship within 23
Colebrook, C. 30, 80, 84, 116
collective ecology 118
colonialism 7, 9, 19, 46, 76, 78, 81, 158 n.4, 163 n.1, 163 n.4
Combahee River Collective, A Black Feminist Statement 55–6
Common Worlds Research Collective 13, 24, 89, 118, 149, 151–3
counterhumanism 48
Covid-19 1, 56
Crawley, A. 153
Crist, E. 7
cruel optimism 24, 62, 146–9
    and angry optimism 148
    extended crisis 147

inevitability 149
reproductive futurism 147
Crutzen, P. 155 n.5

Danowski, D. 84
The Day After Tomorrow (film) 120
De Beers diamond mines 81
decolonization 54, 86, 158 n.4
Deepwater Horizon (2010) oil spill 96, 112
Demos, T. J. 93
Desert (geontology figure) 21, 29–33, 42, 55, 143
Dimaline, C., *The Marrow Thieves* 21, 31, 42–6, 57, 73, 140
disaster films 8, 120
drought (Warrumbungle Shire, New South Wales) 2, 32
Dugas, G. 159 n.6

early childhood education 16, 141, 149–52, 157 n.1
Earth system 1, 5, 68, 73, 116–17, 119, 161 n.6
  human inclusive 118
  science 6, 155 n.5
eco-anxiety 7, 47, 138, 142
ecomodernism 91, 93, 109
Edelman, L. 24, 27, 121, 139, 142, 146
  No Future 14–15, 146
  reproductive futurism 14, 125
educational futures 140, 150–3
  Black children 150
  de-institutionalization of school 150
  early childhood education 141, 149, 152
  human exceptionalism 152
  learning-about 152
  pedagogies for 149
  speculative visioning of 152
Elephant Annie 143–6
Ellsworth, E. 156 n.9
end of the world 1, 7–8, 14, 21–4, 29, 44, 90, 92, 100, 120, 139, 147, 149, 153
  Broken Earth trilogy 69, 74, 83–7
  disaster in 147
  drought 32
  geos-imaginaries 140, 144
  heteronormative family romance 115–16

humanity as whiteness 54
Hushpuppy (*Beasts*) 39
inhuman 83–7
The Marrow Thieves 46
Melanie (*The Girl with All the Gifts*) 48–9
punchy headlines 1
singularity 83
white 53–6, 68
world without us 84–5
Environmental Defence 163 n.2
environmental education 118, 149, 150–1
environmental stewardship 23–4, 121, 131, 133–4
Erasmus, Z. 66–7
Eriksen, C., *Alliances in the Anthropocene* 145
Essun (*The Fifth Season*) 74–6, 85
evolutionary theory (Darwin) 19
Exclusion Zone (Chernobyl Nuclear Power Plant) 143–4

Fanon, F. 20, 55, 64, 102, 158 n.4
  The Wretched of the Earth 158 n.4
Ferguson, A. 85
Ferguson is the Future (Benjamin) 23, 91–2, 97–102, 105–7, 111, 123
  afterlives 100
  Aiyana 97–100, 103, 111, 140
  Black lives matter 102–3
  Black rebel cyborgs 101–5
  healthcare system 98
  Immortocracy 99, 103, 109, 157 n.1
  People's Science Council 97, 99–100, 162 n.7
  Reparations Act 99
  Reparations Movement 97, 100–1
  Revival Ceremony 97–9
The First 48 (A&E network) 99–100
Fisher, B. 107
Foucault, M. 4, 25, 60
Frankencene technologies 92–7
fungible bodies 162 n.7
Futures of Education initiative (UNESCO) 151

Garner, E. 98
gatherings (Anthropocene child) 6, 140–2
  ontological demands 142–6

genome-mapping 98–9
geo-bio-socio assemblages 156 n.9
geo-engineering techno-fixes 148
geontological learning 152
geontology/geontological childhoods 21–2, 25, 29, 31, 88, 109
    Animist 21, 29–31, 34–42, 143
    biontological enclosure of existence 25
    Desert 21, 29–33, 55, 143
    generating 26–9
    Virus 21, 29–31, 42–6, 57, 143
geontopower 72
geopower 72
geos 13, 71–2, 89
    beings and becomings 71–4, 87
    geos-figuring speculative worlds 72–4
geos-childhoods 47
geos-existents, child-figures as 87–90
geosocial formations 82, 87–8
geos-powers 22, 35, 71–2, 75, 86, 90
    in inhuman(e) worlds 76–80
geostories 20–1, 47, 68, 150, 157 n.1
    Broken Earth 74–6
geos-zombification 50
global warming 96, 106, 147–8
Gold Coast 81
Grandin, T. 35
Great Acceleration (1945–2015) 100, 116, 161 n.6
Gross, L., post-apocalyptic stress syndrome 85
Grosz, E., geopower 72

Haraway, D. 60, 67, 102, 111, 153, 159 n.7
    Chthulucene 83
    A Cyborg Manifesto 60–1, 102, 110
    naturecultures 75
    planet and child 119
Hartman, S.
    blackness 78
    slavery afterlife 161–2 n.7
Hoodie-movement 162 n.8
Hornborg, A. 6
human(s)
    anchoring 17–20
    biocentric conception of 19 (*see also* biocentric/biocentrism)
    bios and *mythoi* 20
    dominion 7

enterprise 161 n.6
exceptionalism 28, 53–4, 59, 93, 117, 152
as geologic force 87
homo narrans 20, 61, 64–5
and more than human 60, 139, 153
and nonhuman world 4, 39, 59, 96, 118, 164 n.1
overrepresentation of Man (Wynter) 6, 19–20, 71–2
primitive races 19
Settler/Master(Human) 55
humanity 8–9, 17, 38, 58–60, 62, 66, 76, 87–8, 105, 116, 119, 120, 134
    of child-hungries 50
    and more-than-human world 37
    as whiteness 54
hungries/hungrie-children 22, 48–51, 54, 56, 58, 61–7, 71
hybrid-child/hybrid model of childhood 12, 20, 22

Indigenous Futurisms 10, 15, 149. *See also* Afro-futurisms/Afrofuturisms
Indigenous peoples 18, 22, 26, 33–5, 42–6, 85, 87, 109, 149, 153, 157 n.2, 161 n.5, 163 n.4
Industrial Era (1800–1945), stages 116
inhuman/inhuman worlds 17, 72
    double sense of 81
    geography 140
    geos-powers in 76–80
    monsters and natures 80–7, 89
innocence, childhood 16–17, 50
insensateness 50–1, 158 n.2
Intergovernmental Panel on Climate Change (2018) 2

James, J., Black rebel cyborg 55, 102–5
Jemisin, N. K. 22, 77, 83, 85–6, 89–90. *See also* Broken Earth trilogy (Jemisin)
Johnston, J. 130–1
Joo, H-J. 120
Justice, D. H. 149
    Why Indigenous Literatures Matter 45

Kawash, S. 158–9 n.4
Keystone pipelines 81
King, T. L.

Black fungibility 162 n.7
grammars of suffering 54
Klein, N. 96–7, 137
    kinship of the infertile 92, 112–13, 133
    The Right to Regenerate 112–13
    This Changes Everything: Capitalism vs the Climate 96
Kolbert, E., *The Sixth Extinction* 8
Kruse, J. 156 n.9

language 46
Latimer, H. 124
Latour, B. 23, 92, 108, 115
    Armamis, or Love of Technology 160 n.2
    dismissal of critique 106
    "Love Your Monsters: Why We Must Care for Our Technologies as We Do Our Children" 91–2, 94–7, 107–9, 113, 160 n.1, 160 n.2
    nature *vs.* nurture antagonism 95
    social constructionism 106
    technology 122–3
    We Have Never Been Modern 94, 160 n.1, 160 n.2
Law & Order 126
Lee, E. V., *In Defence of the Wastelands: A Survival Guide* 41
Lewis, T. 18
life 47
    abandonment, iconography 143–4
    beyond survival 41–2
    Life=Childhood formula 27
    v. nonlife 21, 23–31, 34, 42, 46–7, 67, 72, 82, 100, 112, 145, 152, 159 n.4
    possibility of 55
Lothian, A. 116
Lynas, M., *The God Species* 96

MacKendrick, N. 130–1, 163 n.2
Maher, J. 127–9
Malm, A. 6
Malone, K. 13, 118, 139, 142
Margulis, L. 159 n.7
Martin, Trayvon 97, 104–6, 158 n.2
McCarthy, C., *The Girl with All the Gifts* 22, 47–8, 51, 54–9, 65, 68–9, 74, 77, 85, 144, 159 n.5
McDonald, S. N. 138
McNeill, L. 134

Melanie (*The Girl with All the Gifts*) 22, 33, 44, 47, 61, 71, 90, 140–1
    bio-exceptionalism 51
    blackness and monstrosity 48, 55
    child-hungries as inhuman monsters 49, 65
    community through contagion 56–9
    end of the world 48
    fungal pathogens 48–53, 68
    Justineau and Caldwell 49–53, 61–6
    liveable world 53–4
    masking monstrosity 49–50
    Pandora 52, 61–3, 66
    Schrödinger's cat experiment 61, 65
Mellor, A. 161 n.3
Merriman, B. 134
Miigwans 44, 46
Miller, B., *The Handmaid's Tale* 115, 120–1, 163 n.5
    anti-Black slavery 136–7
    bionormative motherhood 122, 126–31
    born pre-polluted 124–6
    "The Bridge" 128
    Commander Fred Waterford 123, 128, 132
    Commander Putman 128
    environmentalization of care 131–4
    fertility crisis 121–4, 131
    Gilead 116, 121–7, 130–8
    Hannah 126, 128–30
    Janine 124, 126, 128
    June 126–30, 137
    Lydia 124, 128
    multiculturalism 137
    Offred 123, 126, 132
    post-racial parenthood 134–8
    regenerative stewardship practices 133–4
    sacrificial love 129
    "Seeds" 163 n.3
    Serena Joy 128, 131–2
    technophobia, Gilead 123
    treatment of blackness 136
    Unbabies and Unwomen of the Colonies 125–6, 132–3, 138, 142
    woman-as-womb 129
    "A Women's Place" 131
Milton, J., *Paradise Lost* 162 n.10

Mitchell, B. 32–3
monsters-children-technologies 107
monstrous geography 82
Mother Earth (*The Marrow Thieves*) 73–4
Muñoz, J. 15, 33

Nakate, V. 154 n.3
Nassun (Broken Earth trilogy) 22, 72, 75–6, 78, 81–2, 85–90, 141
natality 67, 125, 159–60 n.8, 160 n.9
  crisis of 3, 67
nature-cultures 11–13, 75, 95
nature/nurture 11
Neubauer, L. 154 n.3
non-totality 155 n.6
Nordhaus, T. 92, 107
nuclear disaster, iconography 143–5
Nxumalo, F. 149–51
  geotheorizing mountain-child relations 89
Nyong'o, T. 37, 40

Ophiocordyceps unilateralis (*Gifts*) 58
organic child 130–1
origin stories 60–9
orogeny/orogenes 22, 71–2, 74–8
  anti-Black racism 86
  geologic forces 88
  modality of human 80
  oppression of 79, 81
outbreak narrative 58–60, 159 n.6
The Out of the Woods Collective 111

Pandora's Box (myth) 61–3
pan-humanity 6
Parable of the Sower 151
parental stewardship 119–21, 127, 138
partial humanisms 18, 60
Patient Zeros 159 n.6
Peppers, C. 60–1
Piaget, J. 34–5
planet and child 119–21
planetary stewardship 24, 115–19, 127, 130, 138
  human exceptionalism 117–18
  life support system 119
Plante, C. 132
Povinelli, E. 21, 24–6, 29–31, 33–5, 55, 57, 82, 86, 88, 129, 139, 157 n.1.

  See also geontology/geontological childhoods
  biocentric subject of late liberalism 157 n.1
  critical theory 142
  Desert and Virus 42–3
  Geontologies: A Requiem to Late Liberalism 26
  geontopower 72
  metabolic imaginary 47, 157 n.1
power relations 108, 154 n.2, 155 n.4
Prout, A. 12–13
Puig de la Bellacasa, M. 106, 156 n.1
  ethics of care 92, 97, 107–10
  productionism 109
  three layered care formulation 130

race and racism 19, 51–2, 78, 93
  anti-Black racism 76, 86, 101, 103, 105, 111, 162 n.8
  environmental 38, 42, 84, 112, 157 n.1
  systemic 85
  as technology 123
racebending 51
race/reproduction bind 135
racial innocence 15–17, 50–1
real world 149
recapitulation theory 17, 19
recuperation 153
The Red Forest 145
regenerative cyborgs
  care for 110–13
  monstrous love for 105–10
relationship 45, 127, 139, 152
  bionormative parent-child 24
  child-future 3
  reconceptualization 94
  web of human 160 n.8
Reparations Act 99
Reparations Movement 97, 100–1
reproduction, human fantasy of 4
Reser, A. 134
Reuben, S. 163 n.2
Rice, W. 153
Rich, A. 149
Roanhorse, R. 87
Robinson, K. S. 148
ross, kihana miraya 149–51

Save the Children International (2021) 147
Scott, D. C. 157 n.3
Sharpe, C. 15, 39
Sheldon, R. 23, 28, 40, 55, 68, 79, 115, 124, 151
  militarized reproductive futurism 121–2, 125–6
  natality 125
Shellenberger, M. 92, 107
Shelly, M., *Frankenstein* 23, 91–2, 94, 97, 111, 115, 160 n.2, 161 n.3, 162 n.10
Shotwell, A. 161 n.3
Shredder-child 126, 138
slow violence 38, 84, 86, 133, 157 n.1
Smith, A. 15
social construction of childhood 11–12, 20, 27, 106
social dreaming 10
soil care 133
Somerville, M. 13, 139
speculative fiction 7, 21, 23–4, 69, 122, 140
  and anti-blackness 53
  apocalyptic tropes (*see* apocalypse/apocalyptic tropes)
  cruel optimism 146–9
  Frankenfigures 92–7
  imagining of care 42–6
  post-apocalyptic 80
Steffen, W. 116–19, 134
stewardship
  parental 119–21, 127, 138
  planetary 116–19, 127, 130, 138
Stoermer, E. 155 n.5
Stolen Childhoods 163 n.1
Stolen Generation of Indigenous children (Australia) 77
Strathern, M. 101
Sturgeon, N. 154 n.3
superspreaders 159 n.6
Syenite (*The Fifth Season*) 74, 78–80
sympoiesis 67, 159 n.7
systemic racism 85–6

TallBear, K. 161 n.5
Taylor, A. 118, 164 n.2
  alternative conceptualizations 164 n.2
  deconstructive methods 164 n.2
  pedagogical shift 152

technology 92, 107–8, 122, 124, 163 n.1
  Love Your Monsters 92, 96
  and modernization 94
  race as 123
  science and 123
  of unhumaning 81
Thunberg, G. 154 n.3
Tille, L. 154 n.3
Tronto, J. 107
Tsing, A. 56, 59
2012 (film) 120

Unilever 4
  Why Bring a Child into the World campaign 2–3, 93
Unist'ot'en clan 43

Vargas, J. C. 103–5
viral blackness 57–9
Viruru, R. 17
Virus (geontology figure) 21, 29–31, 42–6, 57, 143
Viveiros de Castro, E. 84
Vizenor, G., survivance 157 n.2

Wade, A., viral blackness 57–9
Wald, P. 59
  contagion 58–9
  HIV/AIDS diagnosis 159 n.6
#We Are All Trayvon Martin 162 n.8
Weinbaum, A. E., *Wayward Reproductions* 135
Weisman, A., *The World without Us* 8
Wet'suwet'en peoples 43
whiteness 102–3, 105, 135
  bionormative 127
  end of the world 53–6
  human exceptionalism 54
  humanity as 54
  infecting 48–53
Why Bring a Child into the World campaign 2–3, 93
Wilderson III, F. B. 10
World Children's Day (2014) 2–3
world-destructing events 157 n.1
WRISK project 163 n.2
Wynter, S. 6, 18–19, 48, 56, 60, 157 n.1
  autopoiesis 64, 66
  Man2 157 n.1

origin stories 60–9
overrepresentation of Man 6, 19–20, 71–2
science of the Word 64
theory of sociogeny 64

Yaeger, P., dirty ecology 37–9
Yusoff, K. 17, 72, 76, 82, 89
    anthropogenesis 87
    humanity-as-strata 88

    inhuman, figurations 76, 80–1
    material economy 81

Zeitlin, B. 35. *See also Beasts of the Southern Wild* (Zeitlin)
Ziarek, E. 159 n.8
Ziyad, H. 53–4, 103, 110
zoe (biological substance) 156 n.8
zombie, genealogy 158 n.3

www.ingramcontent.com/pod-product-compliance
Lightning Source LLC
Chambersburg PA
CBHW061831300426
44115CB00013B/2327